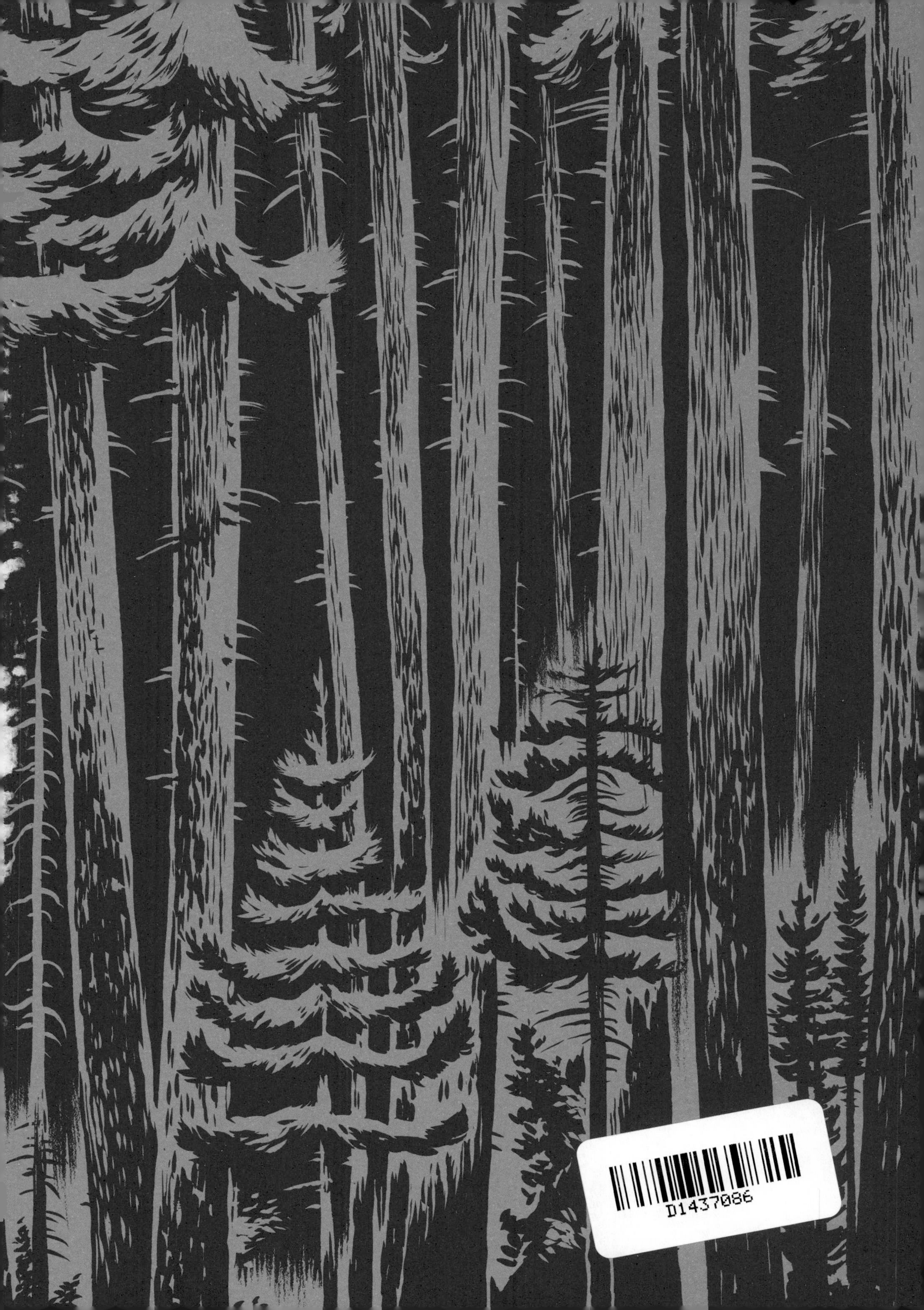

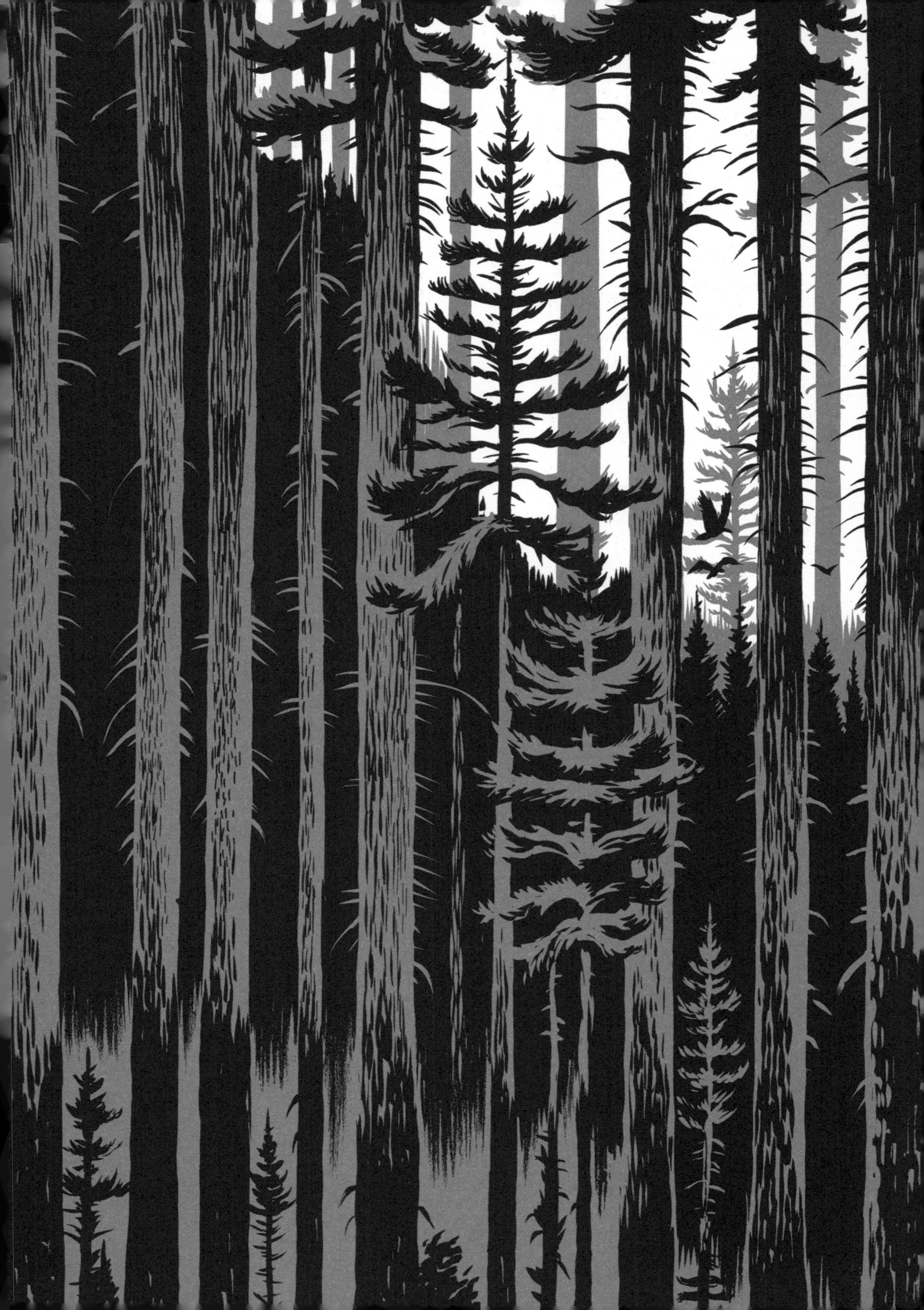

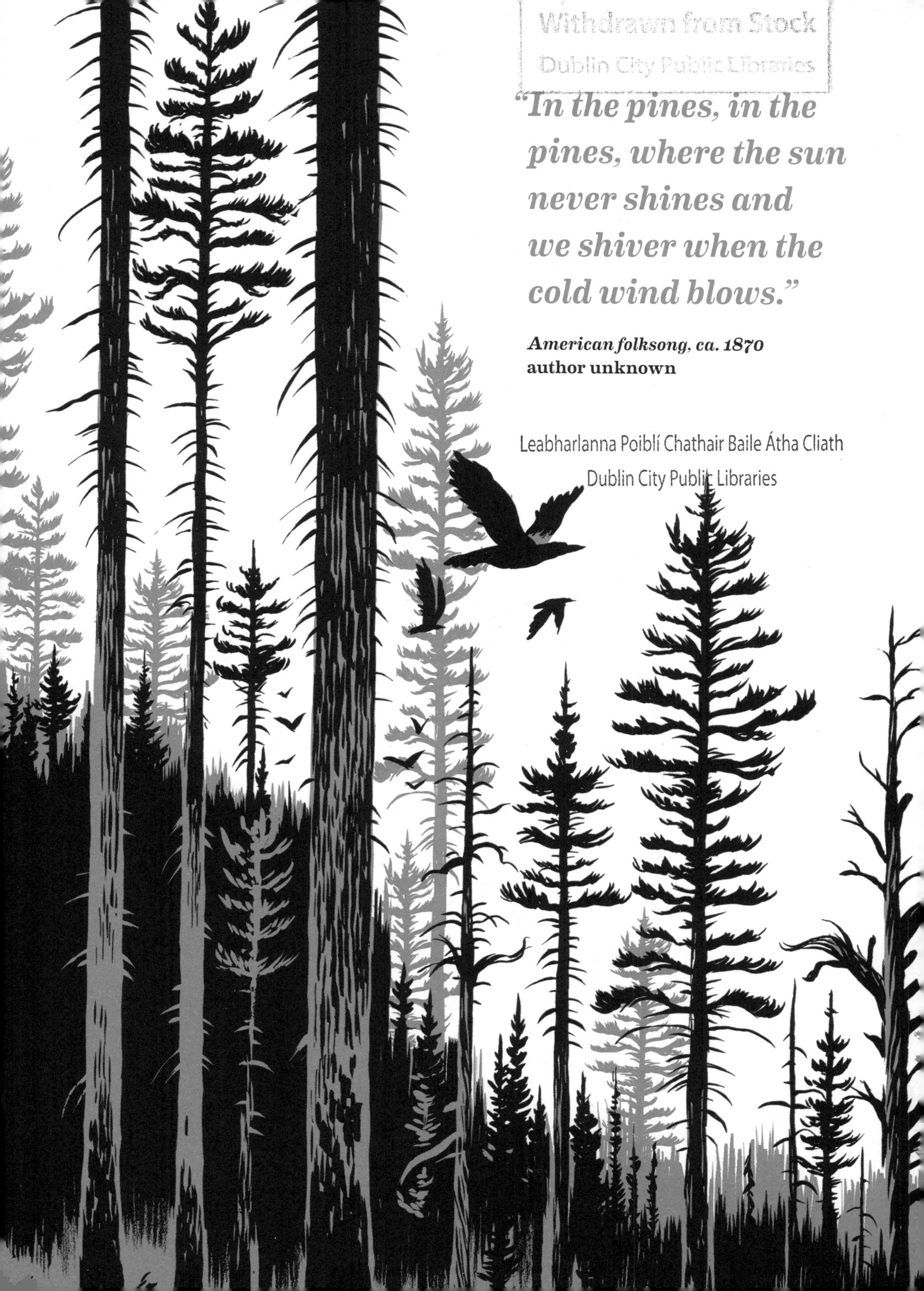

"In the pines, in the pines, where the sun never shines and we shiver when the cold wind blows."

American folksong, ca. 1870
author unknown

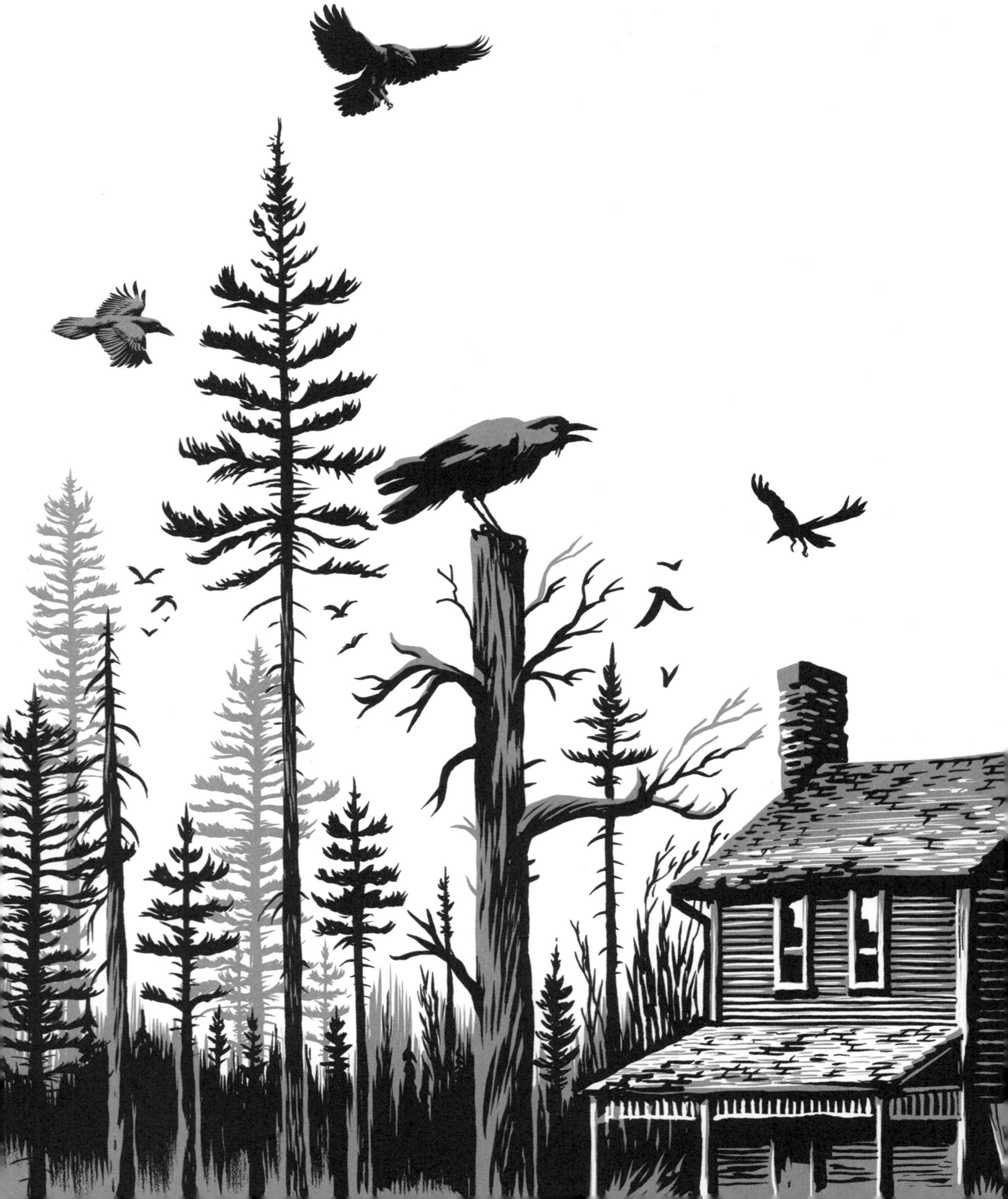

CONTENTS

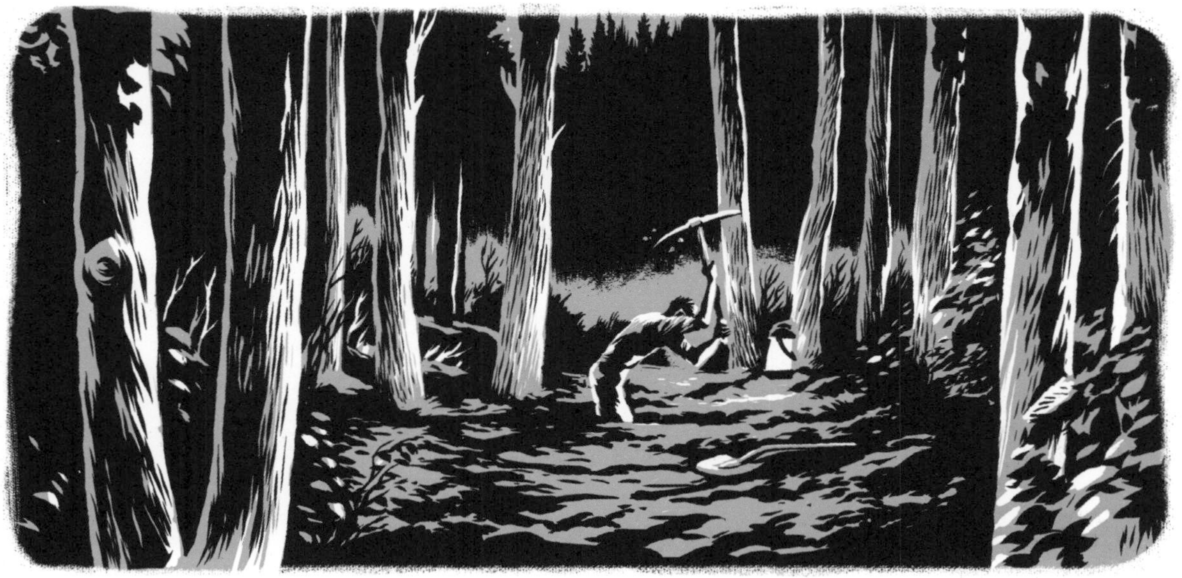

PRETTY POLLY and the SHIP'S CARPENTER

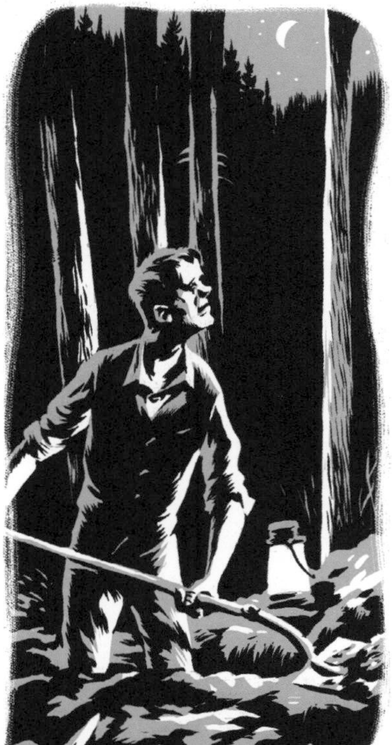

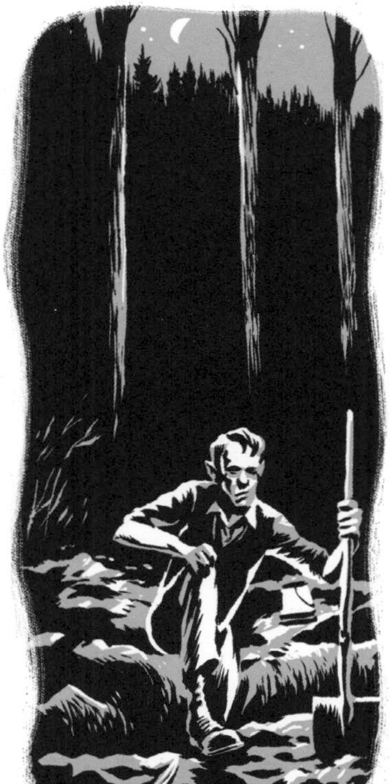

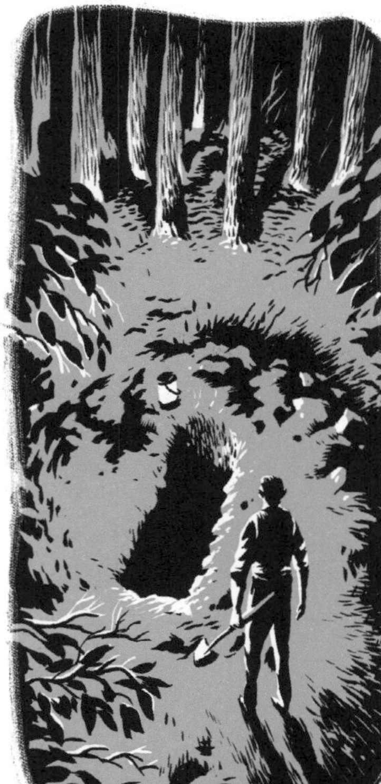

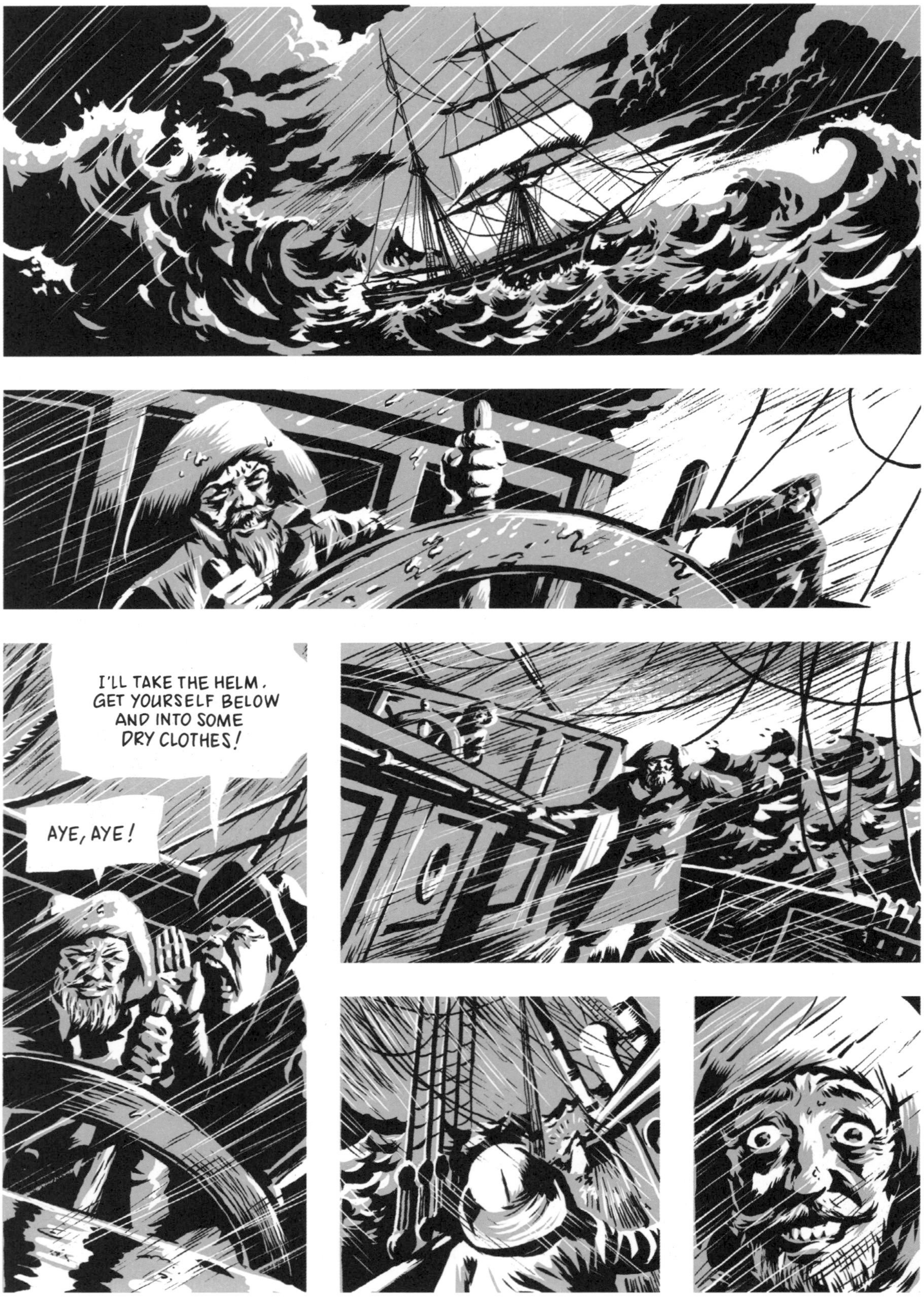
I'LL TAKE THE HELM. GET YOURSELF BELOW AND INTO SOME DRY CLOTHES!
AYE, AYE!

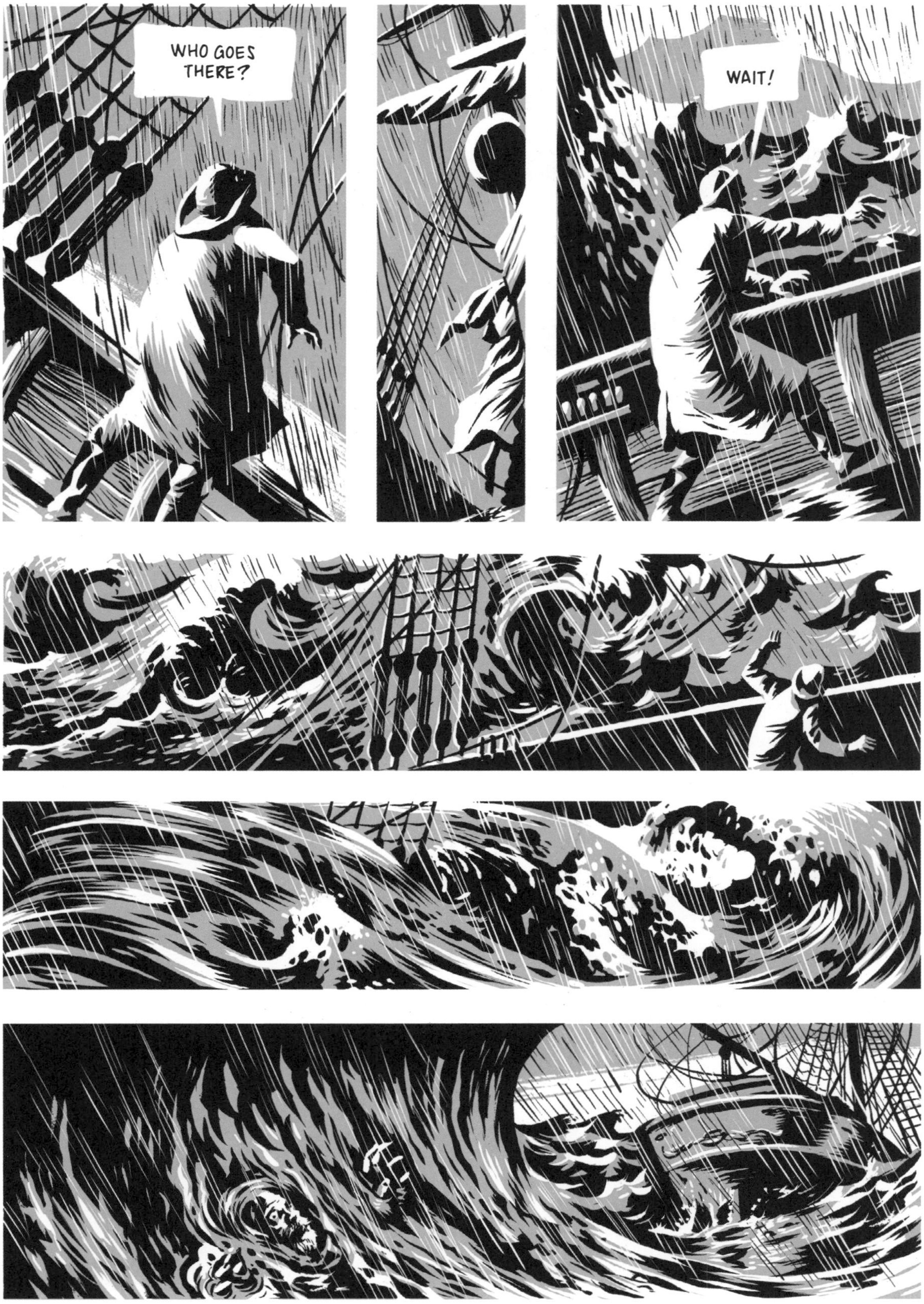
WHO GOES THERE?
WAIT!

ANOTHER ONE?
HOW MANY HAVE WE LOST SO FAR?
THREE, SIR, SINCE THE STORM BEGAN.
WELL, MR. BRIGGS, WE WON'T HAVE A CREW LEFT IF THIS GALE PERSISTS.
MAYBE IF WE STEER SOUTH IT WOULD...
OUT OF THE QUESTION! WE'VE ALL SEEN BAD WEATHER BEFORE.
HAVE SOME HANDS RIG EXTRA SAFETY LINES AND MAN THE PUMPS. THE REST STAY BELOW.
AYE SIR!

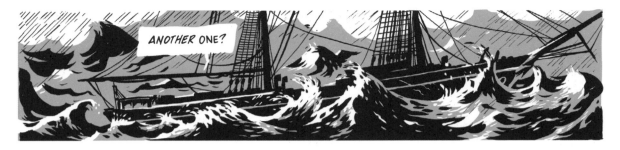

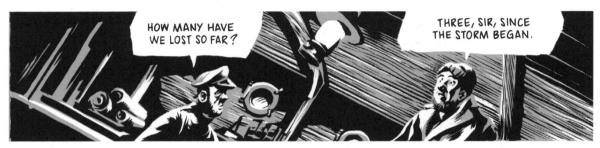

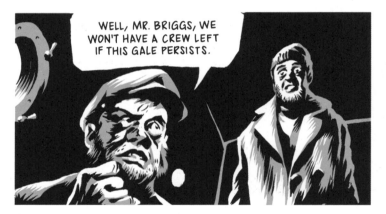

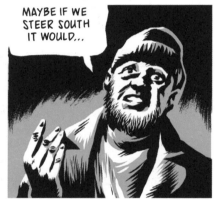

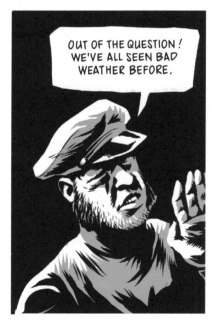

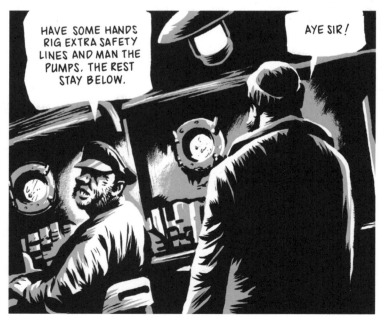

WHAT DID HE SAY?

WE ARE NOT CHANGING OUR COURSE.

DID YOU TELL HIM ABOUT THE GIRL?

I'VE SEEN HER, TOO!

STOP THAT TALK!

THIS SHIP IS CURSED!

HARPER! I WANT YOU TO GO ON DECK AND RIG MORE SAFETY LINES.

AYE AYE!

GET *HIM* TO HELP YOU.

WHO? ME?

YES, YOU, *WILL CLAYTON!* 'BOUT TIME YOU EARNED YOUR PAY!

YOU CAN CONTINUE DAYDREAMING AFTER YOU'VE DONE SOME SERIOUS WORK!

PRETTY POLLY! YOU ACTUALLY CAME.
ARE YOU SURE THAT NOBODY SAW YOU?
YES. I WAS VERY CAREFUL.

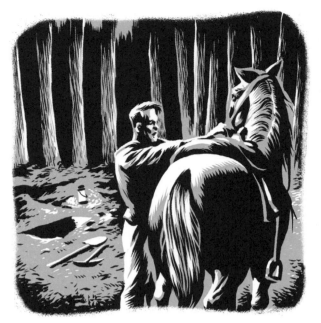

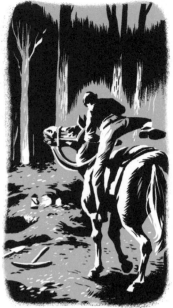

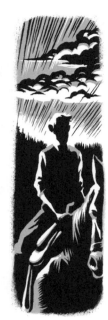

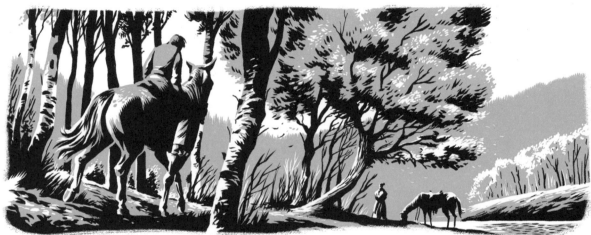

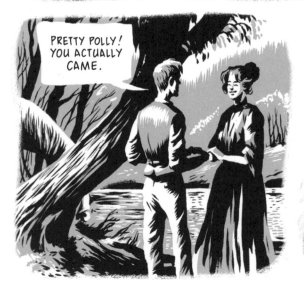

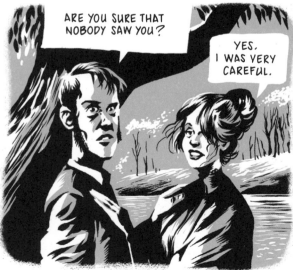

WHAT ON EARTH ARE YOU DOING, WILLIE?
I SMELL OF HORSE. I'M TAKING A BATH.
OH MY, IT'S COLD! HA HA HA!
COME HERE, YOU!

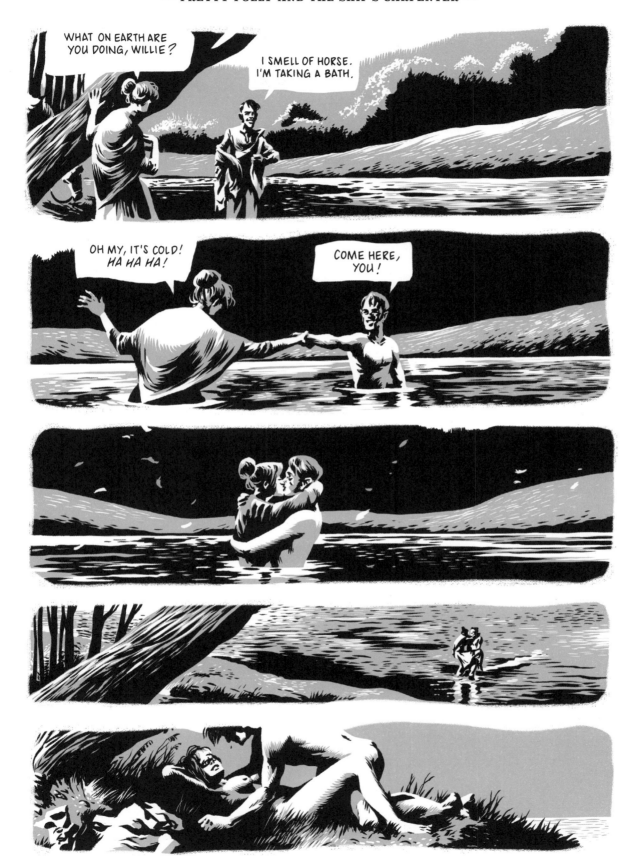

POLLY? LISTEN...

BEFORE WE GET MARRIED I WOULD LIKE...

MARRIED? WE CAN'T GET MARRIED! MY FATHER WOULD *NEVER* ALLOW IT. I THOUGHT WE DISCUSSED THIS.

... I KNOW... I APOLOGIZE. I MEAN... GOD, HOW I *LOVE YOU!*

I KNOW, STUPID BOY! WHY CAN'T WE JUST ENJOY THAT LOVE, HERE AND NOW?

I'VE PREPARED A SURPRISE FOR YOU.

A SURPRISE? FOR ME? HOW SWEET!

WHERE IS IT?

NOT FAR. COME AND I'LL SHOW YOU.

GOD DAMN IT! HARPER!
WHY ARE YOU STILL OUT HERE? HAVE YOU RIGGED THOSE LINES?
AYE, MR. BRIGGS. IT'S JUST...
WHERE THE HELL IS CLAYTON?
HE COULDN'T DO THE WORK. WENT BELOW.
WELL I'LL BE... THAT USELESS KID IS NO SHIP'S CARPENTER! IF HE IS, I'M THE FUCKING POPE!
I'LL SORT HIM OUT LATER. COME ON. LET'S RIG UP THIS LAST ONE!
AYE SIR! THANK YOU!

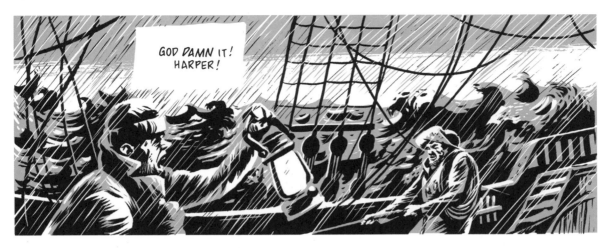

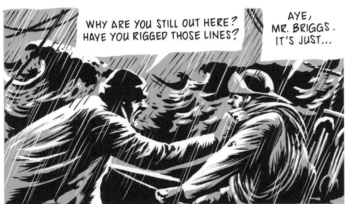

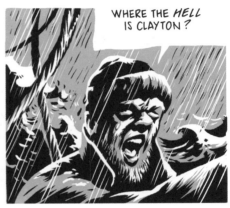

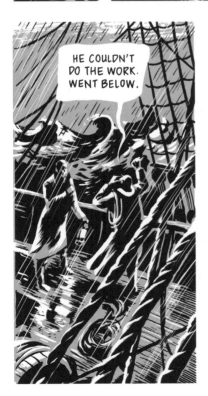

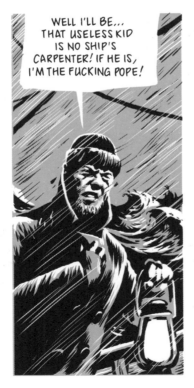

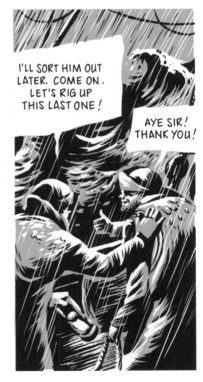

THAT SHOULD DO IT!
NOW, LET'S GO AND FIND CLAYTON. I'LL THRASH HIS SORRY HIDE!
AYE!
STORM'S KICKIN' UP!
HOLD TIGHT!
WHAT'S THAT?
HOLD ON, SIR! LOOK!

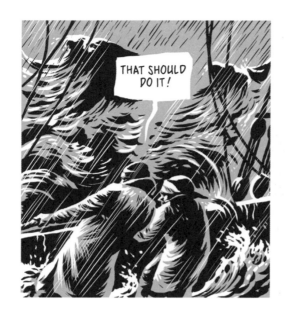

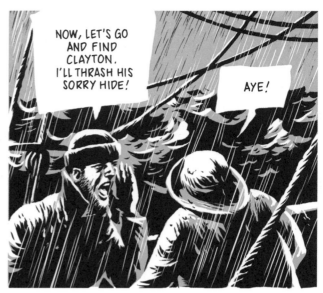

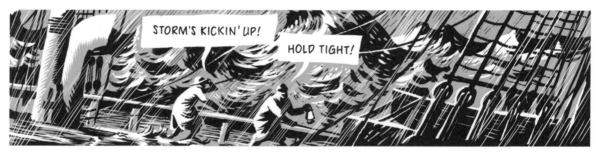

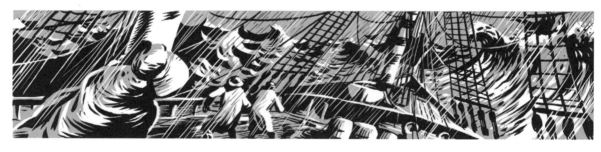

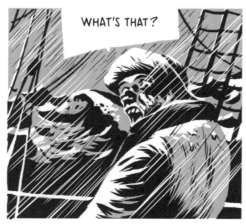

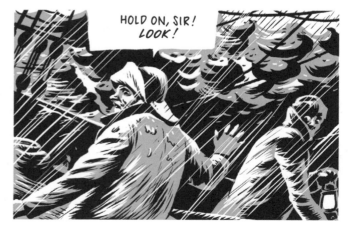

IT'S HER! THE GIRL!
SO IT'S TRUE AFTER ALL!
NO, HARPER! DON'T GET TOO CLOSE. WATCH OUT!

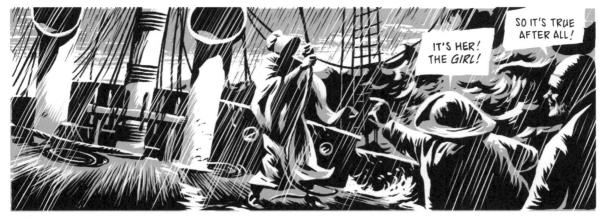

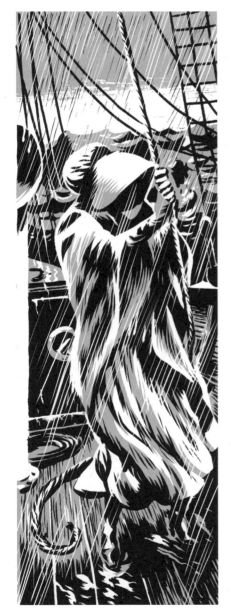

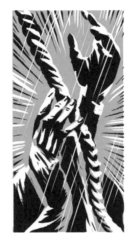

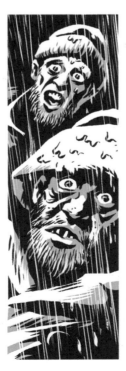

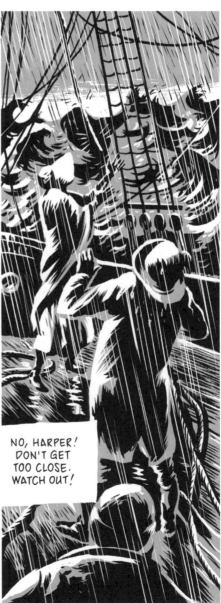

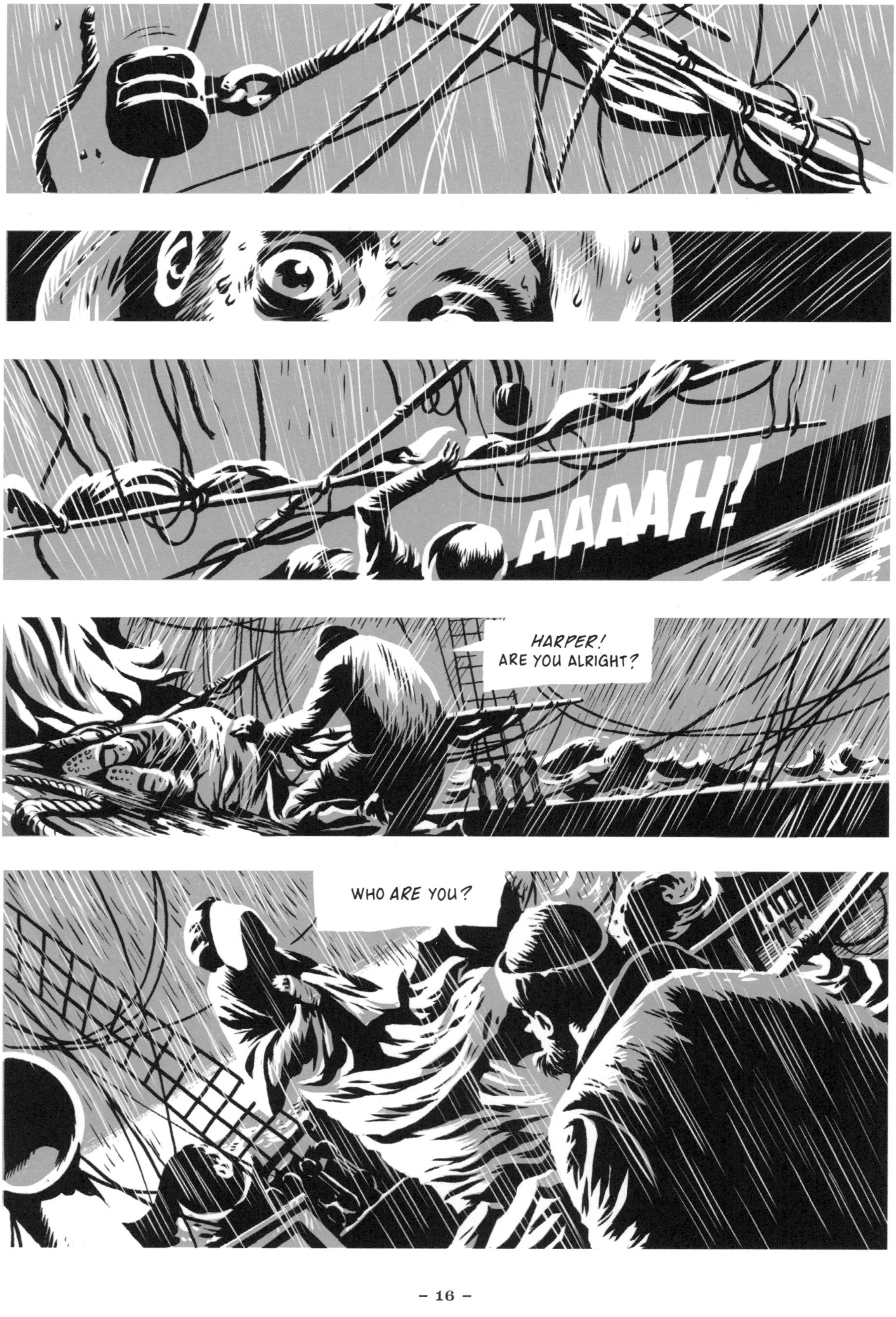
AAAAH!
HARPER! ARE YOU ALRIGHT?
WHO ARE YOU?

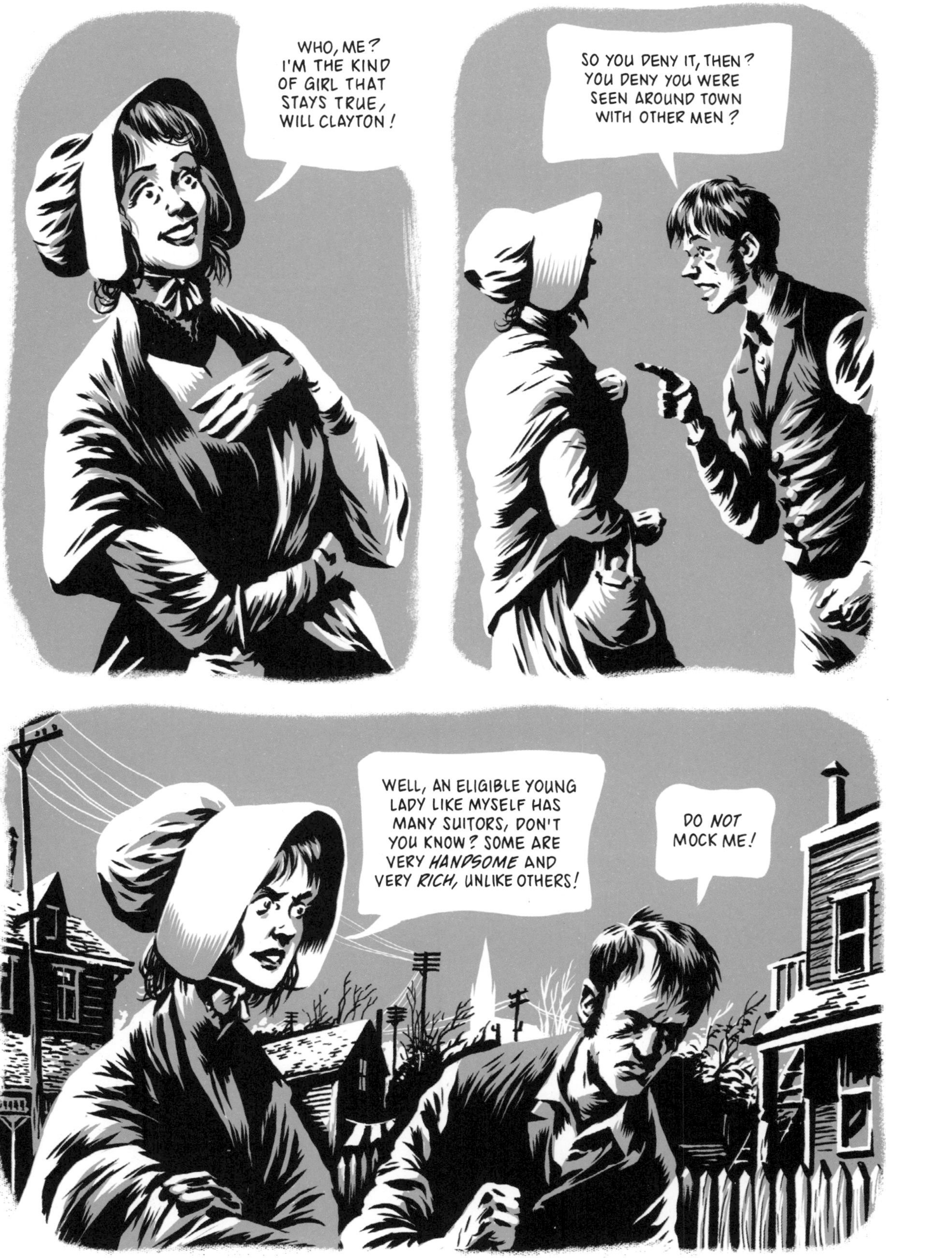
WHO, ME? I'M THE KIND OF GIRL THAT STAYS TRUE, WILL CLAYTON!
SO YOU DENY IT, THEN? YOU DENY YOU WERE SEEN AROUND TOWN WITH OTHER MEN?
WELL, AN ELIGIBLE YOUNG LADY LIKE MYSELF HAS MANY SUITORS, DON'T YOU KNOW? SOME ARE VERY *HANDSOME* AND VERY *RICH,* UNLIKE OTHERS!
DO *NOT* MOCK ME!

DON'T BE SILLY! I'M KIDDING. THERE'S ONLY YOU!

I'M SORRY, IT'S JUST SO HARD SOMETIMES, A GIRL LIKE YOU WITH SOMEONE LIKE ME.

KISS ME. NOW.

NO, I CAN'T! NOT HERE. SOMEONE MIGHT SEE US.

MEET ME BY THE RIVER EARLY TOMORROW MORNING. DO YOU REMEMBER OUR SPOT?

HOW COULD I FORGET? I'LL BE THERE AT DAWN!

I CAN HARDLY WAIT, MY LOVE!

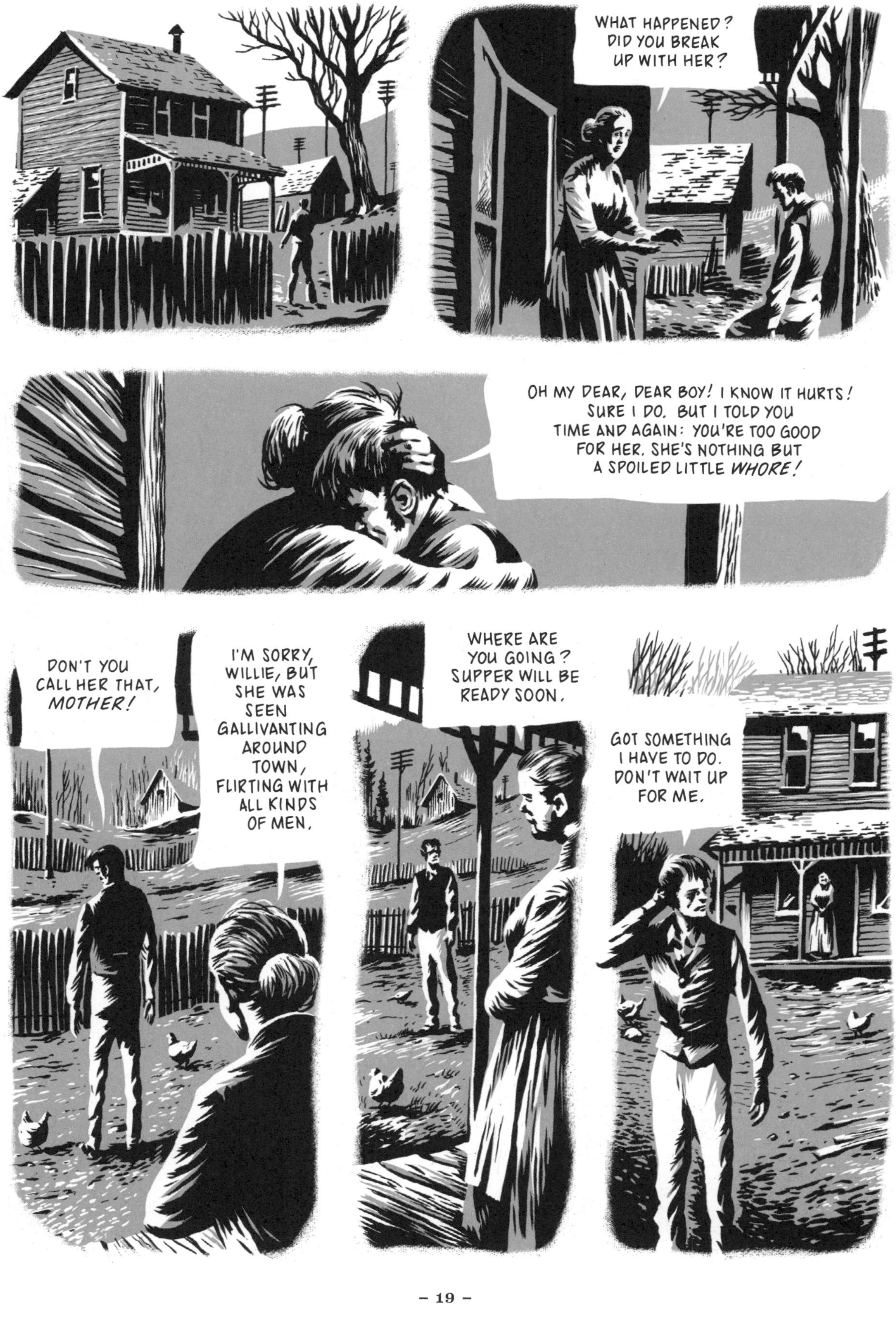
WHAT HAPPENED? DID YOU BREAK UP WITH HER?
OH MY DEAR, DEAR BOY! I KNOW IT HURTS! SURE I DO. BUT I TOLD YOU TIME AND AGAIN: YOU'RE TOO GOOD FOR HER. SHE'S NOTHING BUT A SPOILED LITTLE *WHORE!*
DON'T YOU CALL HER THAT, *MOTHER!*
I'M SORRY, WILLIE, BUT SHE WAS SEEN GALLIVANTING AROUND TOWN, FLIRTING WITH ALL KINDS OF MEN.
WHERE ARE YOU GOING? SUPPER WILL BE READY SOON.
GOT SOMETHING I HAVE TO DO. DON'T WAIT UP FOR ME.

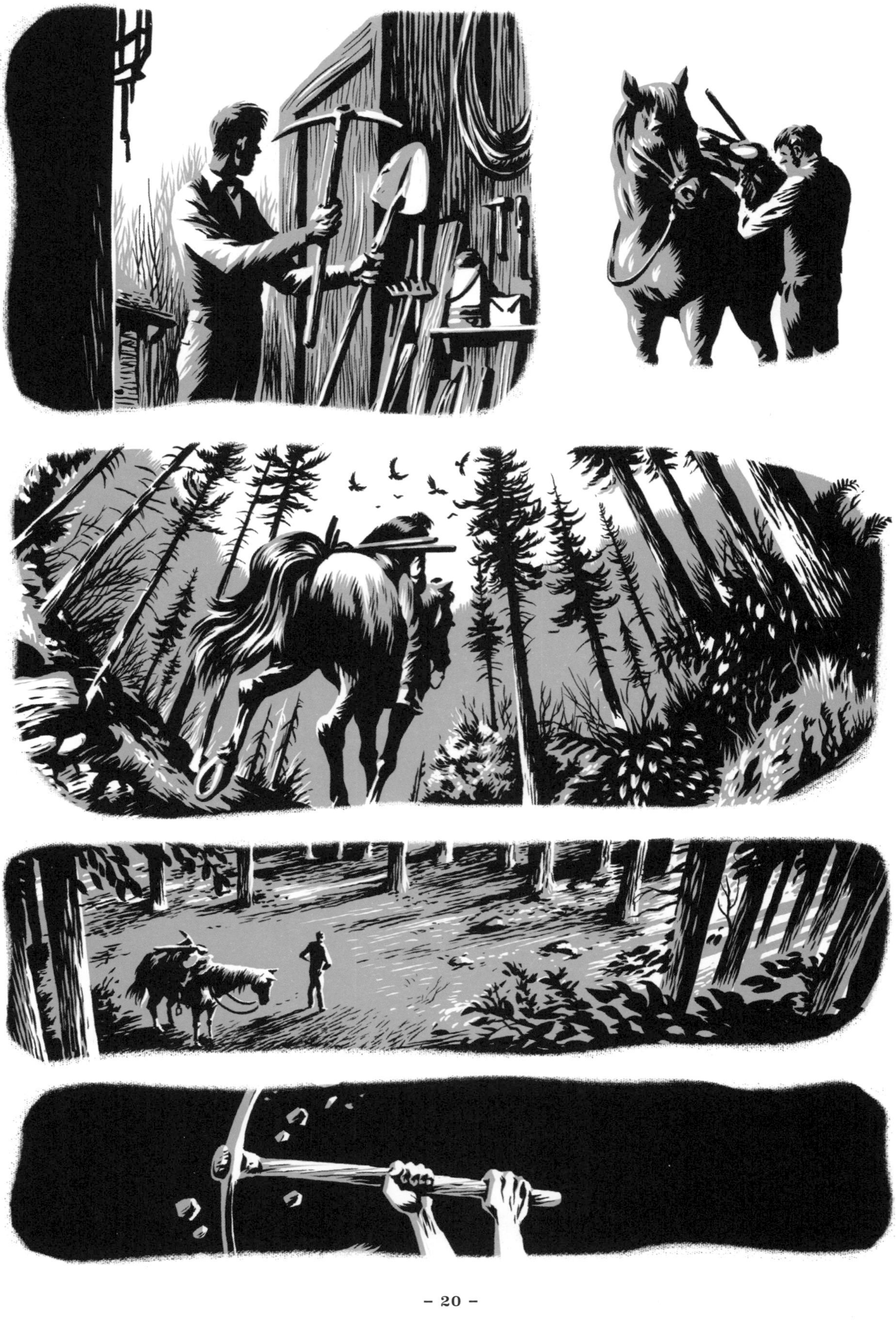

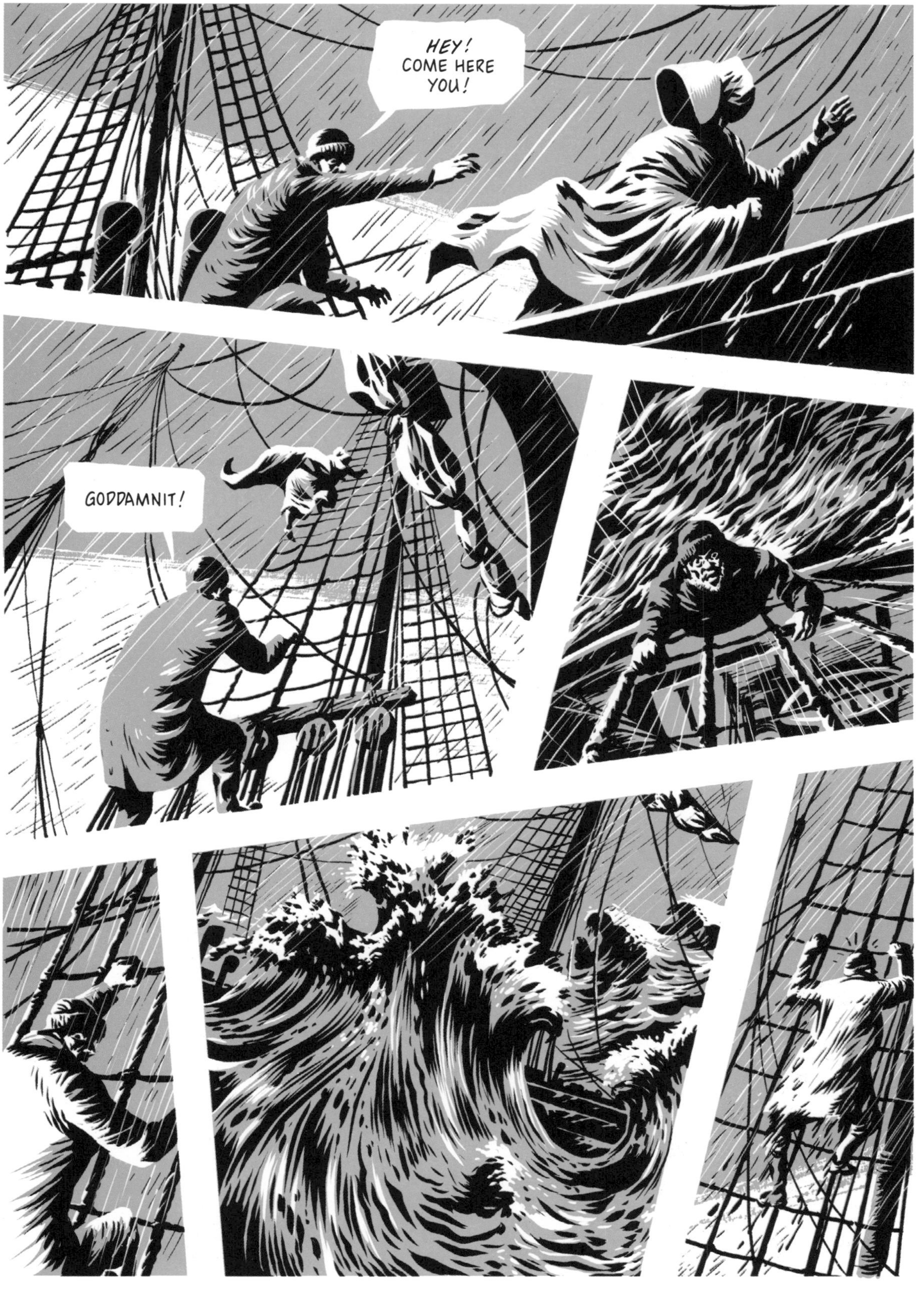
HEY! COME HERE YOU!
GODDAMNIT!

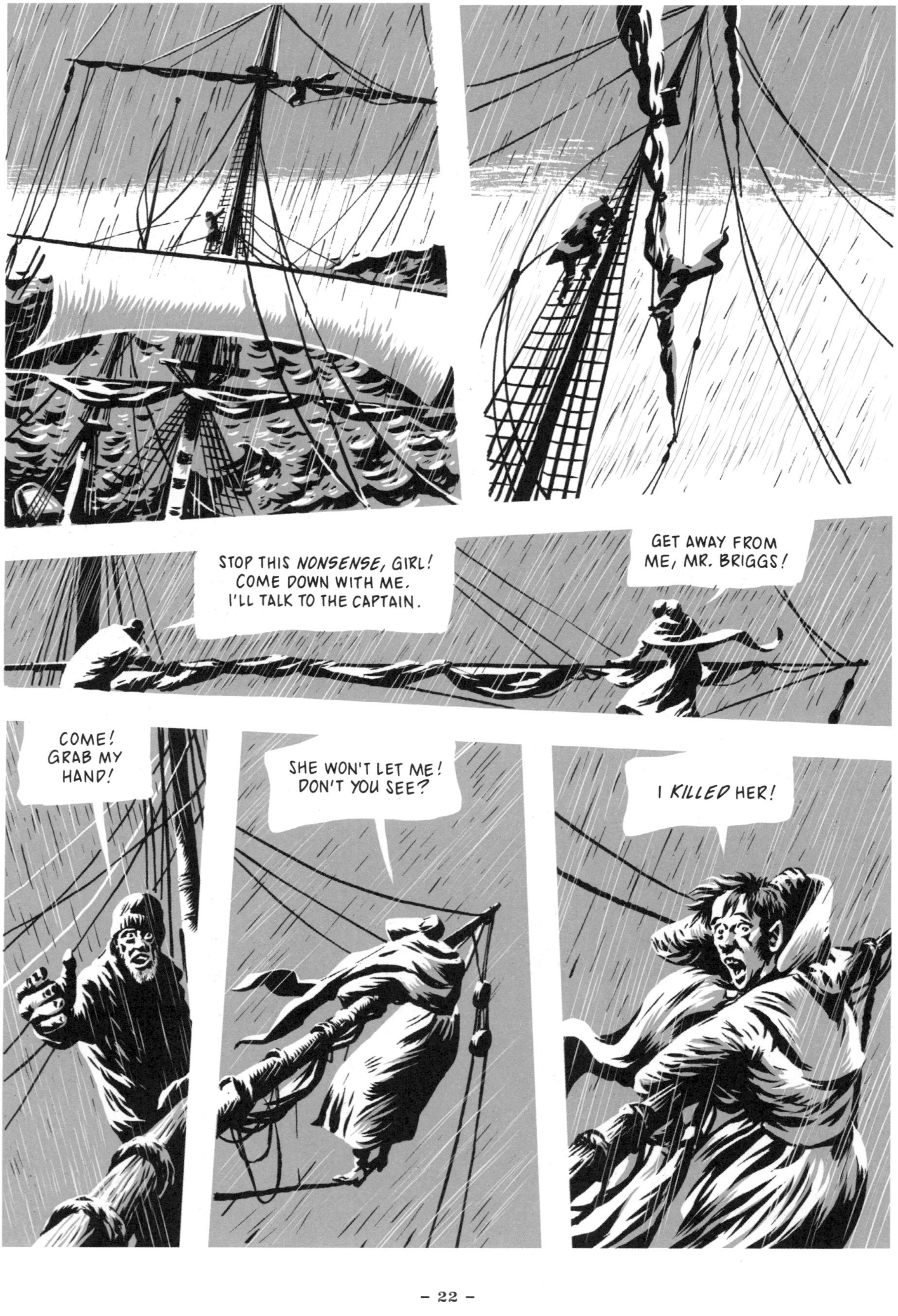
STOP THIS NONSENSE, GIRL! COME DOWN WITH ME. I'LL TALK TO THE CAPTAIN.
GET AWAY FROM ME, MR. BRIGGS!
COME! GRAB MY HAND!
SHE WON'T LET ME! DON'T YOU SEE?
I KILLED HER!

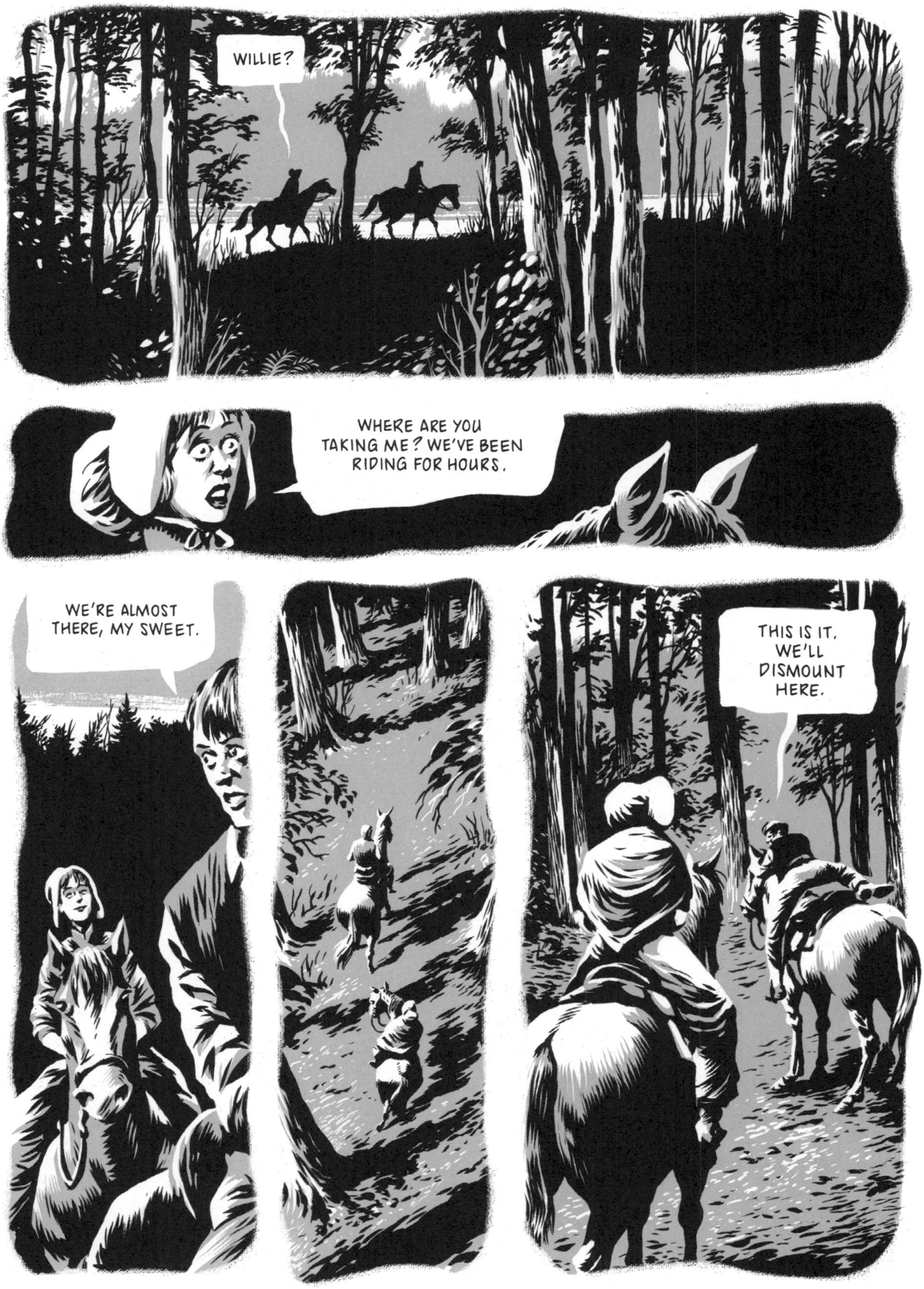
WILLIE?
WHERE ARE YOU TAKING ME? WE'VE BEEN RIDING FOR HOURS.
WE'RE ALMOST THERE, MY SWEET.
THIS IS IT. WE'LL DISMOUNT HERE.

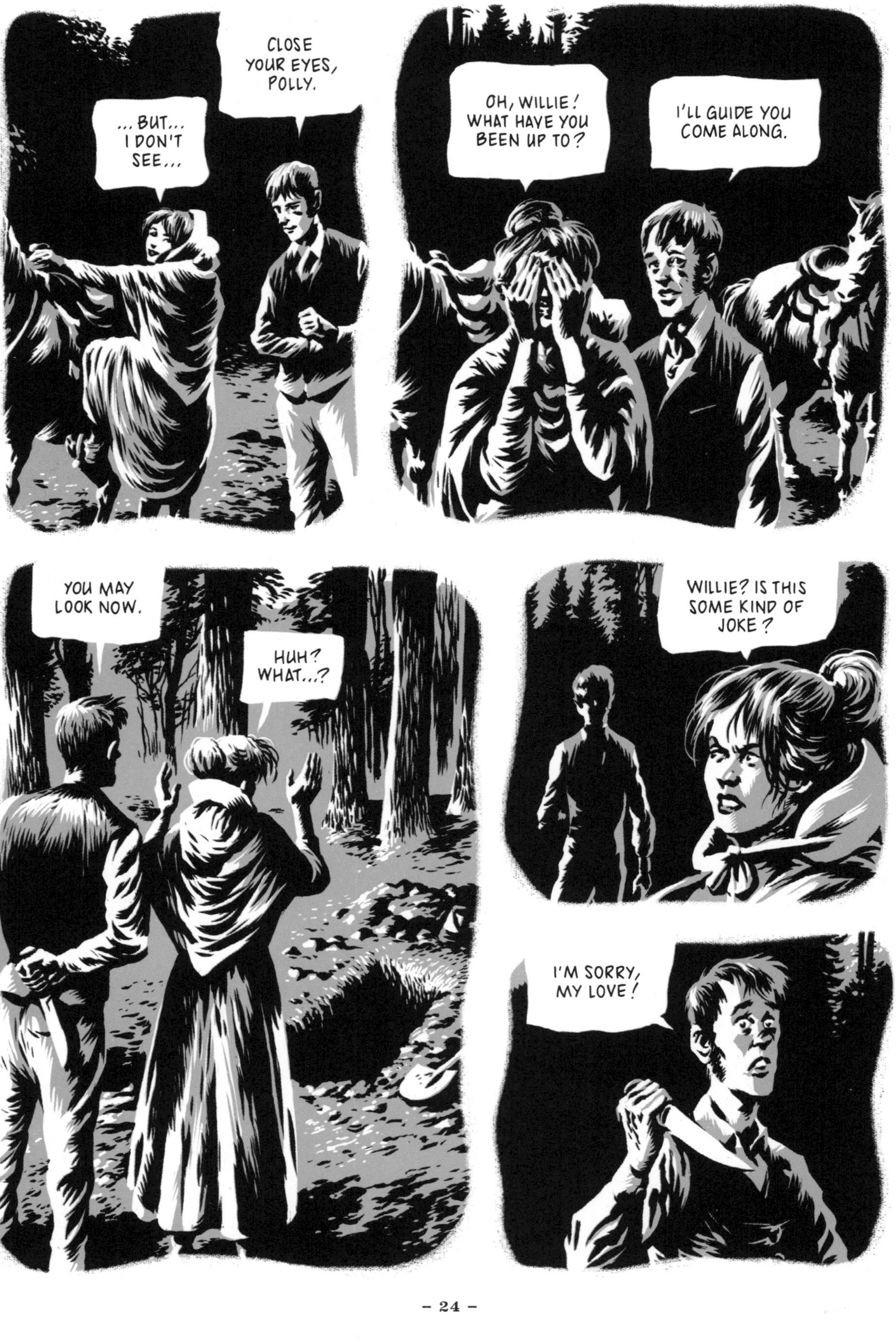
CLOSE YOUR EYES, POLLY.
... BUT... I DON'T SEE...
OH, WILLIE! WHAT HAVE YOU BEEN UP TO?
I'LL GUIDE YOU COME ALONG.
YOU MAY LOOK NOW.
HUH? WHAT...?
WILLIE? IS THIS SOME KIND OF JOKE?
I'M SORRY, MY LOVE!

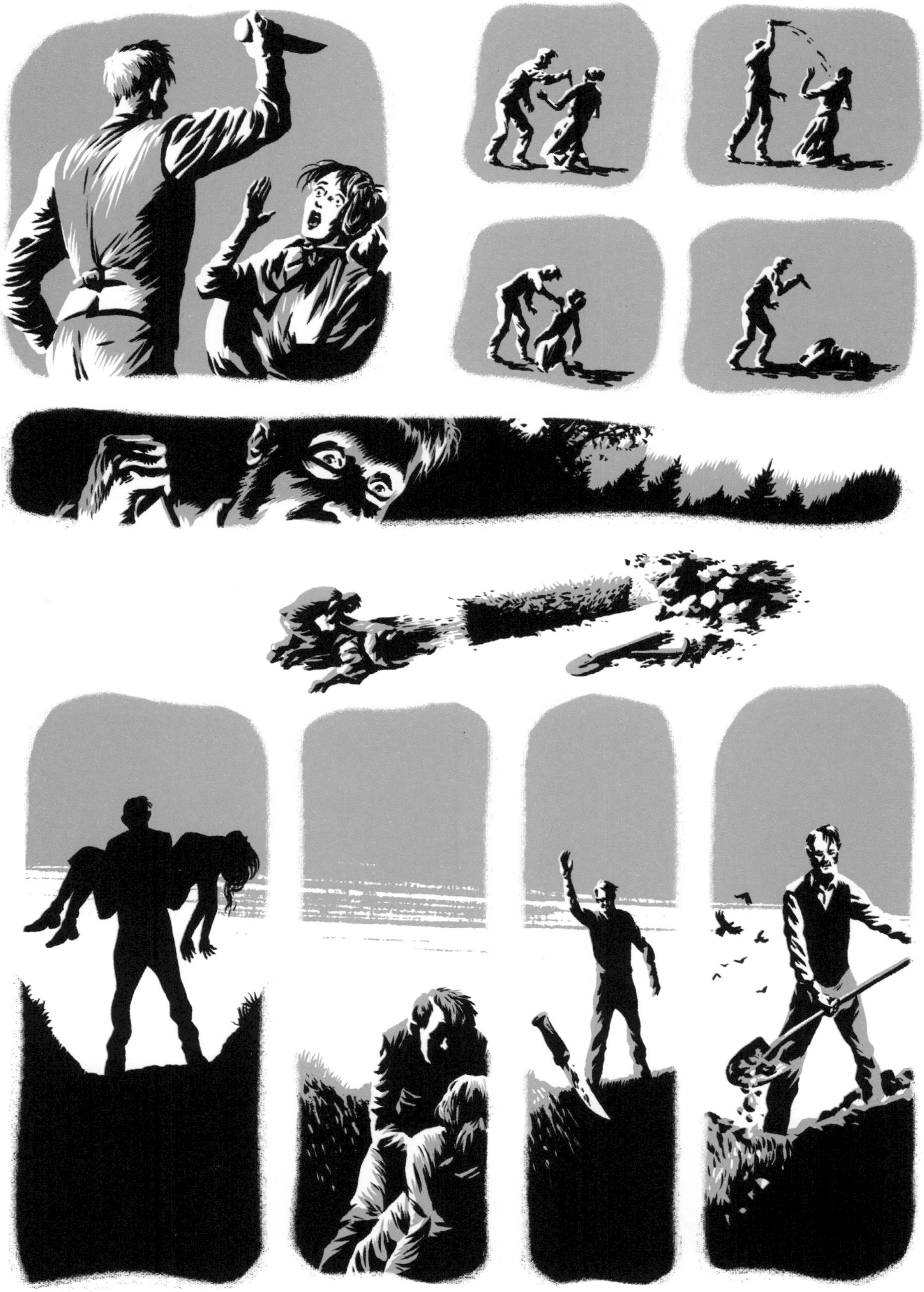

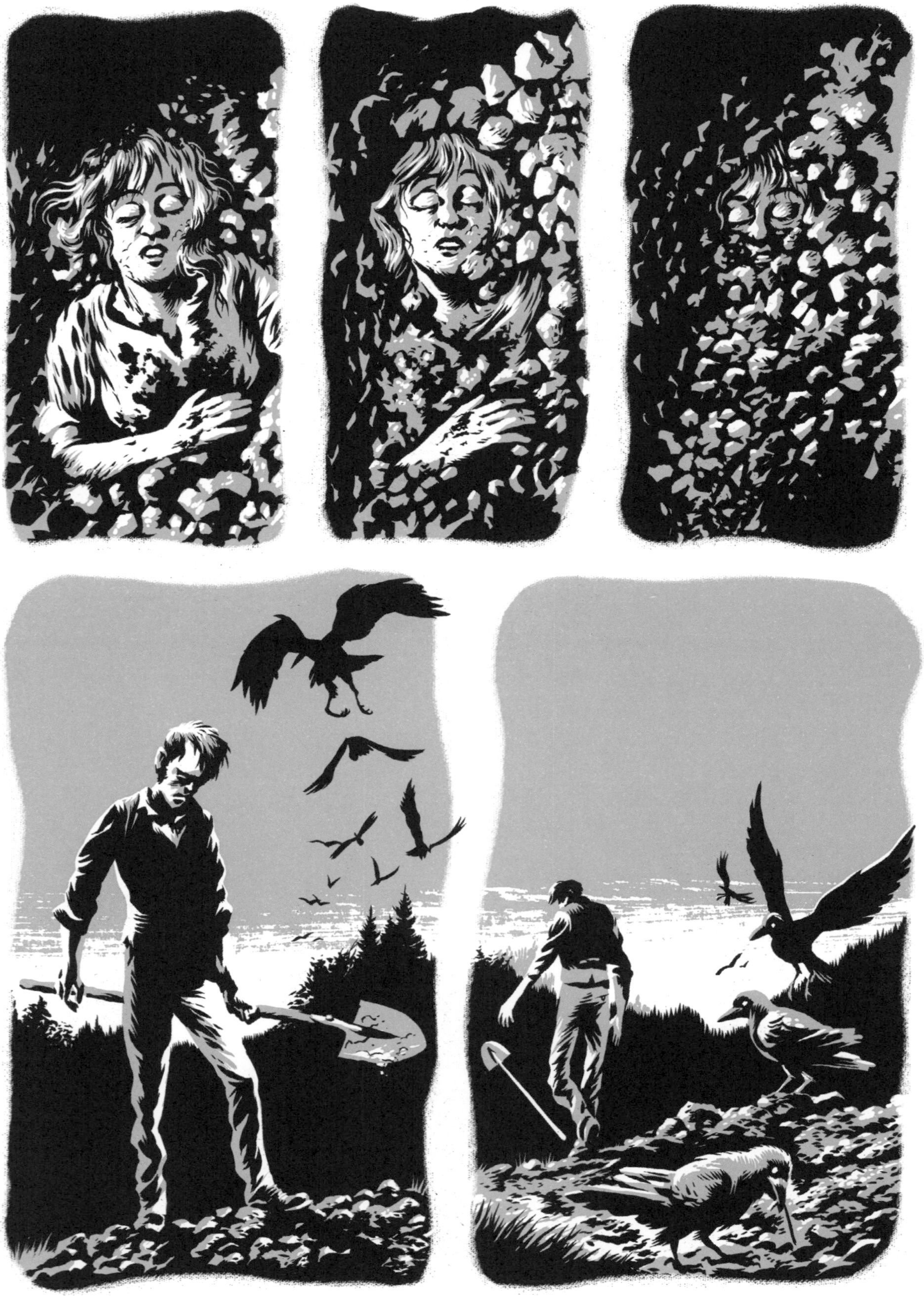

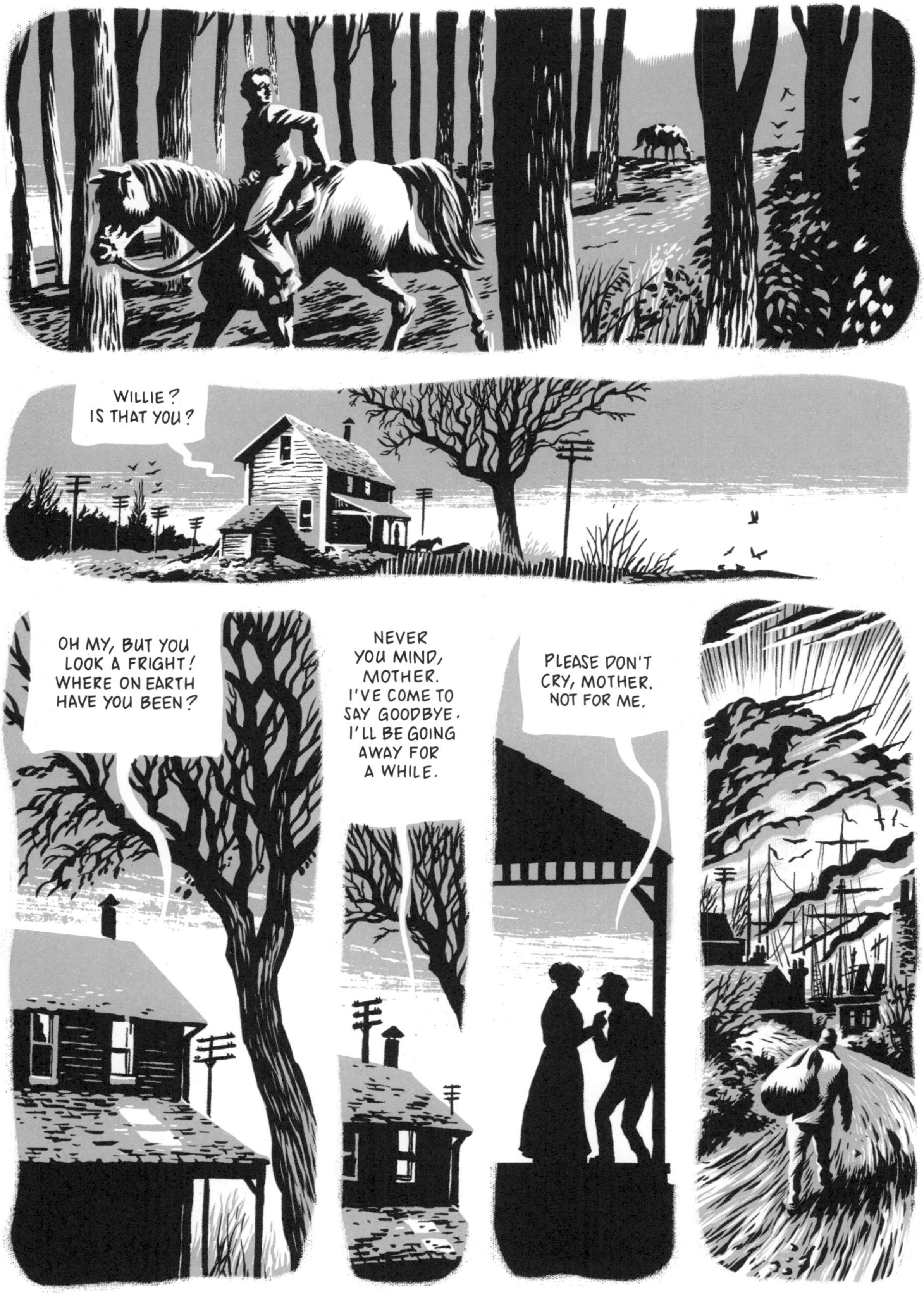
WILLIE? IS THAT YOU?
OH MY, BUT YOU LOOK A FRIGHT! WHERE ON EARTH HAVE YOU BEEN?
NEVER YOU MIND, MOTHER. I'VE COME TO SAY GOODBYE. I'LL BE GOING AWAY FOR A WHILE.
PLEASE DON'T CRY, MOTHER. NOT FOR ME.

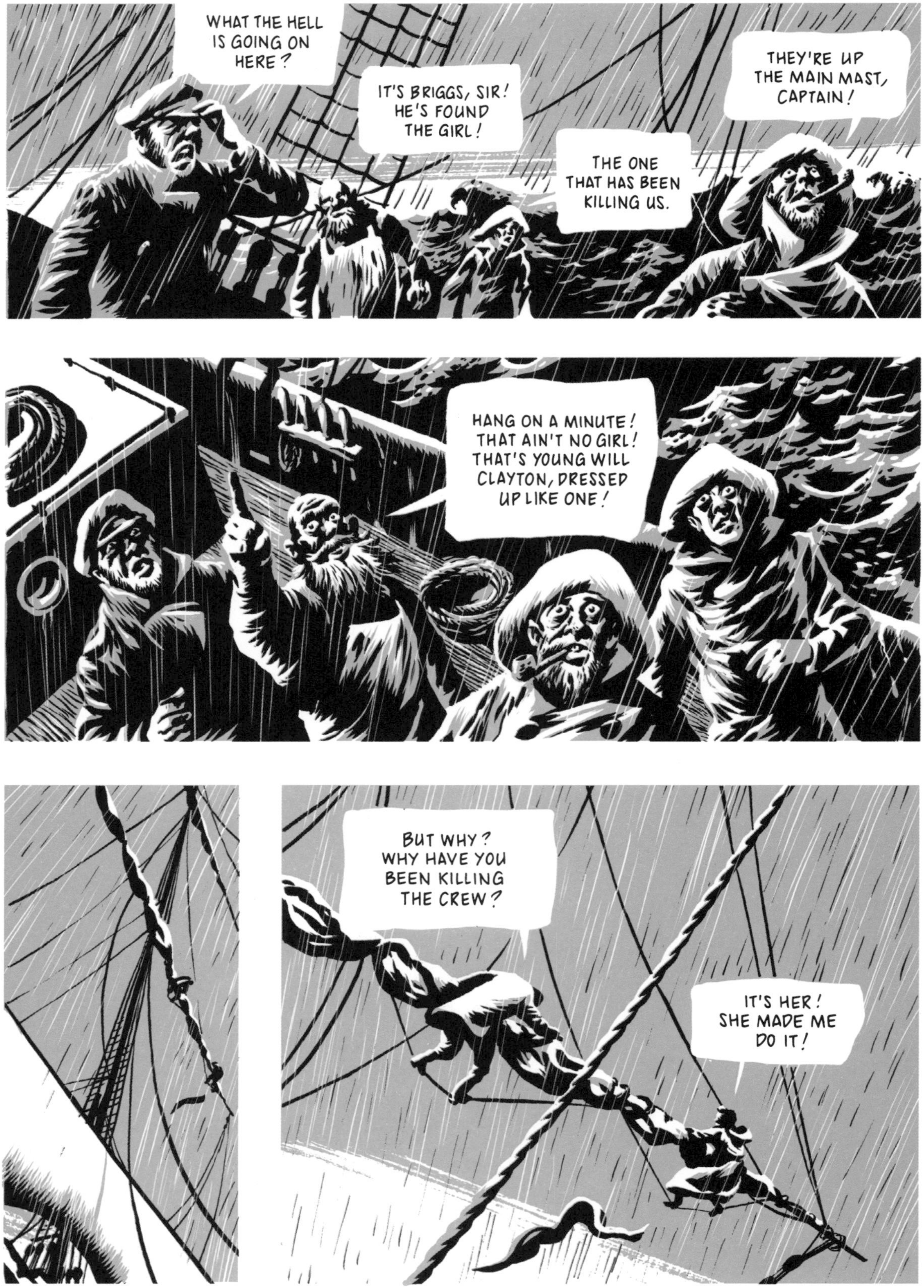
WHAT THE HELL IS GOING ON HERE?
IT'S BRIGGS, SIR! HE'S FOUND THE GIRL!
THE ONE THAT HAS BEEN KILLING US.
THEY'RE UP THE MAIN MAST, CAPTAIN!
HANG ON A MINUTE! THAT AIN'T NO GIRL! THAT'S YOUNG WILL CLAYTON, DRESSED UP LIKE ONE!
BUT WHY? WHY HAVE YOU BEEN KILLING THE CREW?
IT'S HER! SHE MADE ME DO IT!

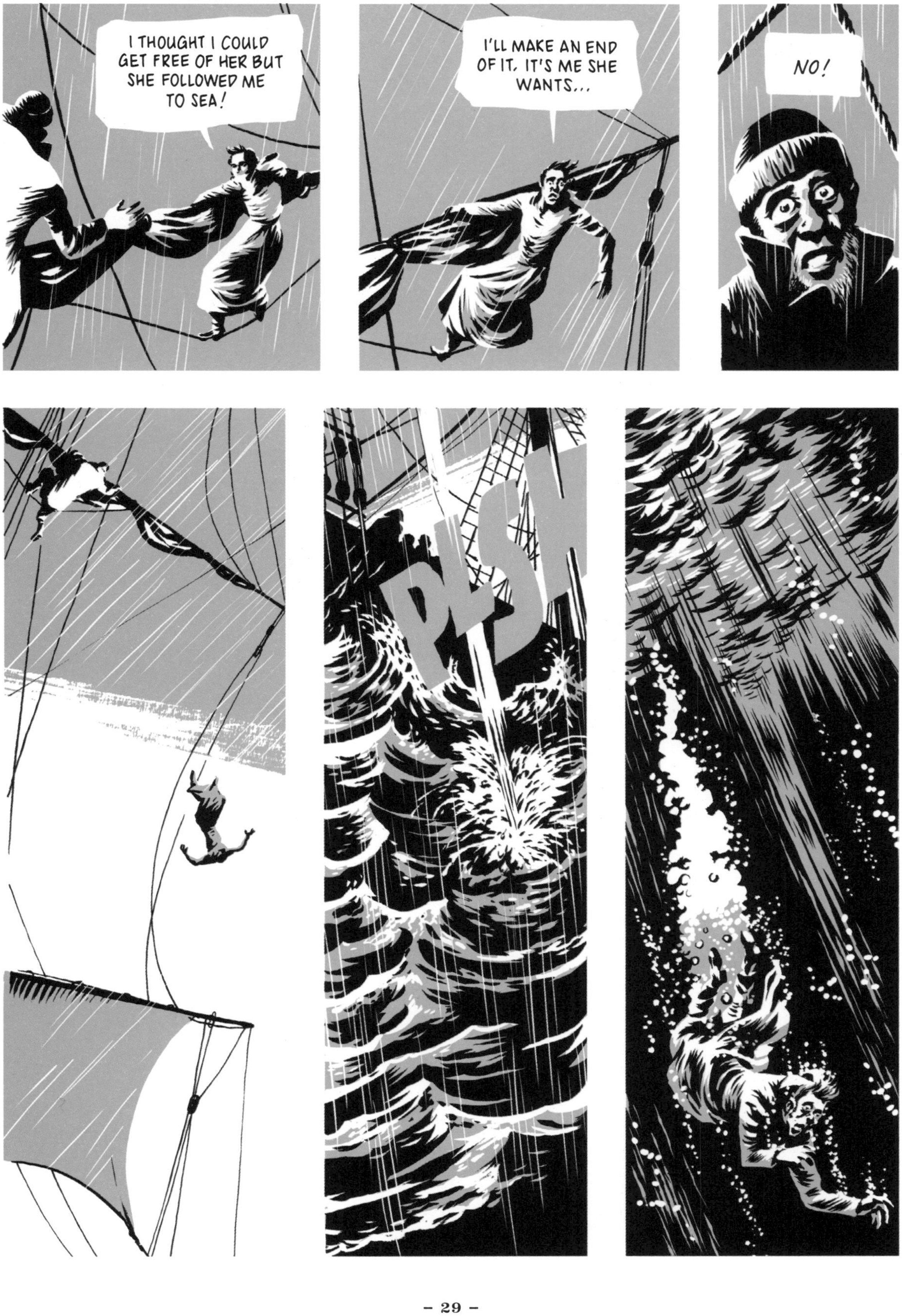
I THOUGHT I COULD GET FREE OF HER BUT SHE FOLLOWED ME TO SEA!
I'LL MAKE AN END OF IT, IT'S ME SHE WANTS...
NO!
PLSH

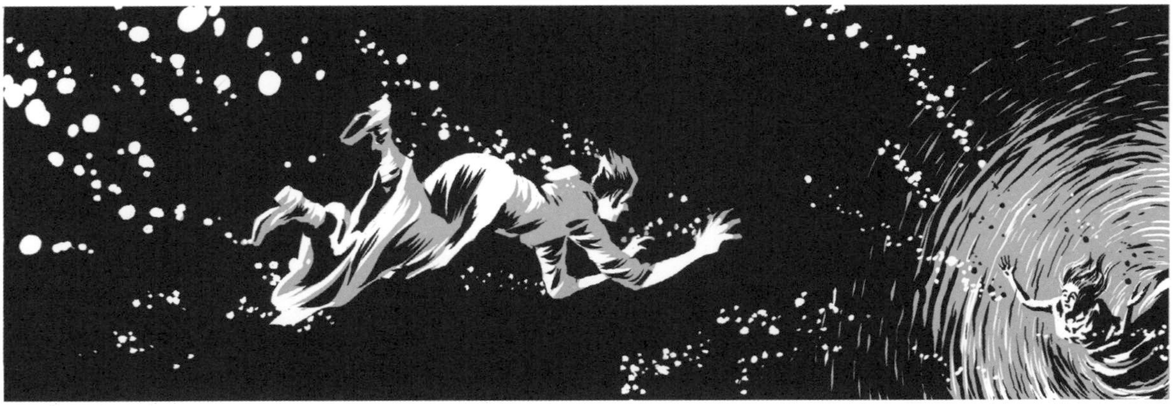

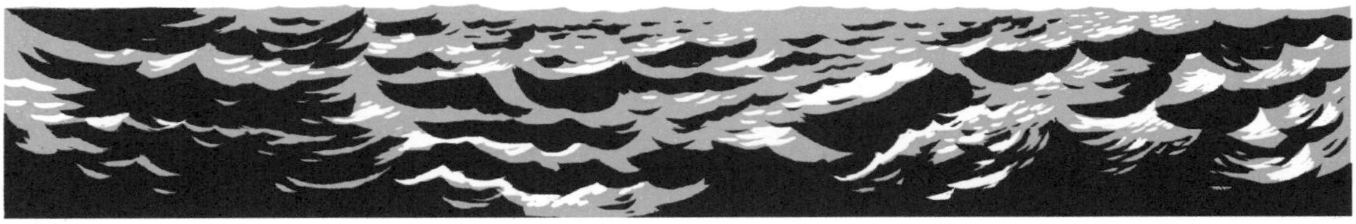

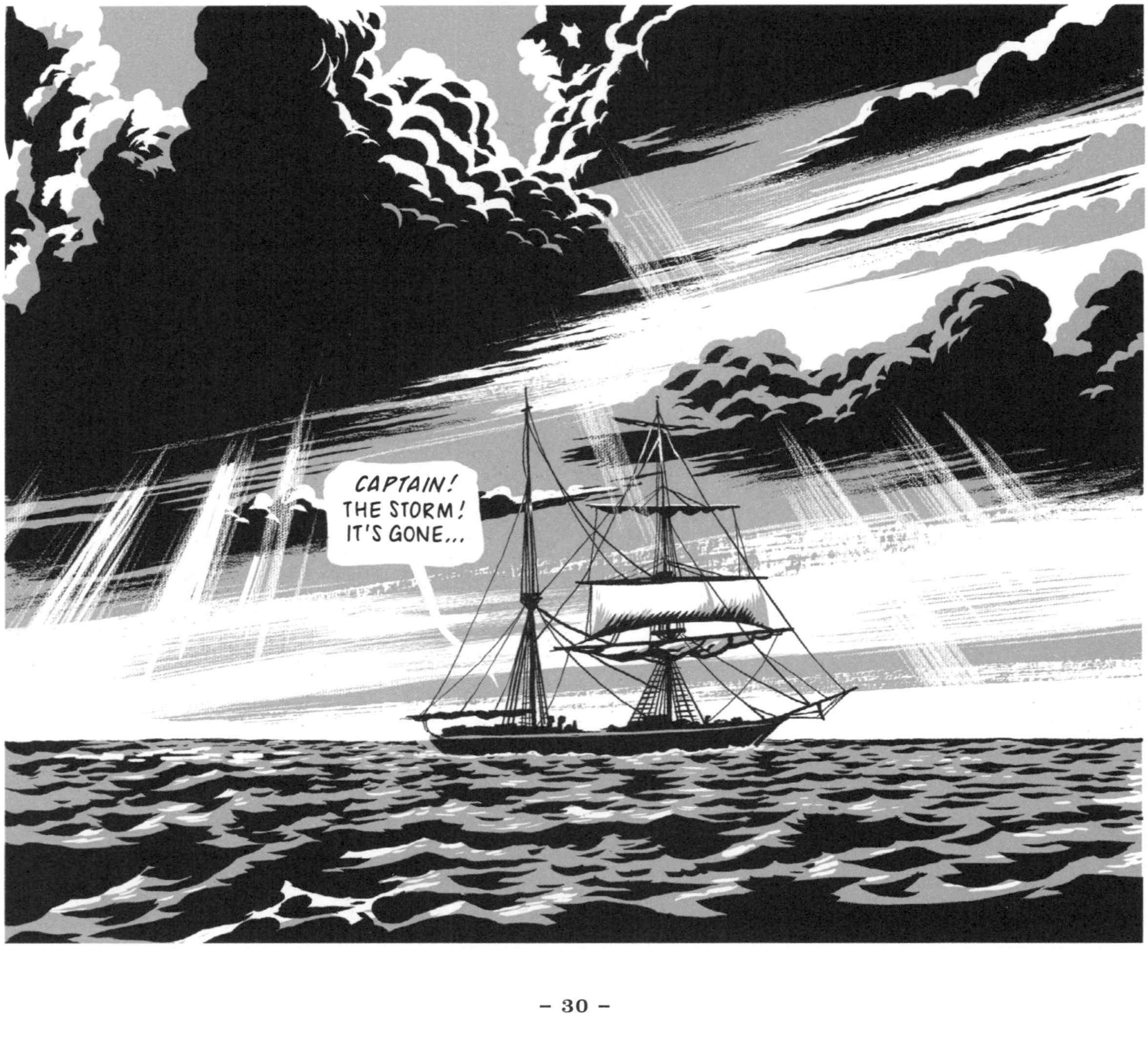
CAPTAIN! THE STORM! IT'S GONE...

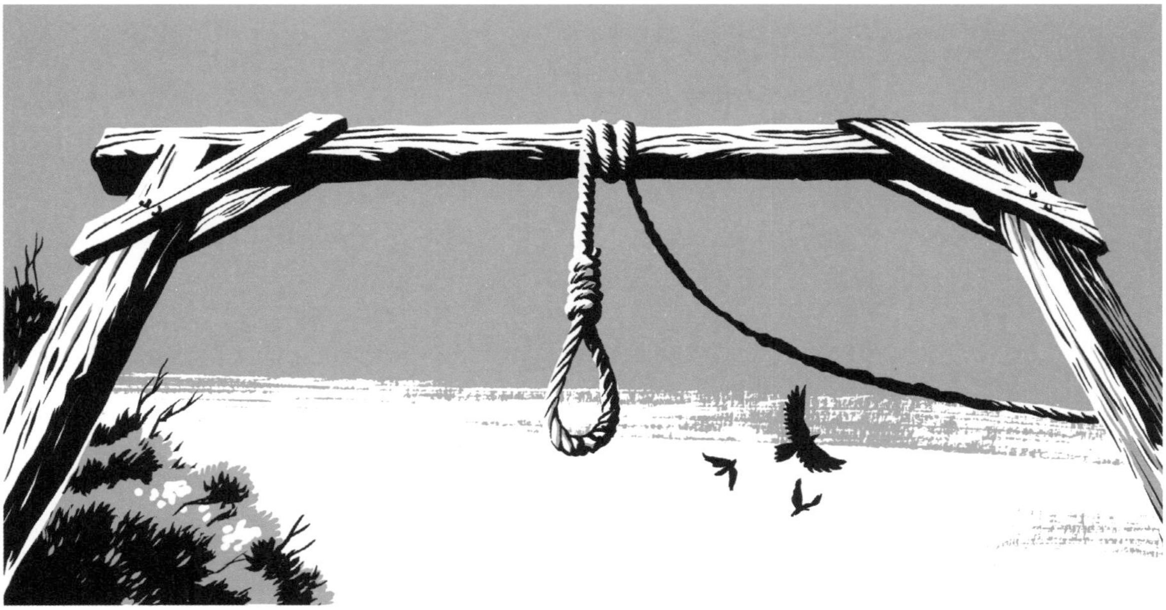

THE LONG BLACK VEIL

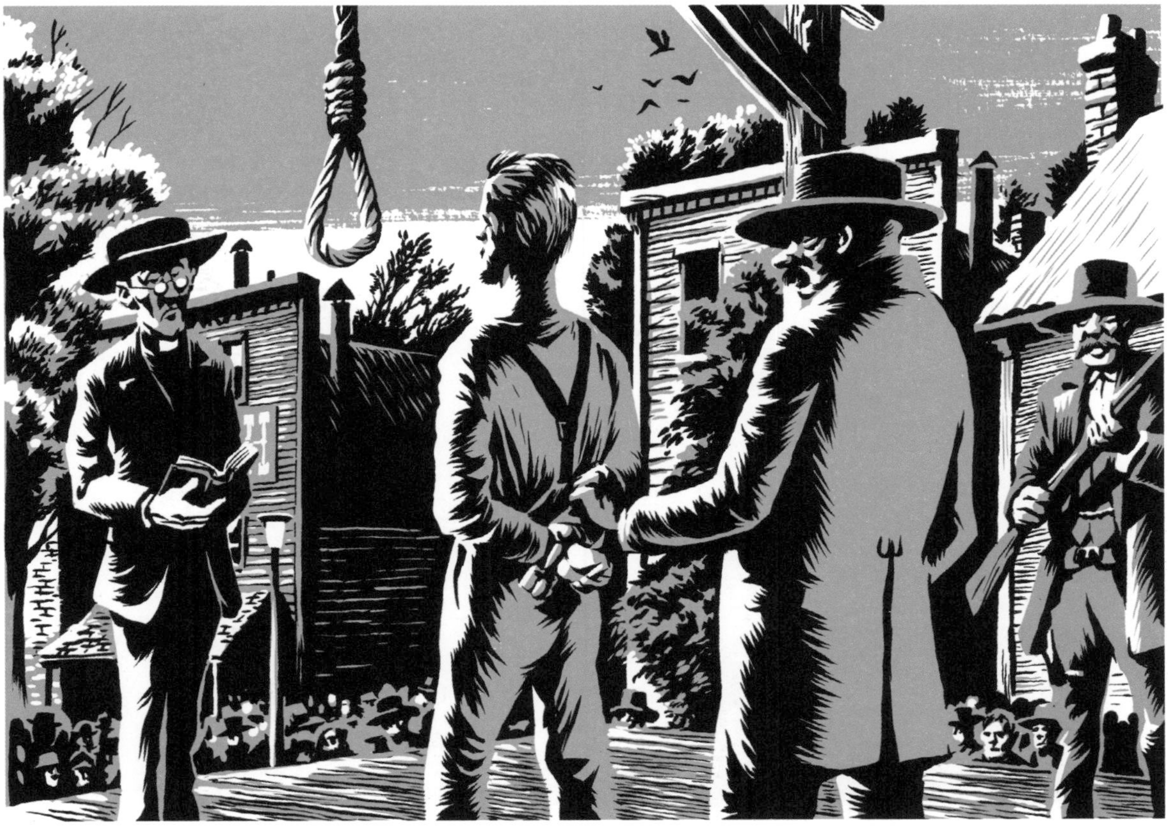

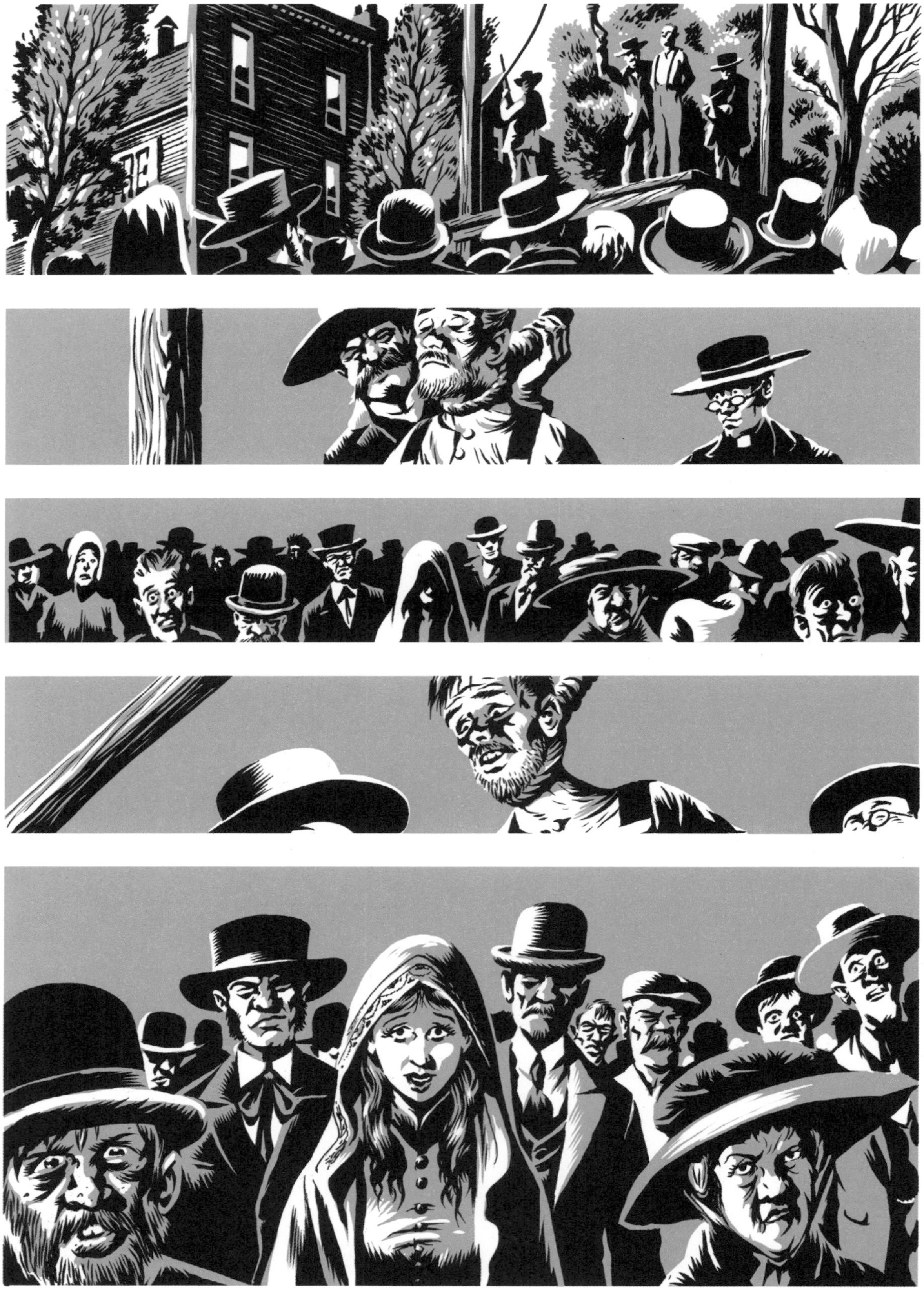
RE

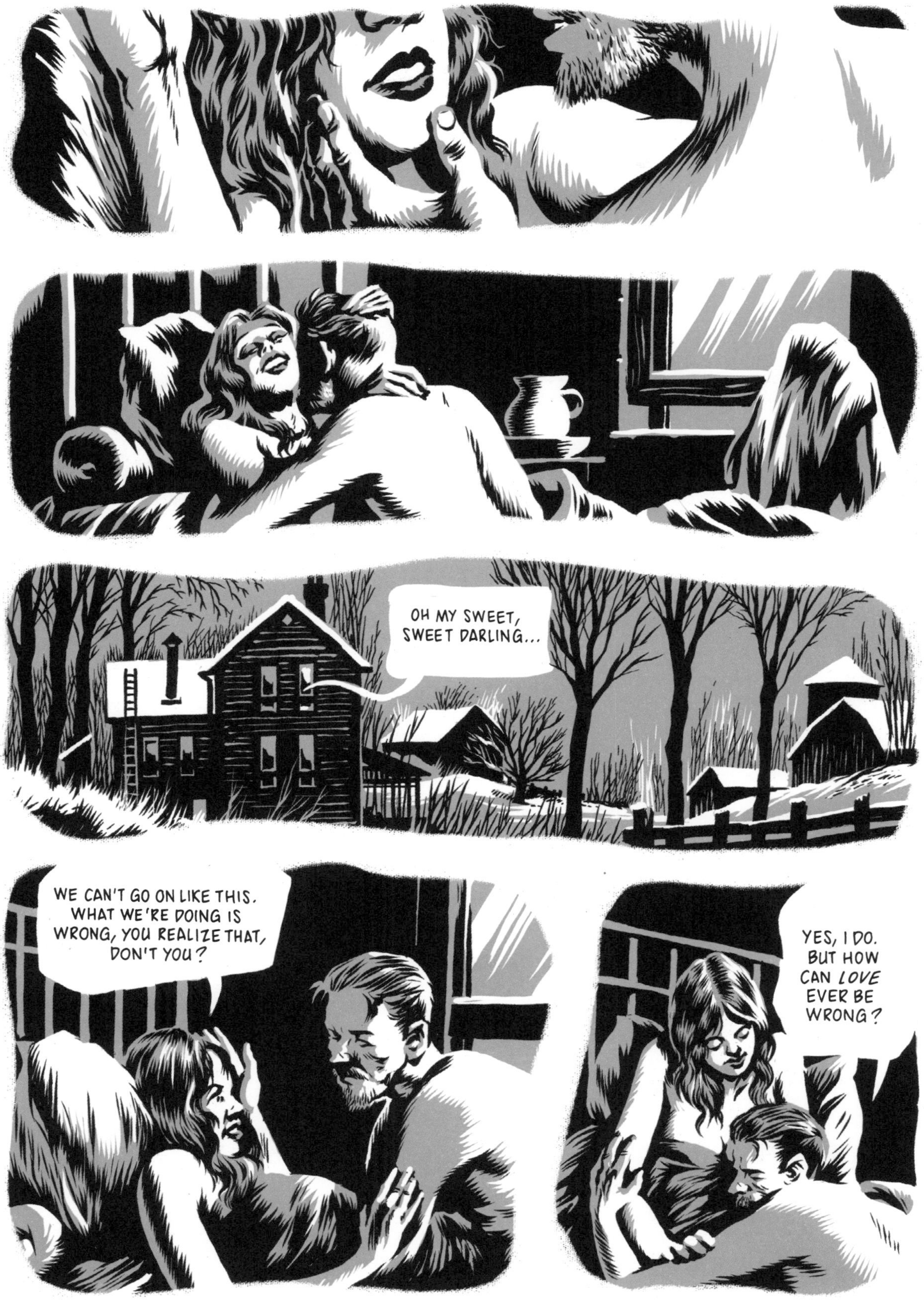
OH MY SWEET,
SWEET DARLING...
WE CAN'T GO ON LIKE THIS. WHAT WE'RE DOING IS WRONG, YOU REALIZE THAT, DON'T YOU?
YES, I DO. BUT HOW CAN *LOVE* EVER BE WRONG?

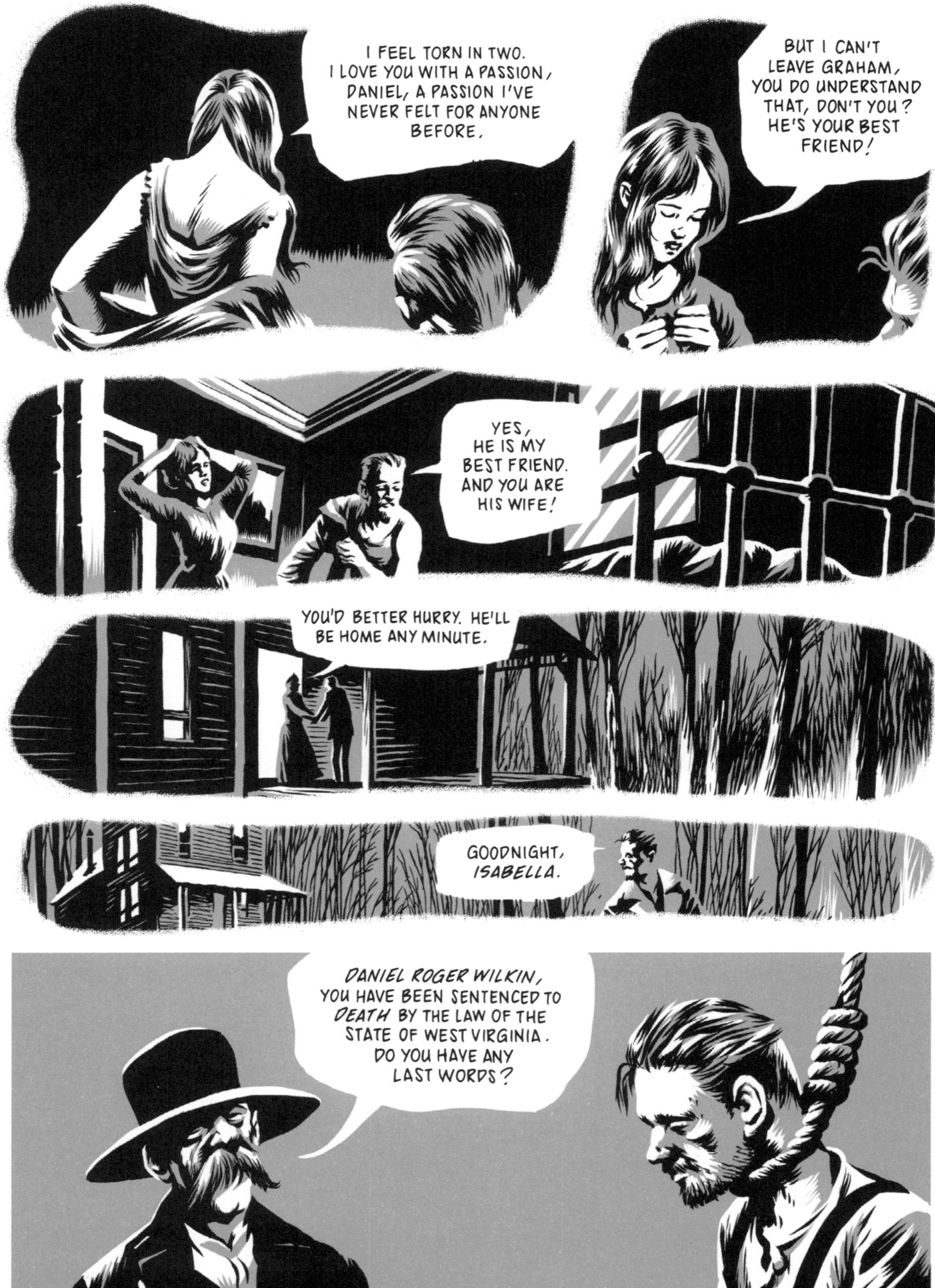
I FEEL TORN IN TWO. I LOVE YOU WITH A PASSION, DANIEL, A PASSION I'VE NEVER FELT FOR ANYONE BEFORE.
BUT I CAN'T LEAVE GRAHAM, YOU DO UNDERSTAND THAT, DON'T YOU? HE'S YOUR BEST FRIEND!
YES, HE IS MY BEST FRIEND. AND YOU ARE HIS WIFE!
YOU'D BETTER HURRY. HE'LL BE HOME ANY MINUTE.
GOODNIGHT, *ISABELLA*.
DANIEL ROGER WILKIN, YOU HAVE BEEN SENTENCED TO *DEATH* BY THE LAW OF THE STATE OF WEST VIRGINIA. DO YOU HAVE ANY LAST WORDS?

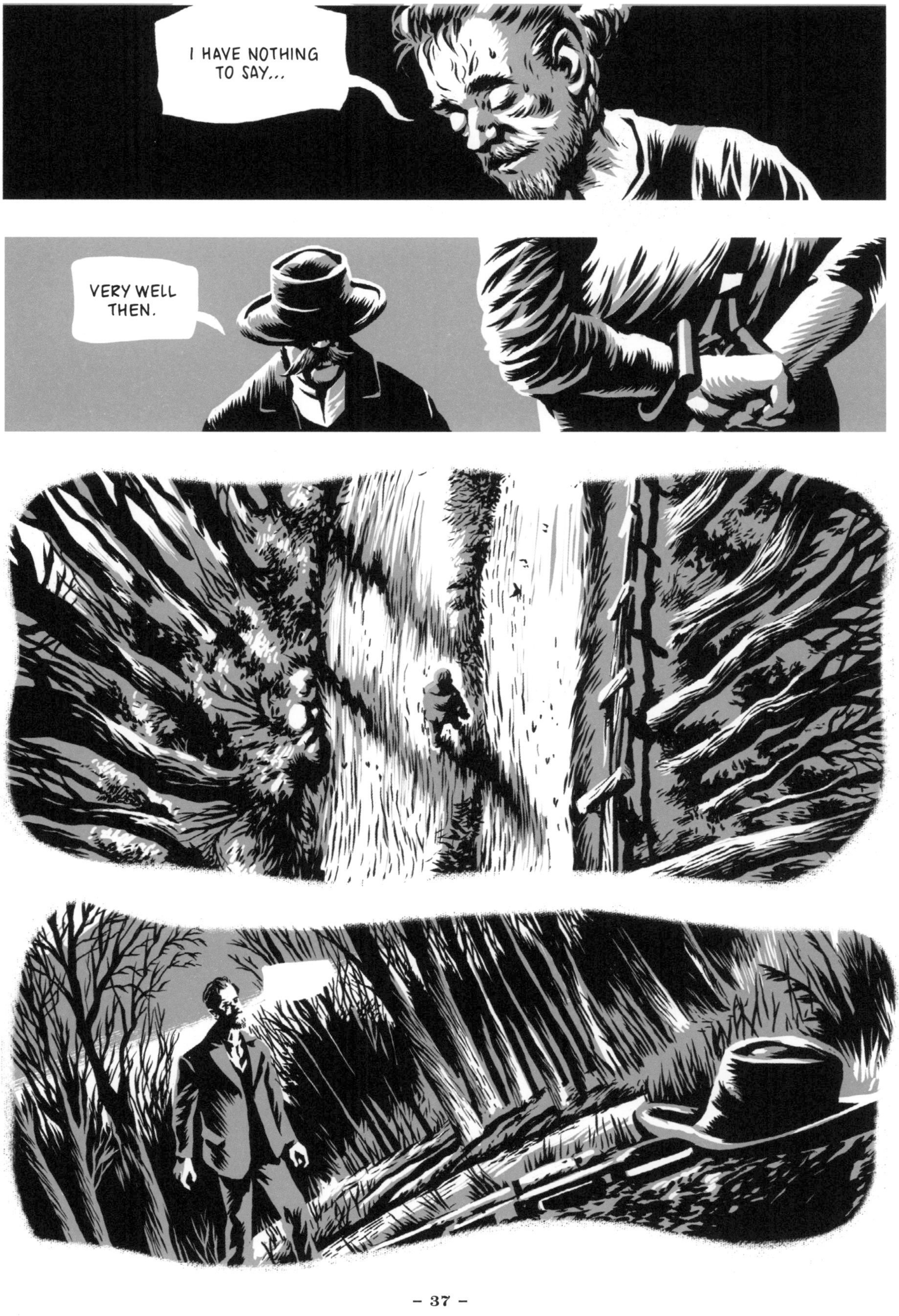
I HAVE NOTHING TO SAY...
VERY WELL THEN.

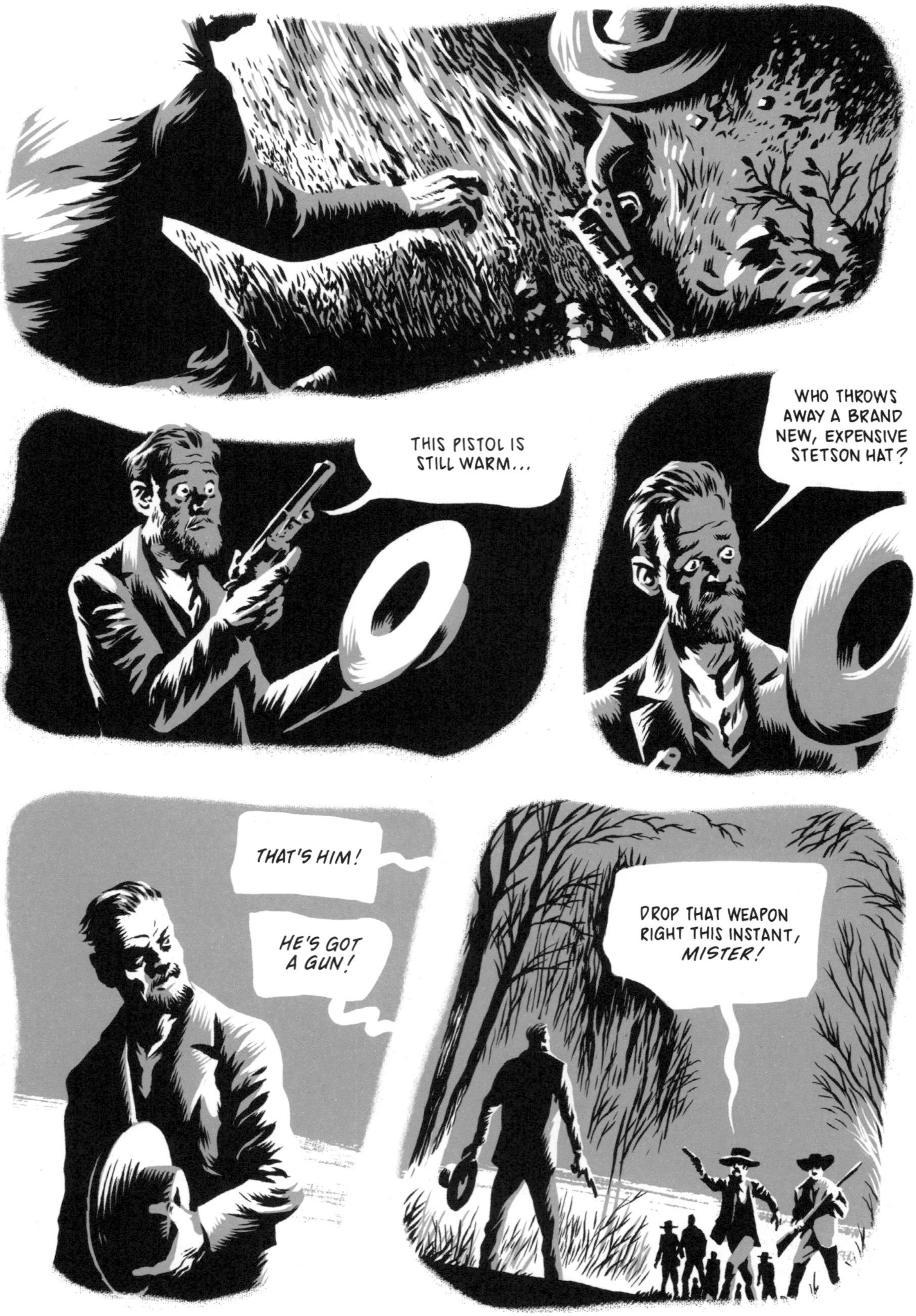
THIS PISTOL IS STILL WARM...
WHO THROWS AWAY A BRAND NEW, EXPENSIVE STETSON HAT?
THAT'S HIM!
HE'S GOT A GUN!
DROP THAT WEAPON RIGHT THIS INSTANT, MISTER!

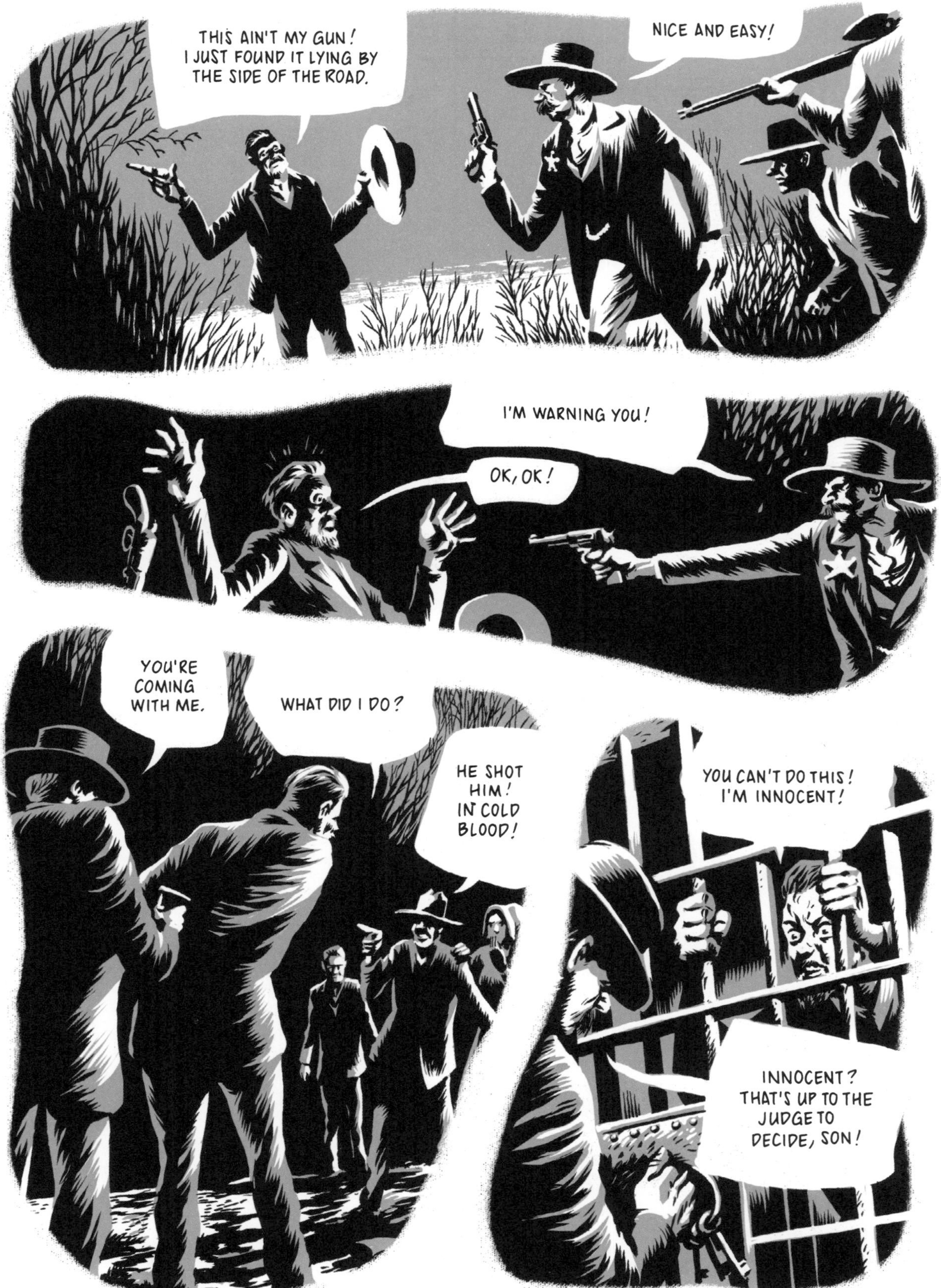
THIS AIN'T MY GUN! I JUST FOUND IT LYING BY THE SIDE OF THE ROAD.
NICE AND EASY!
I'M WARNING YOU!
OK, OK!
YOU'RE COMING WITH ME.
WHAT DID I DO?
HE SHOT HIM! IN COLD BLOOD!
YOU CAN'T DO THIS! I'M INNOCENT!
INNOCENT? THAT'S UP TO THE JUDGE TO DECIDE, SON!

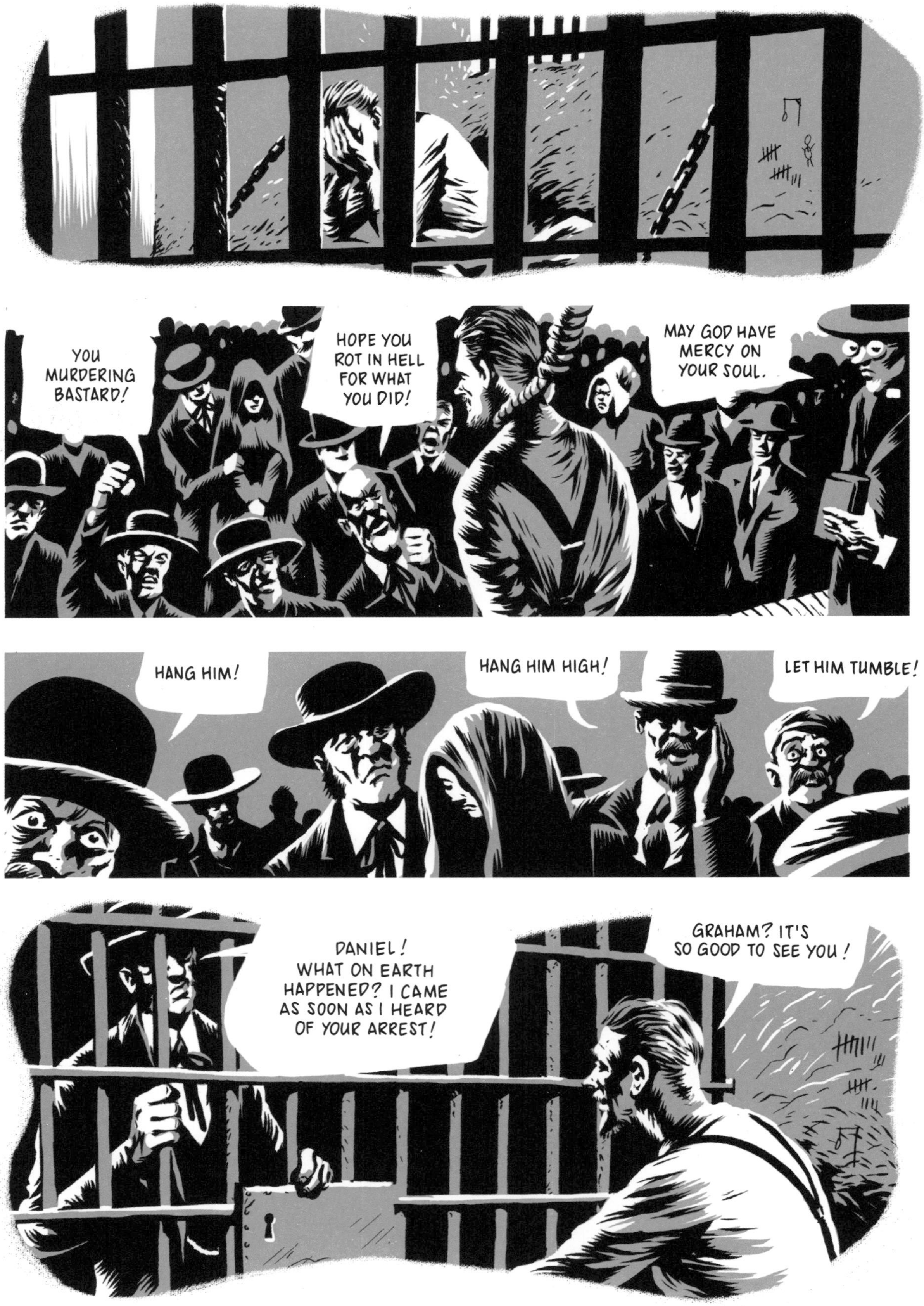
YOU MURDERING BASTARD!
HOPE YOU ROT IN HELL FOR WHAT YOU DID!
MAY GOD HAVE MERCY ON YOUR SOUL.
HANG HIM!
HANG HIM HIGH!
LET HIM TUMBLE!
DANIEL! WHAT ON EARTH HAPPENED? I CAME AS SOON AS I HEARD OF YOUR ARREST!
GRAHAM? IT'S SO GOOD TO SEE YOU!

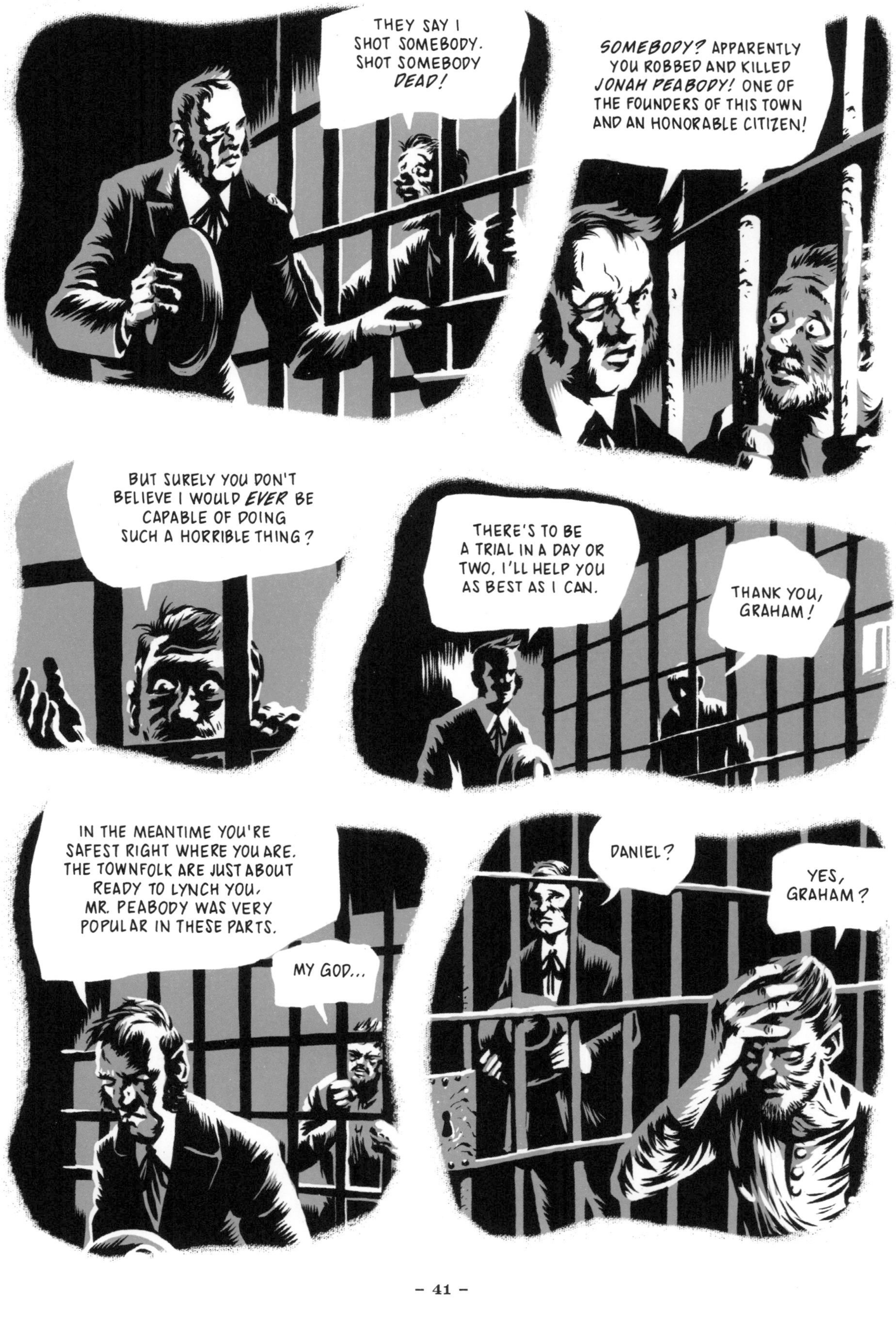
THEY SAY I SHOT SOMEBODY. SHOT SOMEBODY *DEAD!*
SOMEBODY? APPARENTLY YOU ROBBED AND KILLED *JONAH PEABODY!* ONE OF THE FOUNDERS OF THIS TOWN AND AN HONORABLE CITIZEN!
BUT SURELY YOU DON'T BELIEVE I WOULD *EVER* BE CAPABLE OF DOING SUCH A HORRIBLE THING?
THERE'S TO BE A TRIAL IN A DAY OR TWO. I'LL HELP YOU AS BEST AS I CAN.
THANK YOU, GRAHAM!
IN THE MEANTIME YOU'RE SAFEST RIGHT WHERE YOU ARE. THE TOWNFOLK ARE JUST ABOUT READY TO LYNCH YOU. MR. PEABODY WAS VERY POPULAR IN THESE PARTS.
MY GOD...
DANIEL?
YES, GRAHAM?

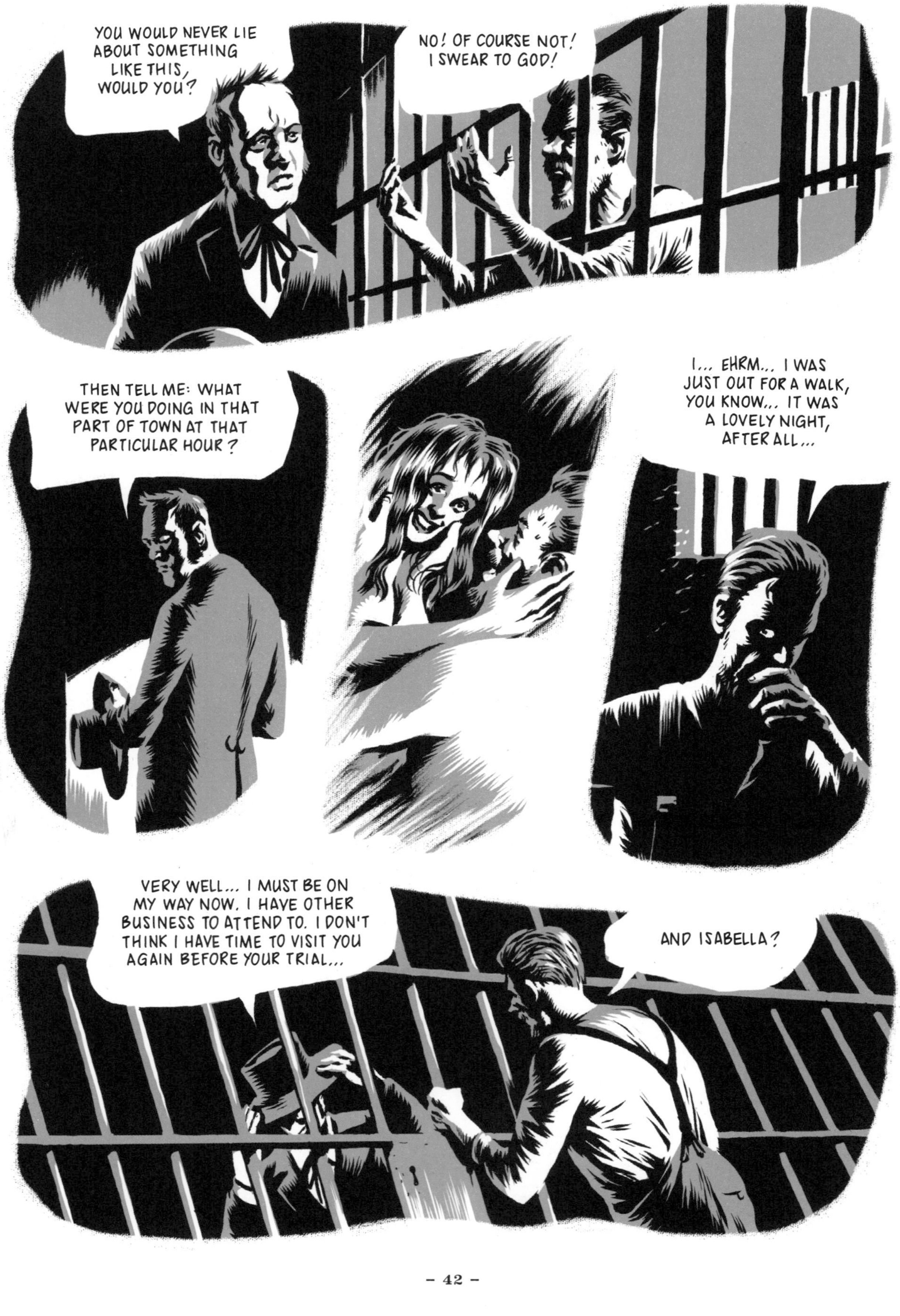
YOU WOULD NEVER LIE ABOUT SOMETHING LIKE THIS, WOULD YOU?
NO! OF COURSE NOT! I SWEAR TO GOD!
THEN TELL ME: WHAT WERE YOU DOING IN THAT PART OF TOWN AT THAT PARTICULAR HOUR?
I... EHRM... I WAS JUST OUT FOR A WALK, YOU KNOW... IT WAS A LOVELY NIGHT, AFTER ALL...
VERY WELL... I MUST BE ON MY WAY NOW. I HAVE OTHER BUSINESS TO ATTEND TO. I DON'T THINK I HAVE TIME TO VISIT YOU AGAIN BEFORE YOUR TRIAL...
AND ISABELLA?

WHAT ABOUT ISABELLA?
I... HM... I MEAN... HOW IS SHE? WILL YOU GIVE HER MY REGARDS?
SHE WAS DEVASTATED WHEN SHE HEARD YOU WERE IN HERE. SHE'S ALWAYS BEEN VERY FOND OF YOU, YOU KNOW. I'LL MAKE SURE TO GIVE HER YOUR REGARDS. GOODNIGHT, DANIEL.
GOODNIGHT, GRAHAM. AND THANK YOU.

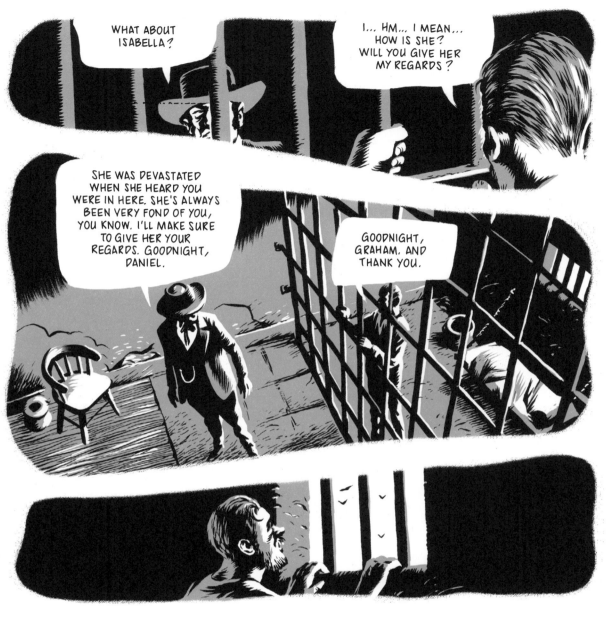

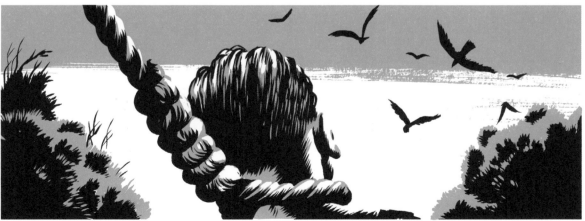

LOOK, SON, I'VE GOT SEVEN WITNESSES THAT HAVE TESTIFIED THEY SAW YOU SHOOT AND KILL MR. PEABODY.

THEY LATER RECOGNIZED YOUR BLACK STETSON HAT AND THE COLT NAVY PISTOL FOUND ON YOUR PERSON THAT EVENING.

YOU CLAIM THAT YOU WERE SOMEWHERE ELSE WHEN THE KILLING TOOK PLACE. CAN YOU PRODUCE AN ALIBI?

NO, YOUR HONOR. AS I HAVE STATED BEFORE, I WAS JUST OUT FOR A STROLL.

'OUT FOR A STROLL'. ARE YOU QUITE SURE THAT IS ALL YOU WANT TO TELL THE COURT?
YES, YOUR HONOR. I MEAN: NO, YOUR HONOR, I'M *INNOCENT!*
VERY WELL THEN. HAS THE JURY REACHED A VERDICT?
YES, YOUR HONOR. WE FIND THE DEFENDANT *GUILTY.*
THANK YOU, MEMBERS OF THE JURY. *DANIEL ROGER WILKIN,* YOU HAVE BEEN FOUND GUILTY OF COLD-BLOODED MURDER. I HEREBY SENTENCE YOU TO DEATH BY HANGING, THREE DAYS FROM NOW.
THE DEFENDANT WILL BE TAKEN BACK TO HIS CELL TO AWAIT HIS EXECUTION. THIS COURT IS ADJOURNED!
JUSTICE HAS BEEN DONE!
KILLER!

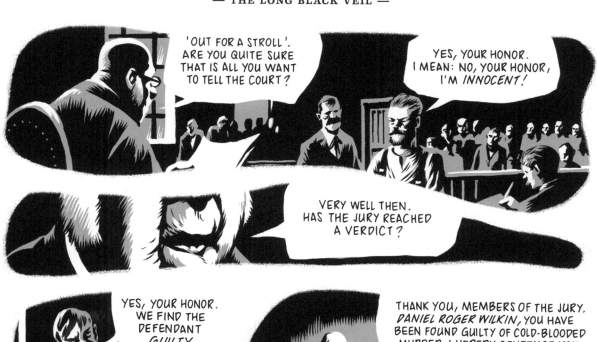

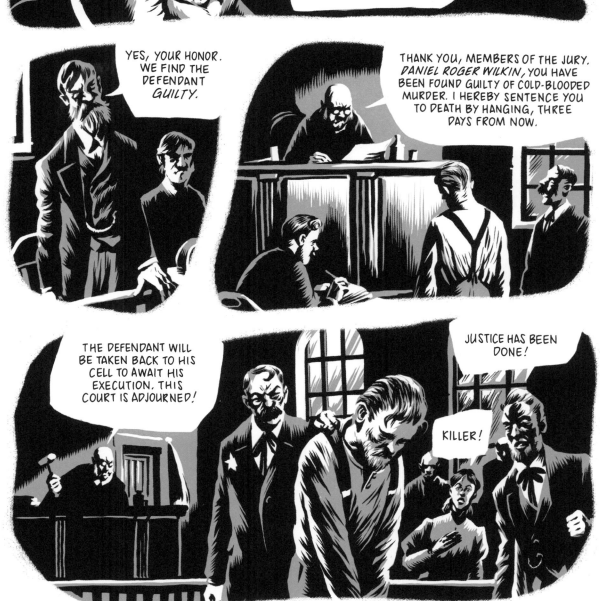

KRK

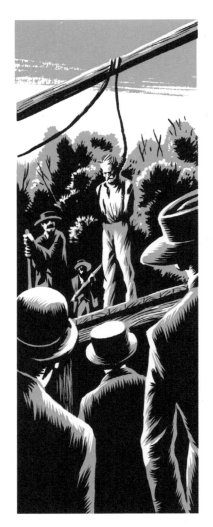

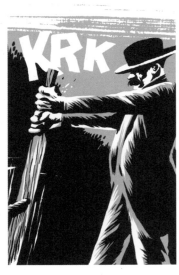

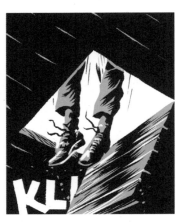

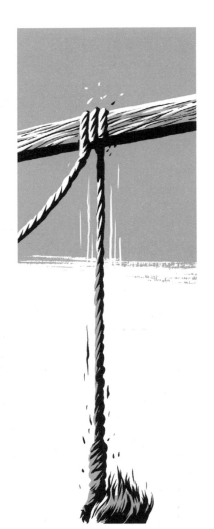

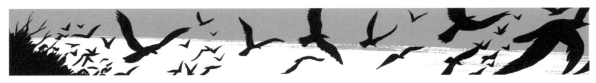

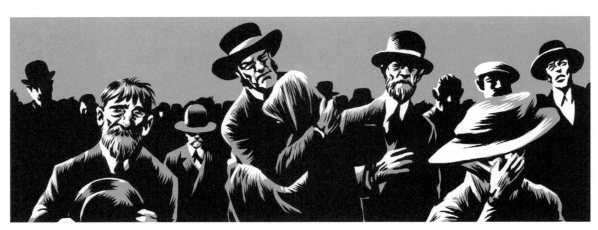

I WISH I COULD HAVE DONE MORE TO HELP HIM.

IN THE END HE ALMOST SEEMED RESIGNED TO HIS FATE.

WHO COULD HAVE THOUGHT THAT *DANIEL*, OF ALL PEOPLE, COULD BE CAPABLE OF SUCH A TERRIBLE DEED?

I GUESS YOU NEVER *REALLY* GET TO KNOW FOLKS. NOT EVEN THE ONES THAT ARE CLOSEST TO YOU.

WHERE WERE YOU? I EXPECTED YOU HOME HOURS AGO!

...SORRY, MY DARLIN'... I DIDN'T WANT TO WAKE YOU...

WHY DON'T YOU GO BACK TO SLEEP?
TAKE YOUR CLOTHES OFF BEFORE YOU COME TO BED. YOU SMELL OF SMOKE AND WHISKEY.
WHERE'S YOUR HAT? WE JUST BOUGHT IT A COUPLE OF DAYS AGO. IT DIDN'T COME CHEAP, IF I REMEMBER RIGHTLY.
I'M SORRY, SWEETIE! I LOST THE HAT IN TONIGHT'S POKER GAME. BUT DON'T FRET! I CAN BUY A DOZEN NEW ONES WITH THE MONEY I WON!
GOODNIGHT... ZZZ

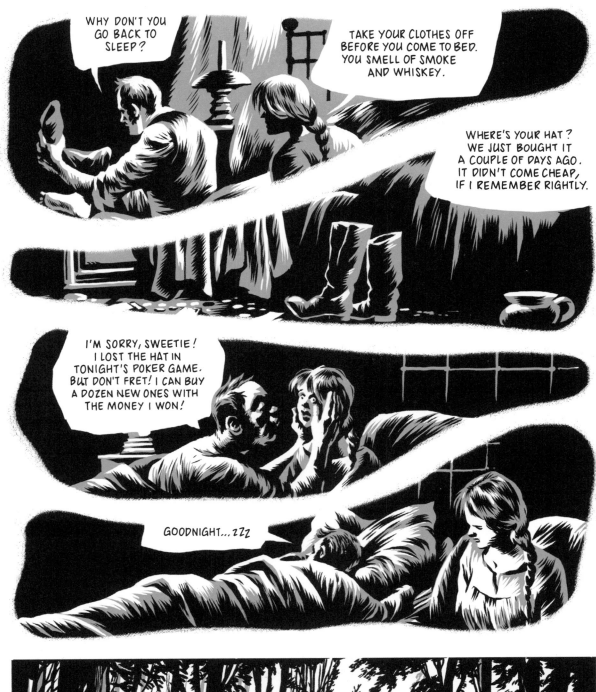

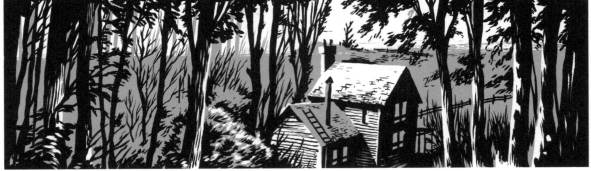

LOVING HUSBAND
WILLIAM ORVILLE
DANIEL ROGER WILKIN
18 63

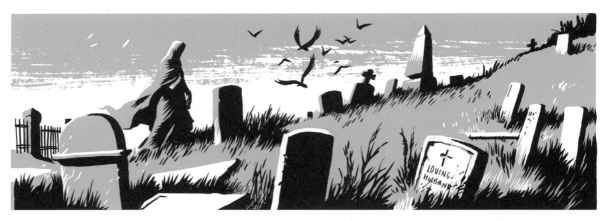

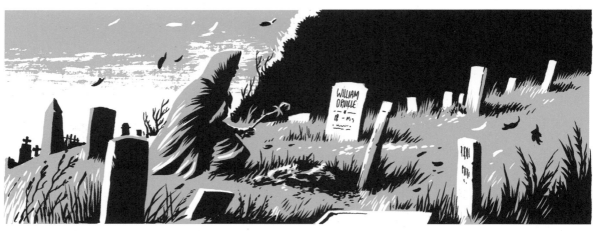

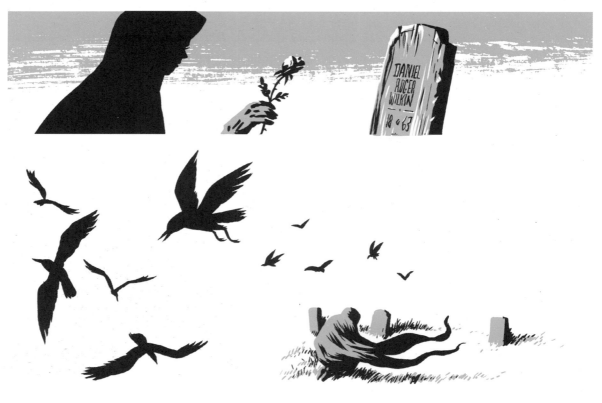

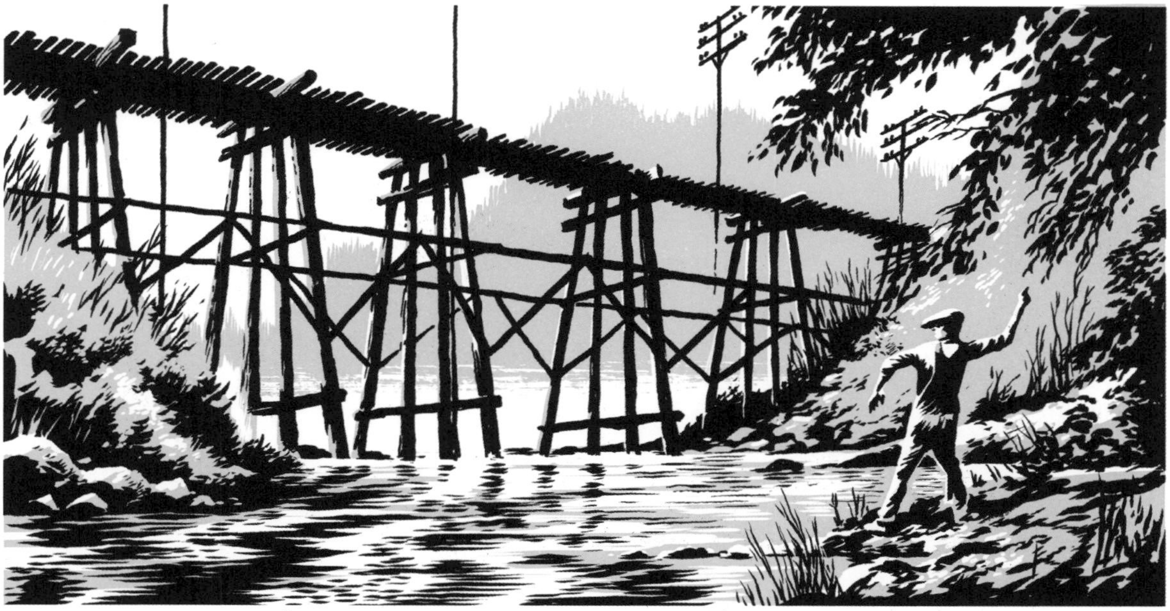

TANEYTOWN

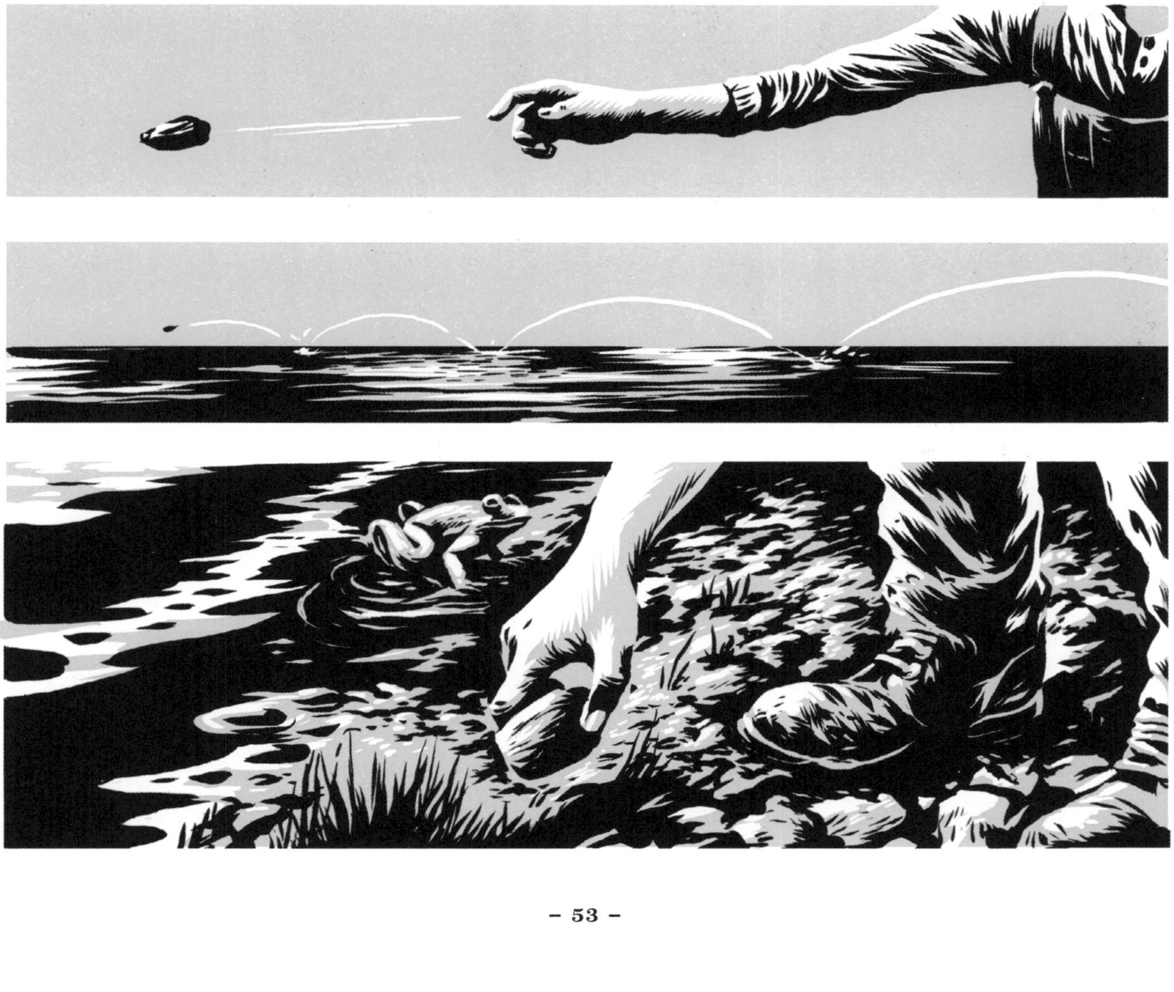

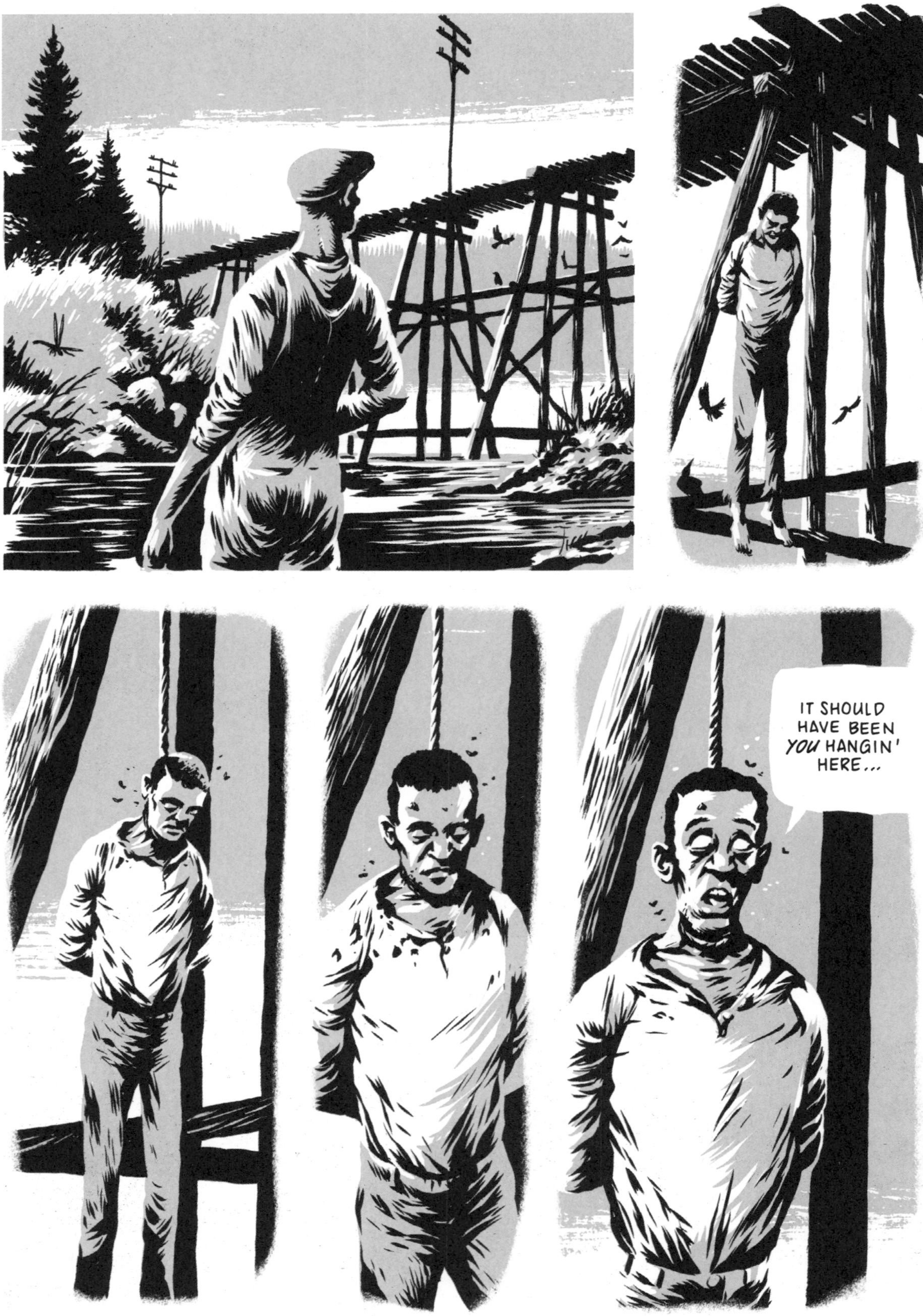
IT SHOULD
HAVE BEEN
YOU HANGIN'
HERE...

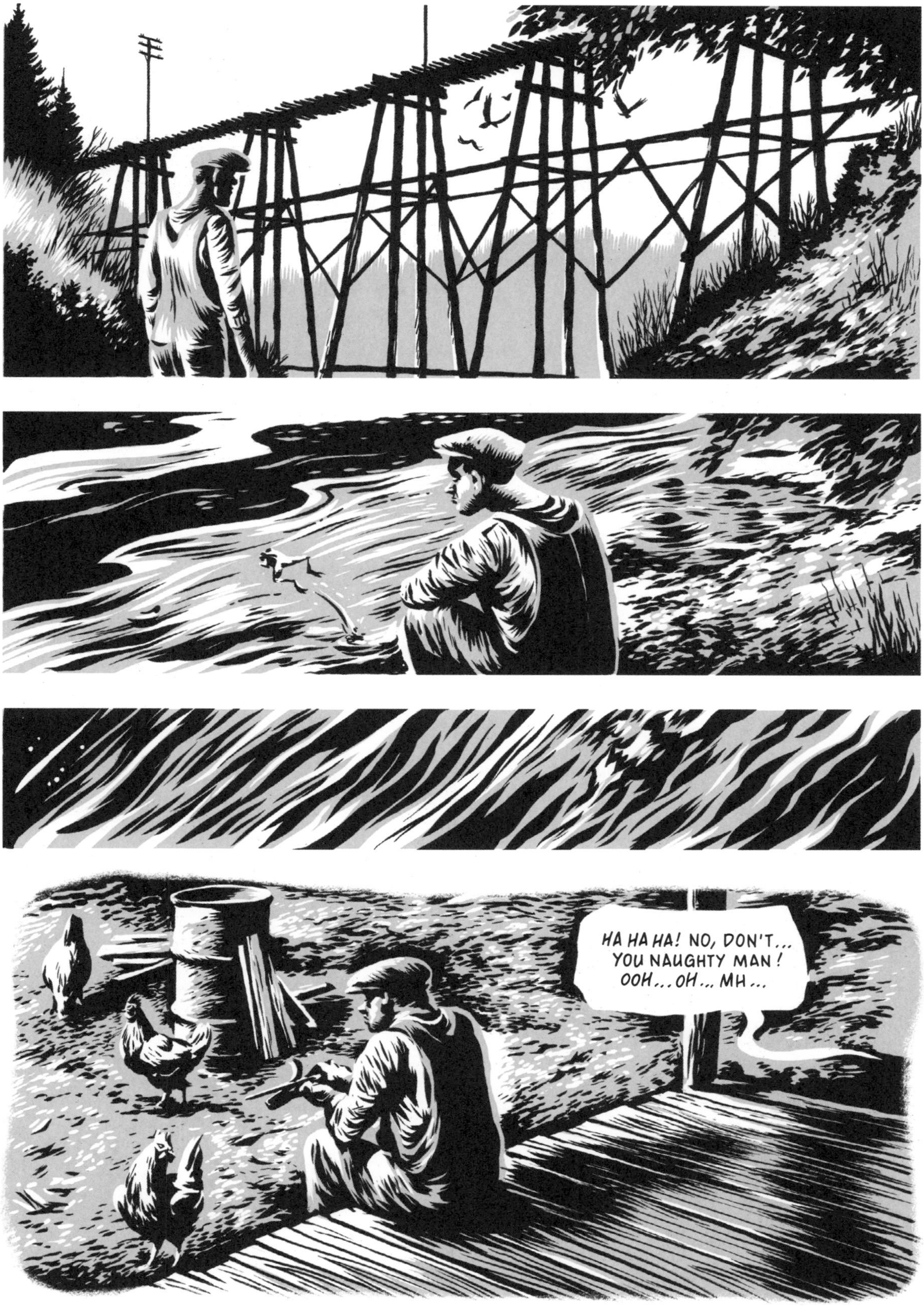
HA HA HA! NO, DON'T...
YOU NAUGHTY MAN!
OOH... OH... MH...

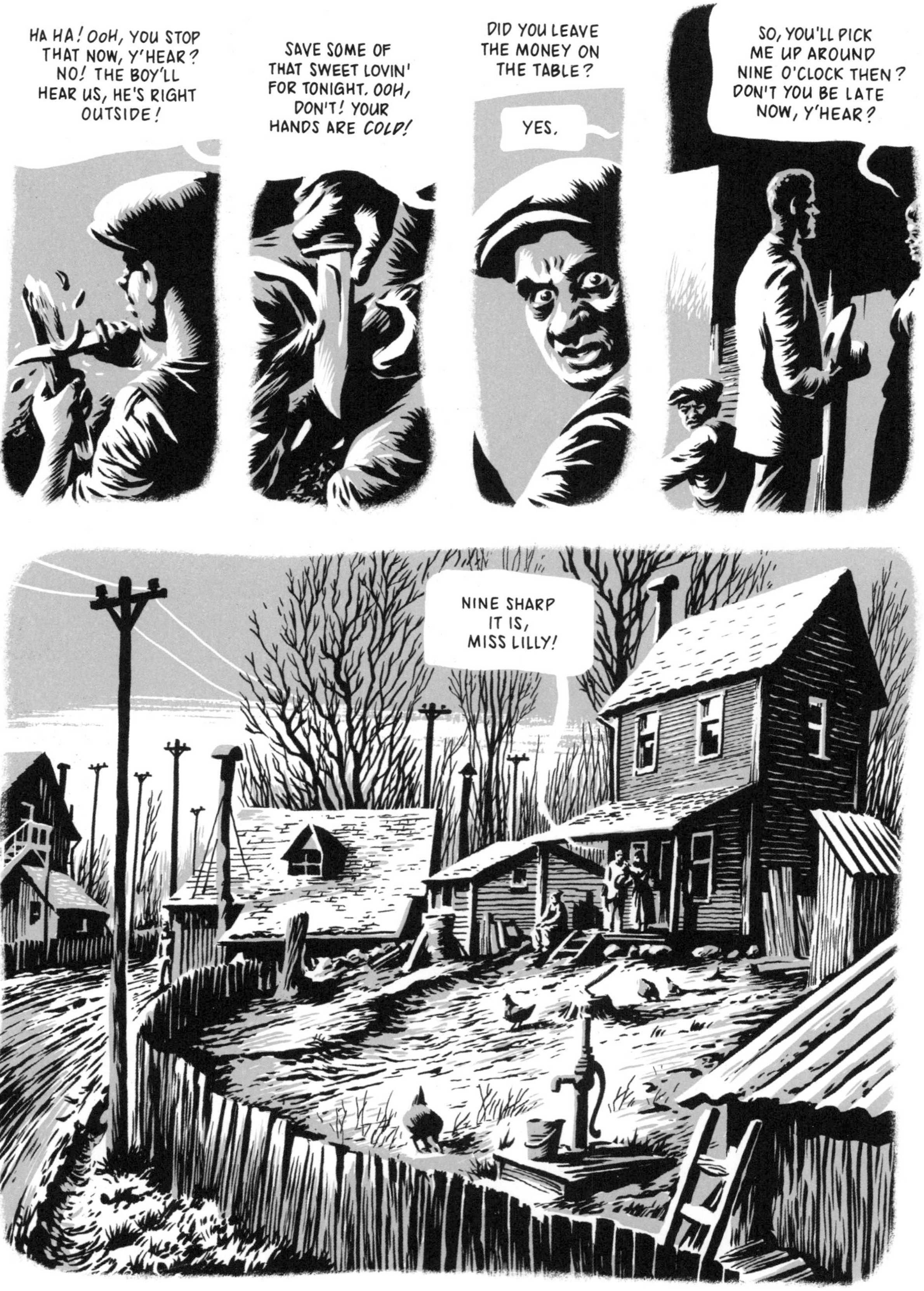
HA HA! OOH, YOU STOP THAT NOW, Y'HEAR? NO! THE BOY'LL HEAR US, HE'S RIGHT OUTSIDE!
SAVE SOME OF THAT SWEET LOVIN' FOR TONIGHT. OOH, DON'T! YOUR HANDS ARE COLD!
DID YOU LEAVE THE MONEY ON THE TABLE?
YES.
SO, YOU'LL PICK ME UP AROUND NINE O'CLOCK THEN? DON'T YOU BE LATE NOW, Y'HEAR?
NINE SHARP IT IS, MISS LILLY!

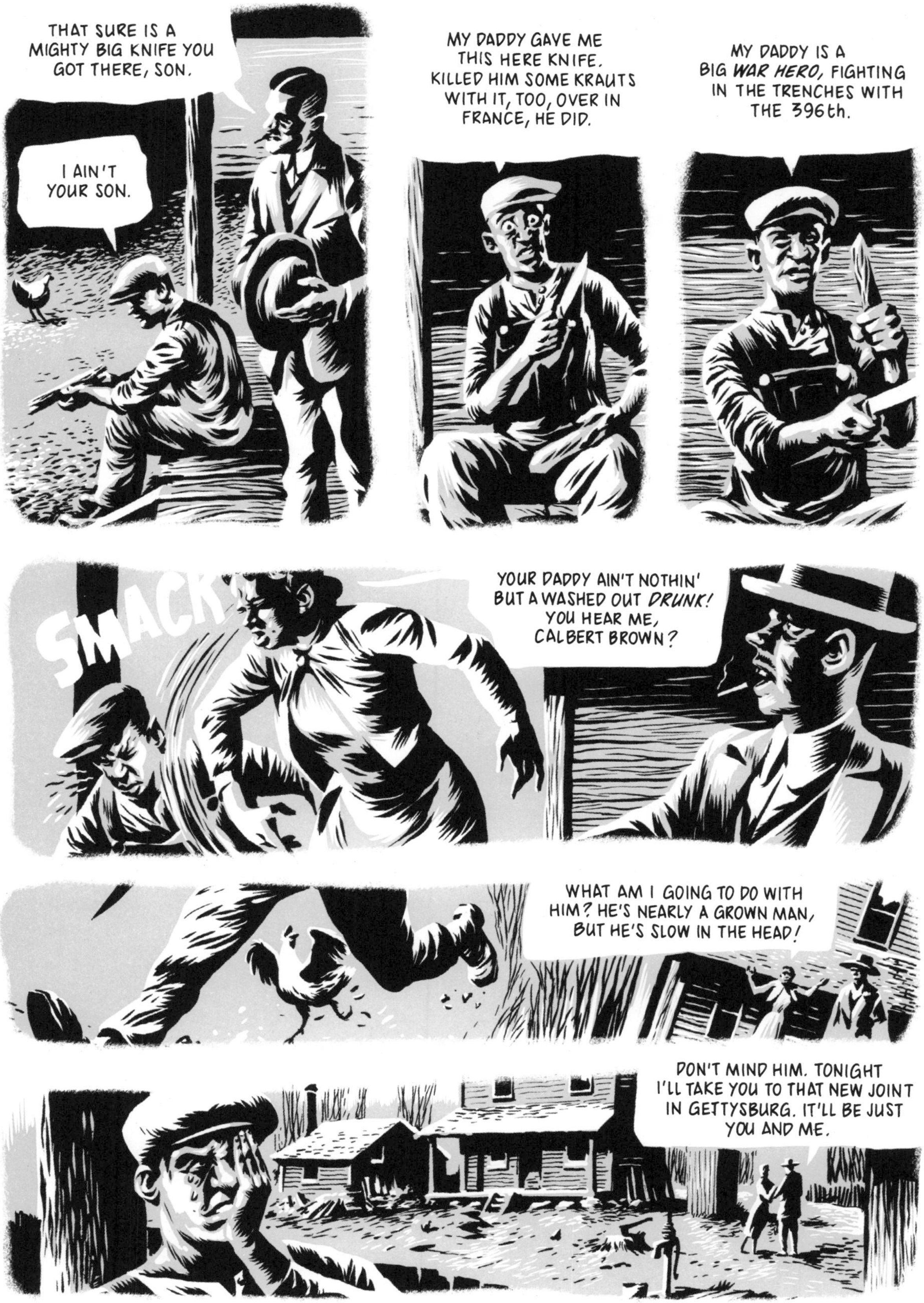
THAT SURE IS A MIGHTY BIG KNIFE YOU GOT THERE, SON.
I AIN'T YOUR SON.
MY DADDY GAVE ME THIS HERE KNIFE. KILLED HIM SOME KRAUTS WITH IT, TOO, OVER IN FRANCE, HE DID.
MY DADDY IS A BIG WAR HERO, FIGHTING IN THE TRENCHES WITH THE 396th.
SMACK
YOUR DADDY AIN'T NOTHIN' BUT A WASHED OUT DRUNK! YOU HEAR ME, CALBERT BROWN?
WHAT AM I GOING TO DO WITH HIM? HE'S NEARLY A GROWN MAN, BUT HE'S SLOW IN THE HEAD!
DON'T MIND HIM. TONIGHT I'LL TAKE YOU TO THAT NEW JOINT IN GETTYSBURG. IT'LL BE JUST YOU AND ME.

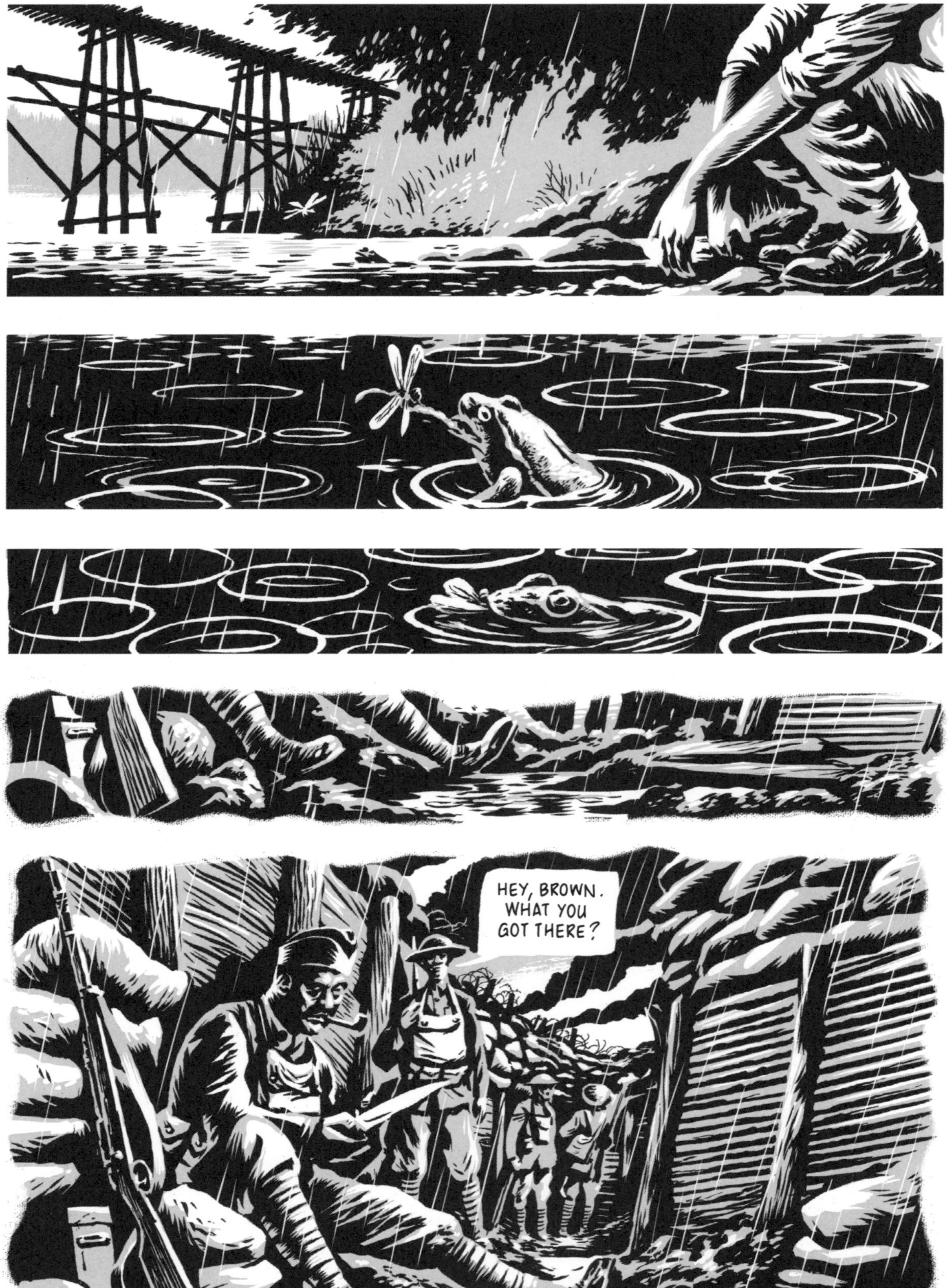
HEY, BROWN. WHAT YOU GOT THERE?

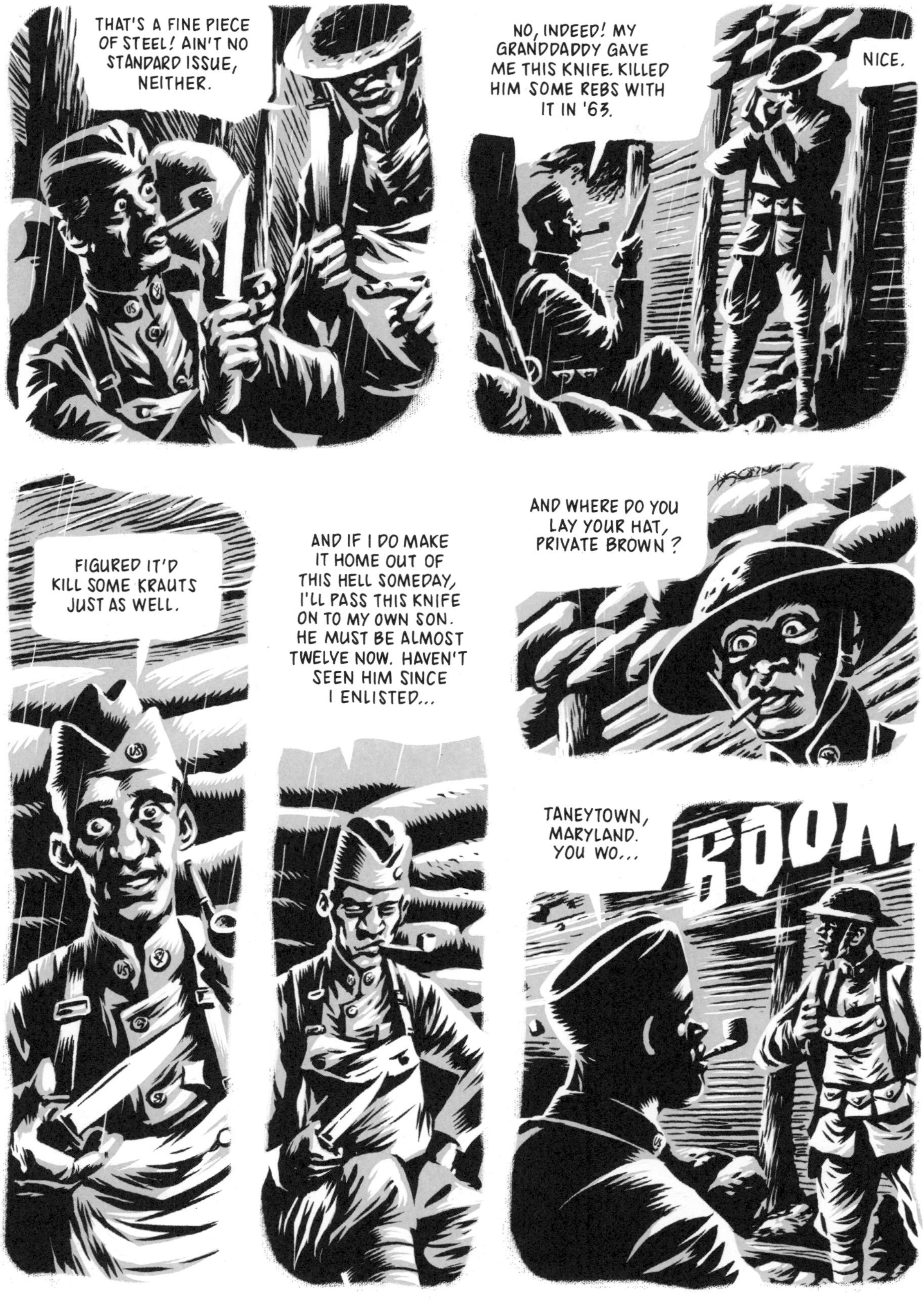
THAT'S A FINE PIECE OF STEEL! AIN'T NO STANDARD ISSUE, NEITHER.
NO, INDEED! MY GRANDDADDY GAVE ME THIS KNIFE. KILLED HIM SOME REBS WITH IT IN '63.
NICE.
FIGURED IT'D KILL SOME KRAUTS JUST AS WELL.
AND IF I DO MAKE IT HOME OUT OF THIS HELL SOMEDAY, I'LL PASS THIS KNIFE ON TO MY OWN SON. HE MUST BE ALMOST TWELVE NOW. HAVEN'T SEEN HIM SINCE I ENLISTED...
AND WHERE DO YOU LAY YOUR HAT, PRIVATE BROWN?
TANEYTOWN, MARYLAND. YOU WO...
BOOM

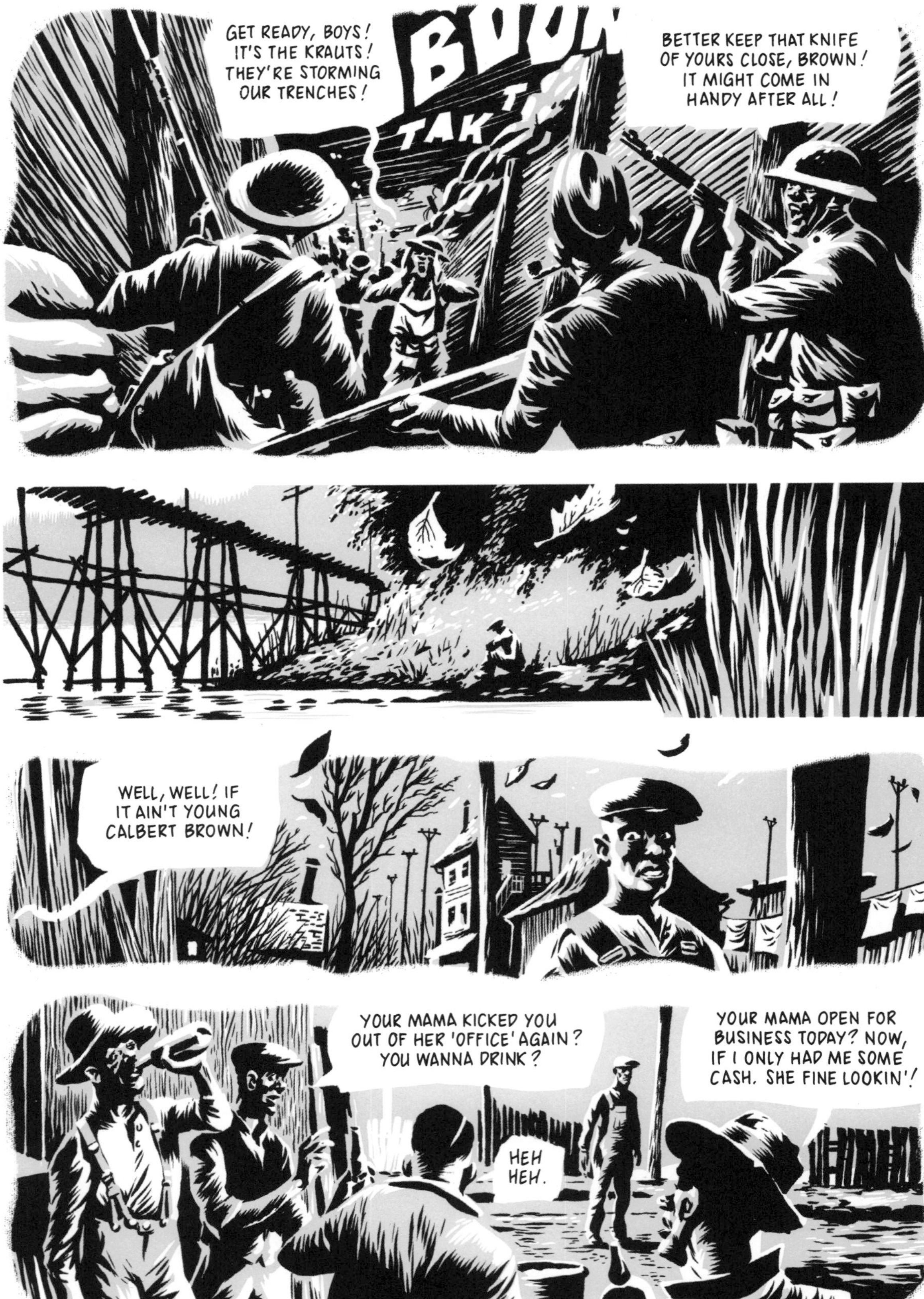
GET READY, BOYS! IT'S THE KRAUTS! THEY'RE STORMING OUR TRENCHES!
TAK
BETTER KEEP THAT KNIFE OF YOURS CLOSE, BROWN! IT MIGHT COME IN HANDY AFTER ALL!
WELL, WELL! IF IT AIN'T YOUNG CALBERT BROWN!
YOUR MAMA KICKED YOU OUT OF HER 'OFFICE' AGAIN? YOU WANNA DRINK?
HEH HEH.
YOUR MAMA OPEN FOR BUSINESS TODAY? NOW, IF I ONLY HAD ME SOME CASH. SHE FINE LOOKIN'!

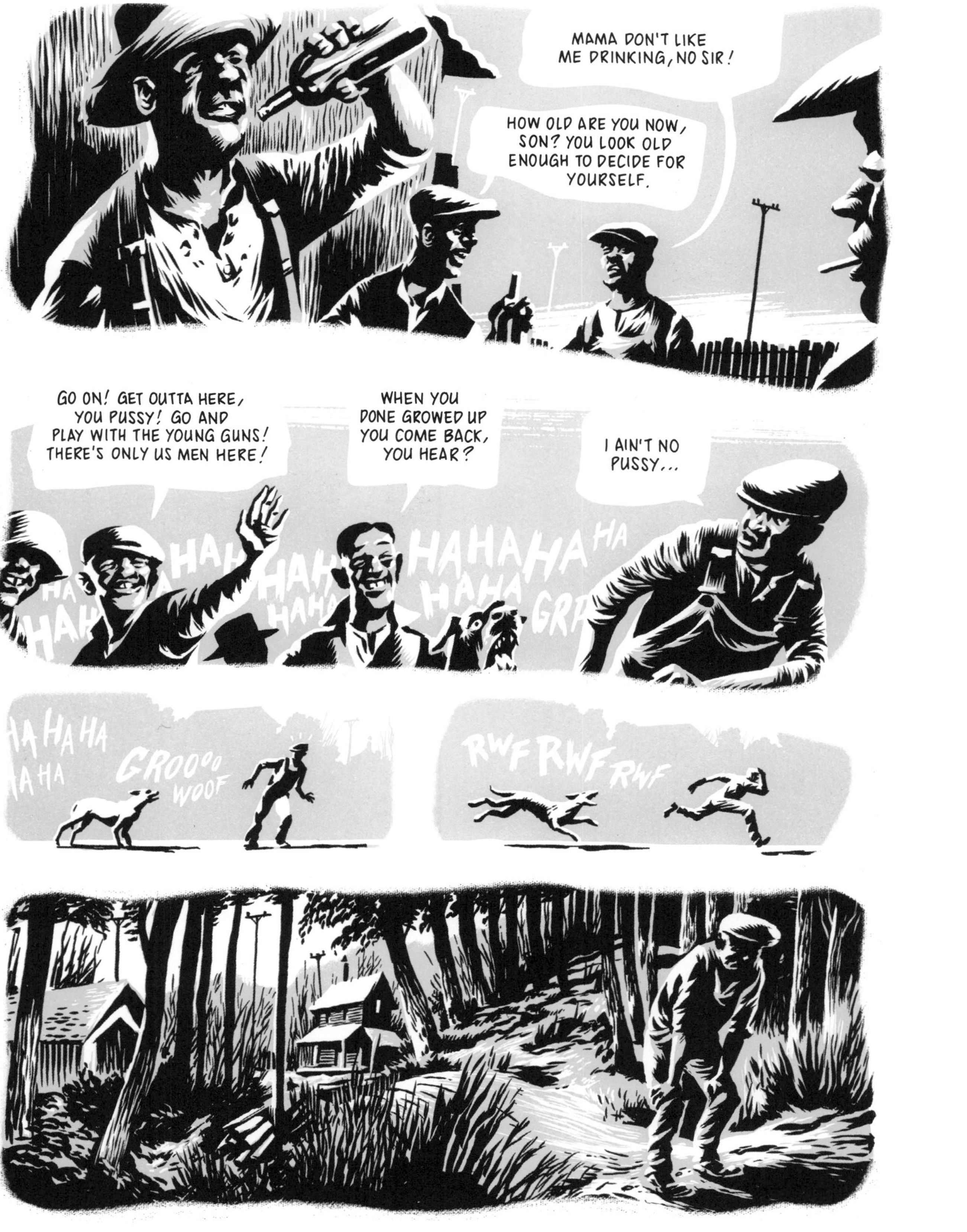
MAMA DON'T LIKE ME DRINKING, NO SIR!
HOW OLD ARE YOU NOW, SON? YOU LOOK OLD ENOUGH TO DECIDE FOR YOURSELF.
GO ON! GET OUTTA HERE, YOU PUSSY! GO AND PLAY WITH THE YOUNG GUNS! THERE'S ONLY US MEN HERE!
WHEN YOU DONE GROWED UP YOU COME BACK, YOU HEAR?
I AIN'T NO PUSSY...
HAHAHAHA HA
GROOOO WOOF
RWF RWF RWF

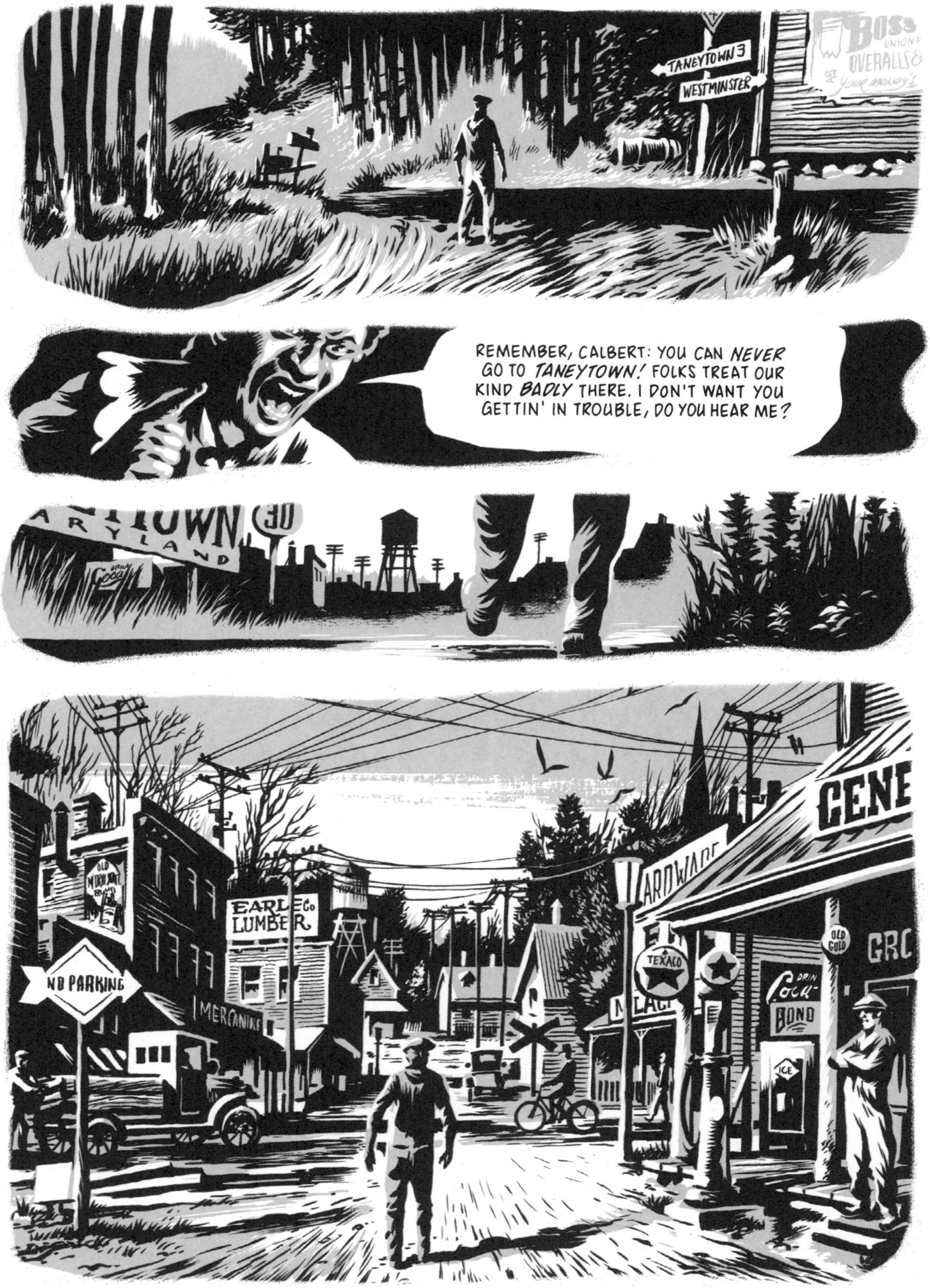
TANEYTOWN 3
WESTMINSTER
BOSS
OVERALLS &
REMEMBER, CALBERT: YOU CAN *NEVER* GO TO *TANEYTOWN!* FOLKS TREAT OUR KIND *BADLY* THERE. I DON'T WANT YOU GETTIN' IN TROUBLE, DO YOU HEAR ME?
TOWN
ARYLAND
30
NO PARKING
EARLE Co LUMBER
MERCANTILE
TEXACO
OLD GOLD
BOND
ICE

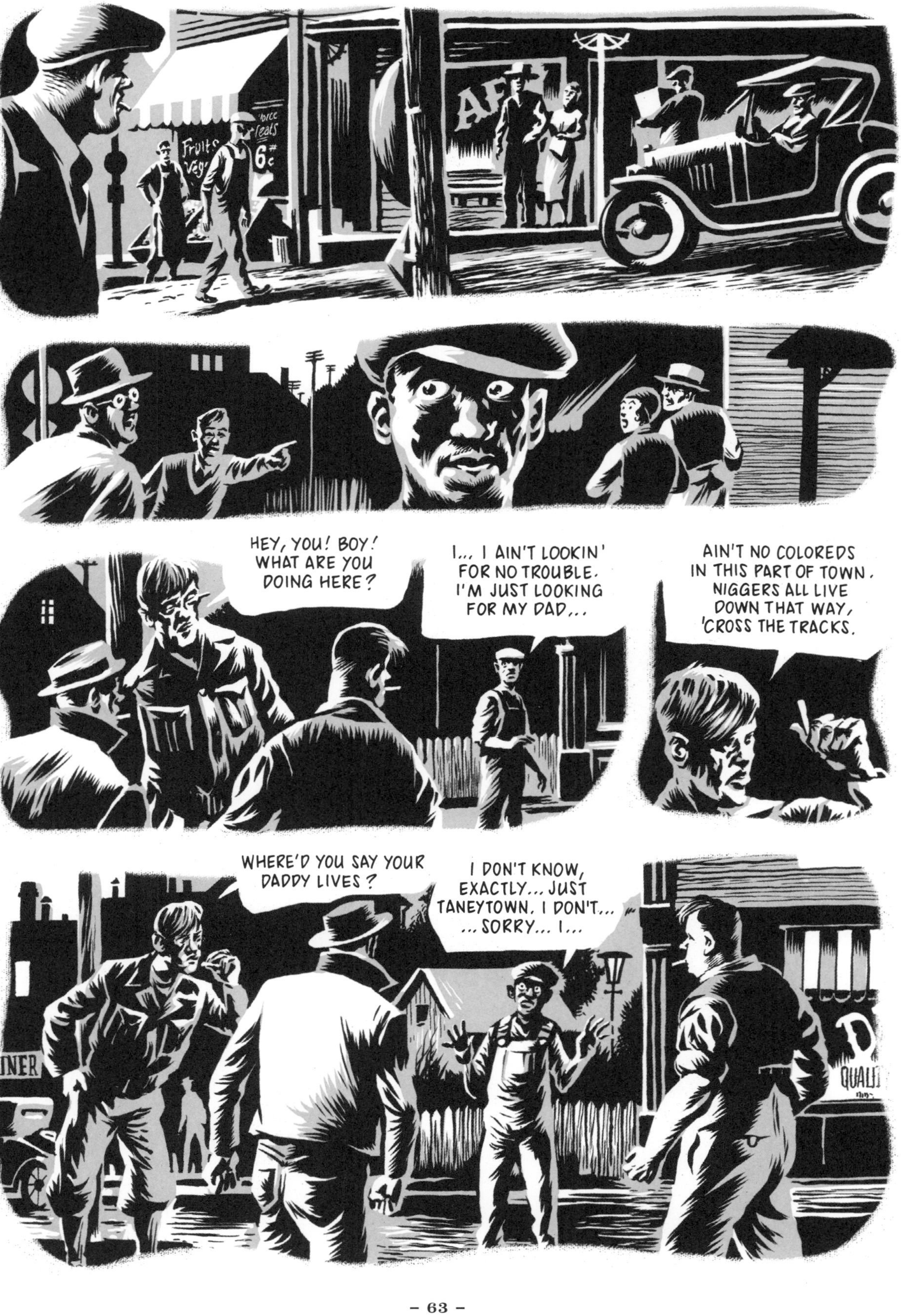
HEY, YOU! BOY! WHAT ARE YOU DOING HERE?
I.., I AIN'T LOOKIN' FOR NO TROUBLE. I'M JUST LOOKING FOR MY DAD...
AIN'T NO COLOREDS IN THIS PART OF TOWN. NIGGERS ALL LIVE DOWN THAT WAY, 'CROSS THE TRACKS.
WHERE'D YOU SAY YOUR DADDY LIVES?
I DON'T KNOW, EXACTLY... JUST TANEYTOWN. I DON'T... ...SORRY... I...

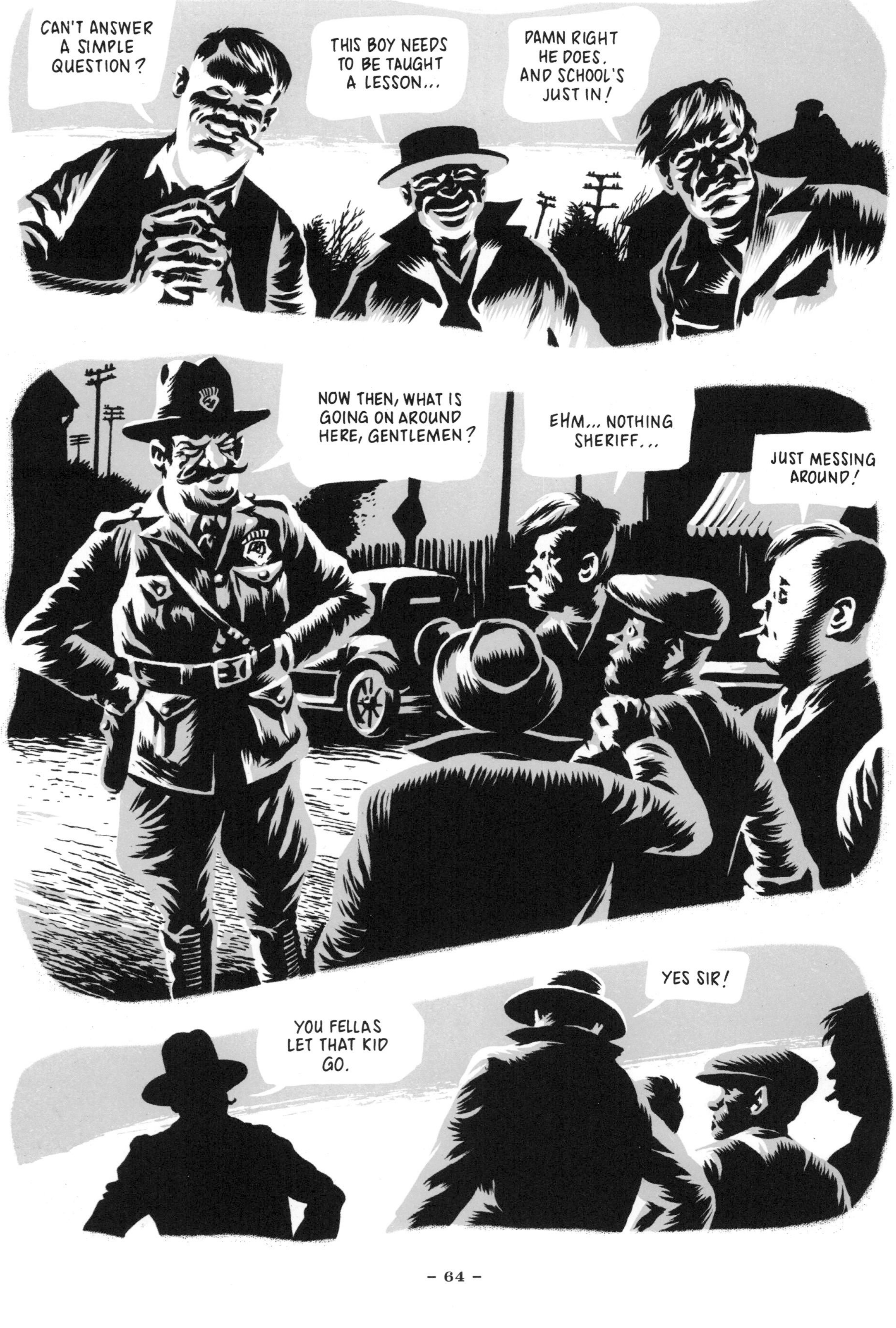
CAN'T ANSWER A SIMPLE QUESTION?
THIS BOY NEEDS TO BE TAUGHT A LESSON...
DAMN RIGHT HE DOES. AND SCHOOL'S JUST IN!
NOW THEN, WHAT IS GOING ON AROUND HERE, GENTLEMEN?
EHM... NOTHING SHERIFF...
JUST MESSING AROUND!
YOU FELLAS LET THAT KID GO.
YES SIR!

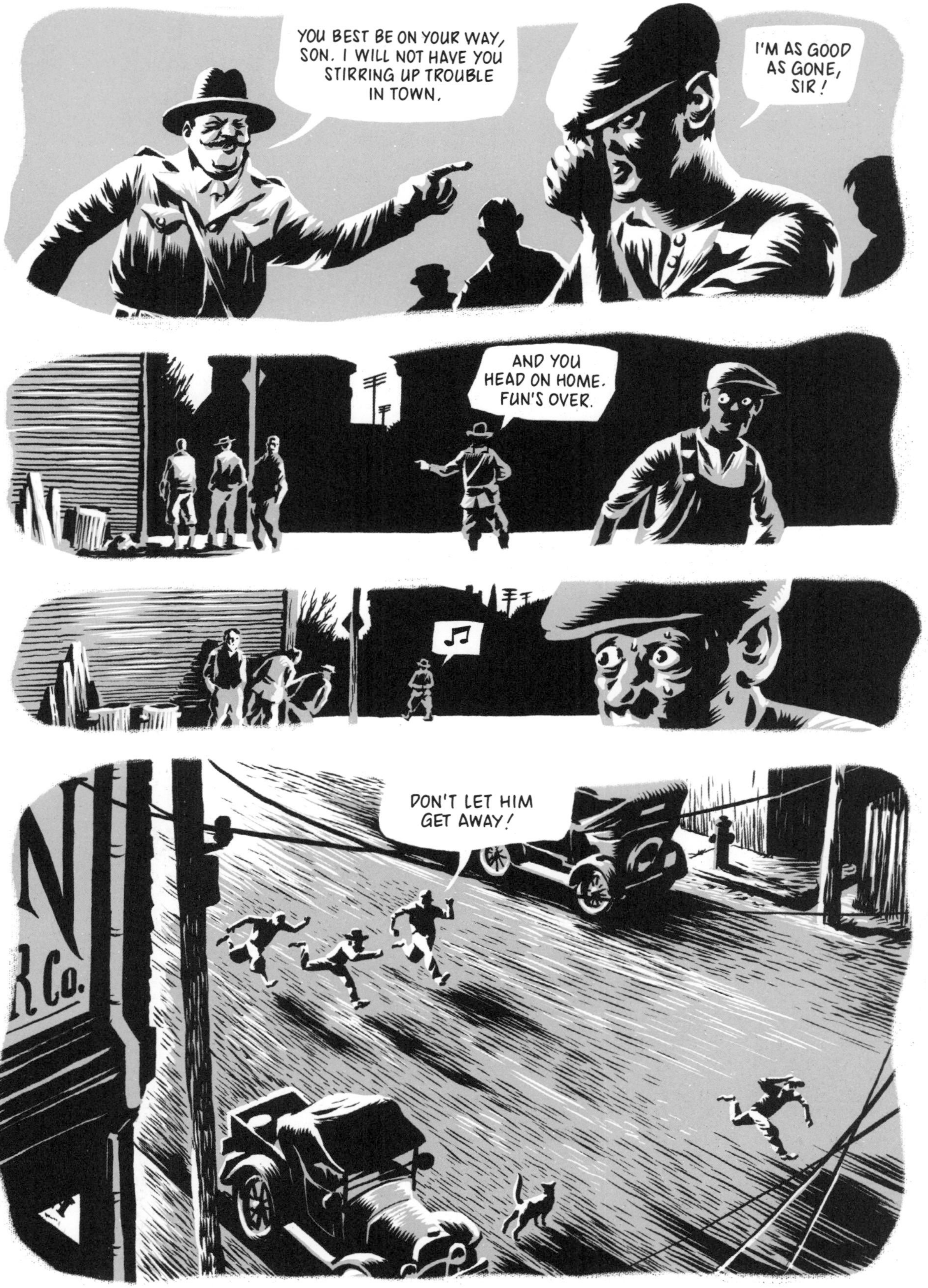
YOU BEST BE ON YOUR WAY, SON. I WILL NOT HAVE YOU STIRRING UP TROUBLE IN TOWN.
I'M AS GOOD AS GONE, SIR!
AND YOU HEAD ON HOME. FUN'S OVER.
♫
DON'T LET HIM GET AWAY!

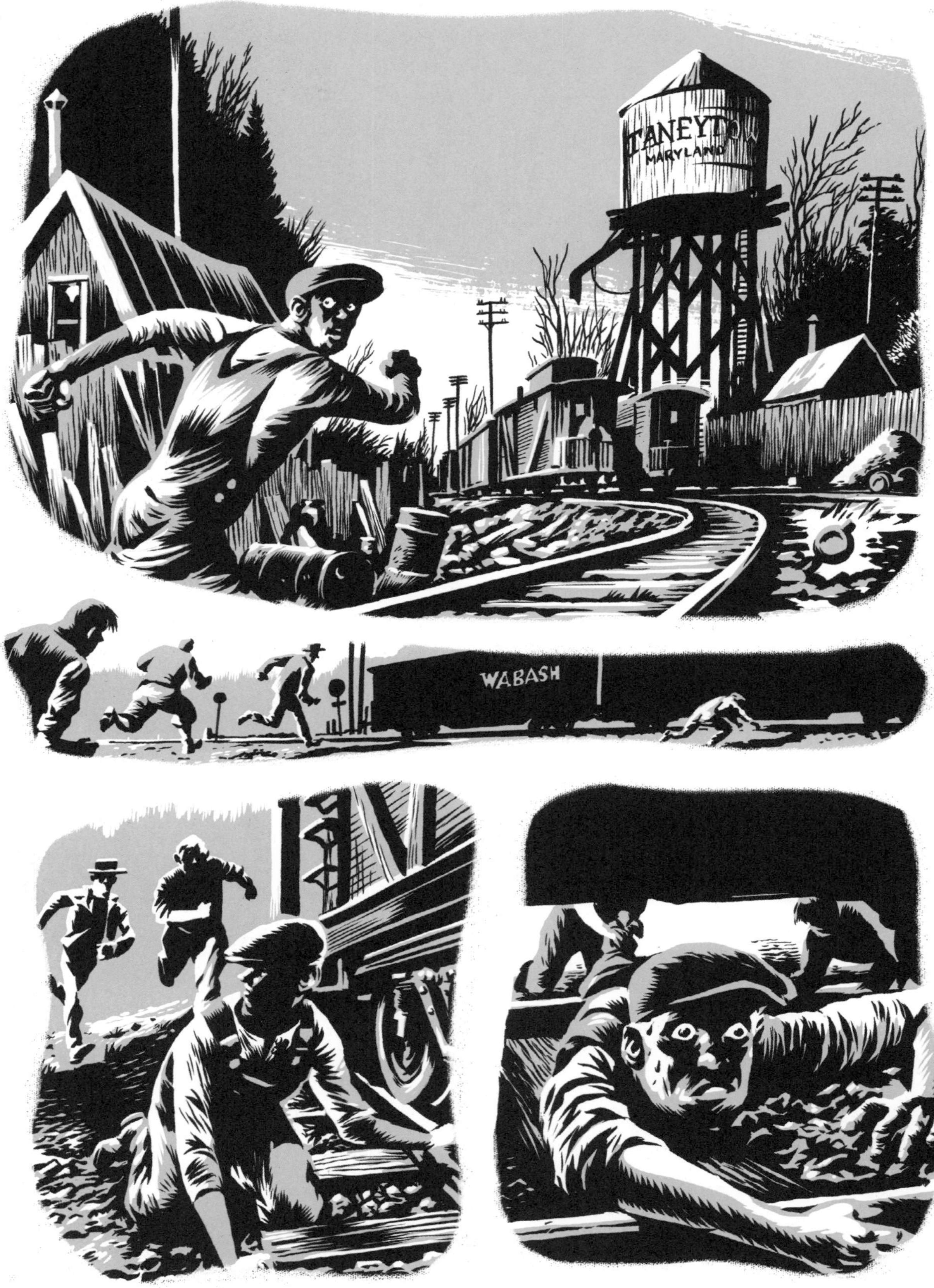
TANEYTOW
MARYLAND
WABASH

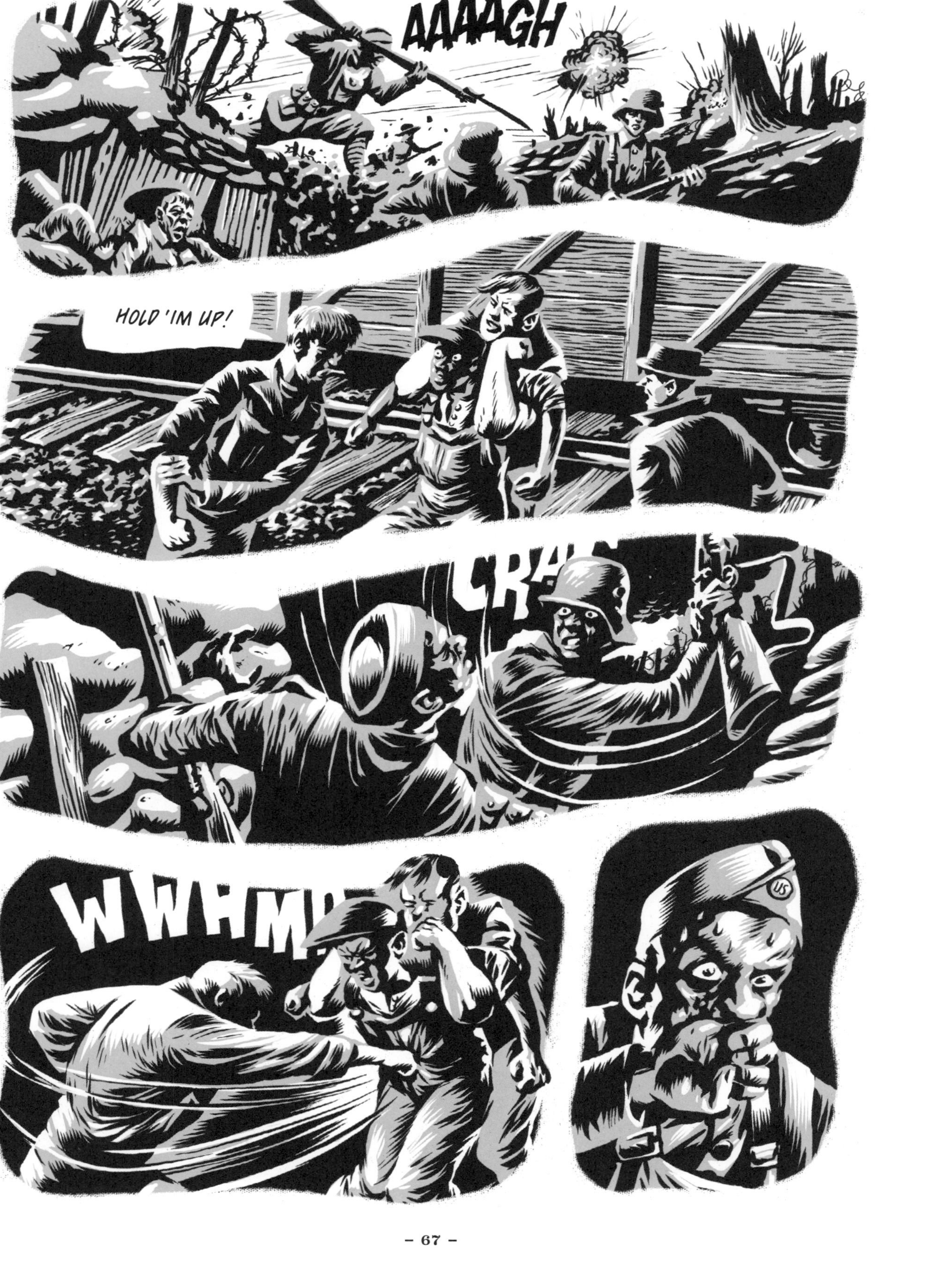
AAAAGH
HOLD 'IM UP!
CRA
WWHAM
US

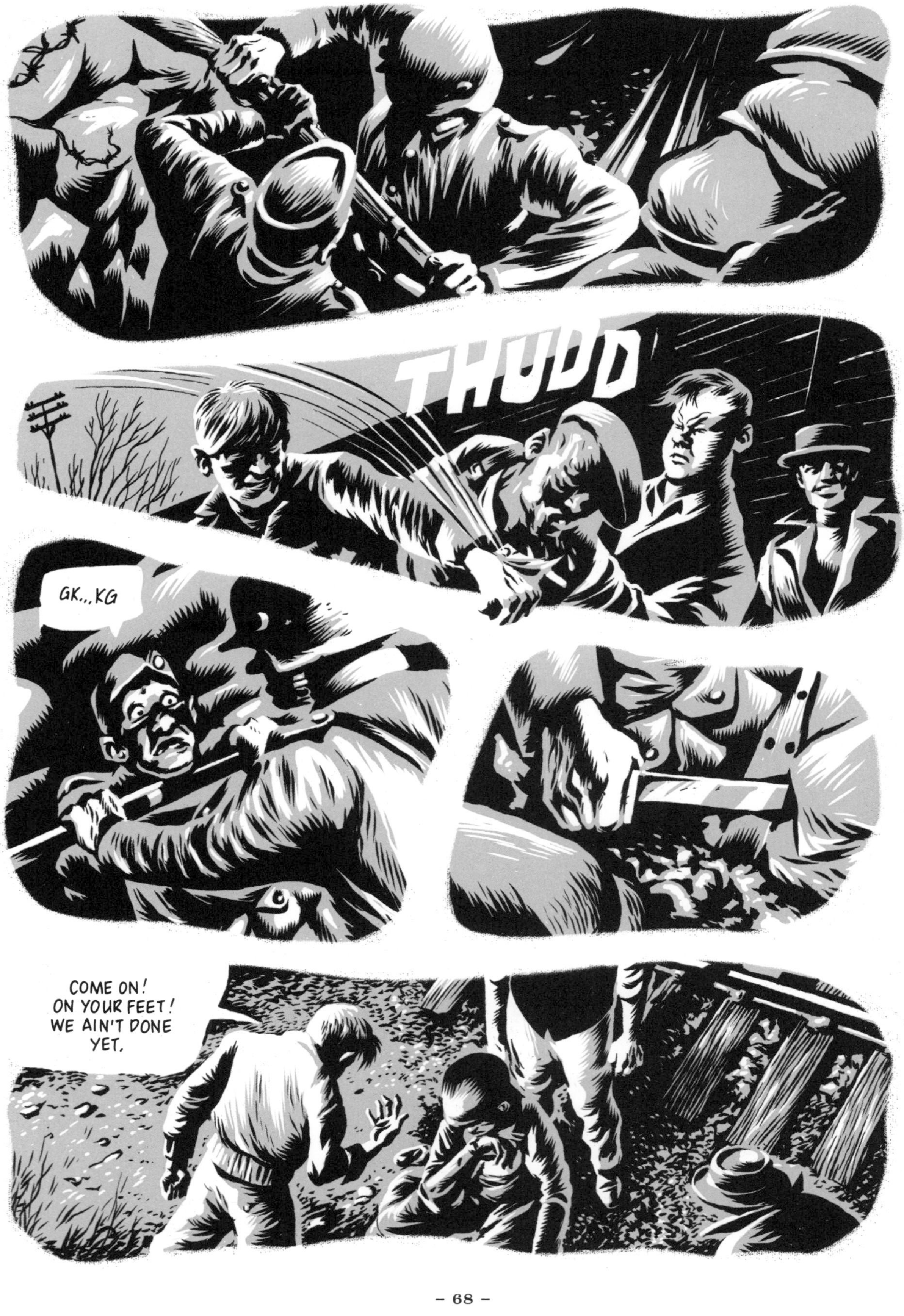
THUDD
GK...KG
COME ON! ON YOUR FEET! WE AIN'T DONE YET.

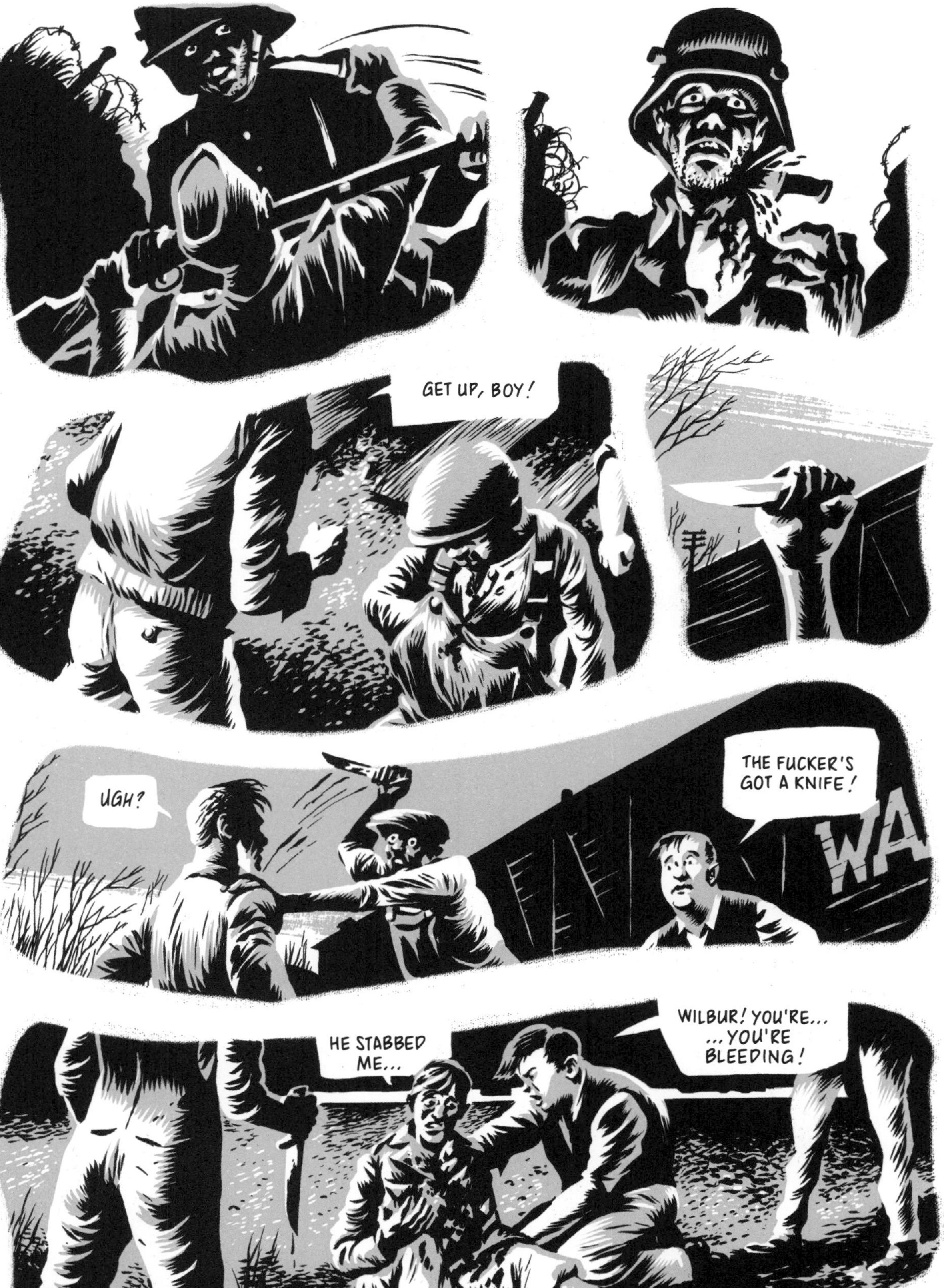
GET UP, BOY!
UGH?
THE FUCKER'S GOT A KNIFE!
WA
HE STABBED ME...
WILBUR! YOU'RE... ...YOU'RE BLEEDING!

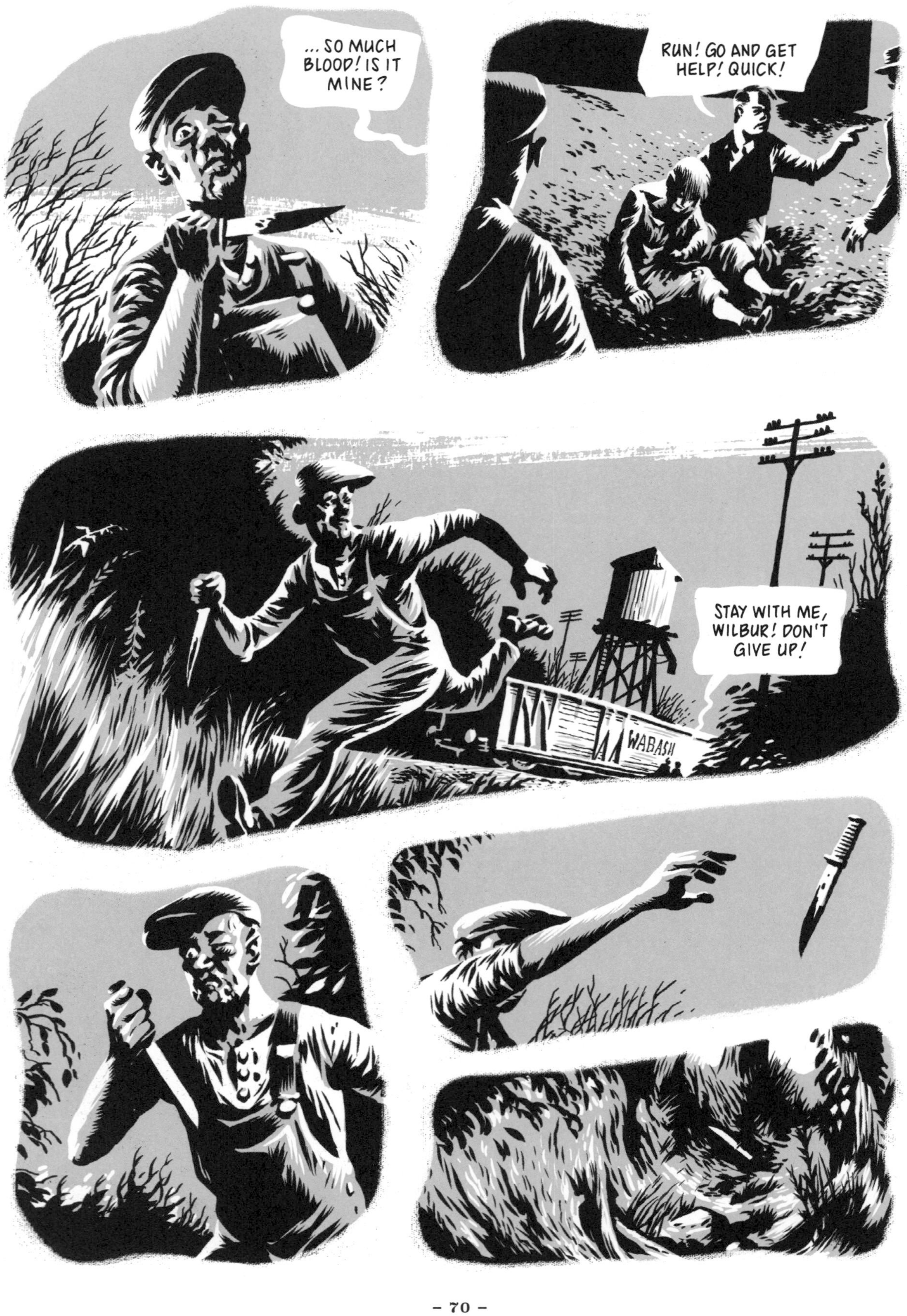
...SO MUCH BLOOD! IS IT MINE?
RUN! GO AND GET HELP! QUICK!
STAY WITH ME, WILBUR! DON'T GIVE UP!
WABASH

HAHAHA! SHHT, QUIET! YOU'LL WAKE CALBERT.
MOMMA? 'S THAT YOU?

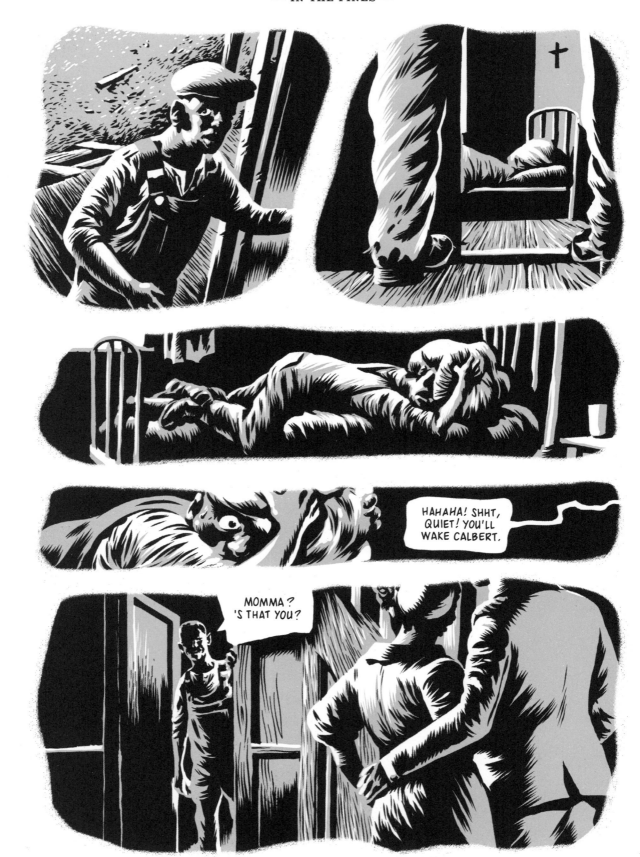

CALBERT! WHY ARE YOU STILL UP?
WHAT DID YOU DO? WALK INTO A POST? YOU LOOK LIKE HELL BOY!
I'M GOING TO BED. AND YOU SHOULD, TOO.
DON'T FORGET YOUR CHORES IN THE MORNING!
NO, MA'AM.
AND DON'T WAKE ME BEFORE TEN!

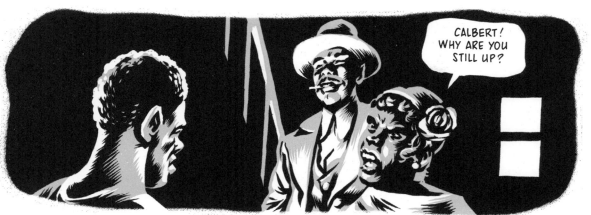

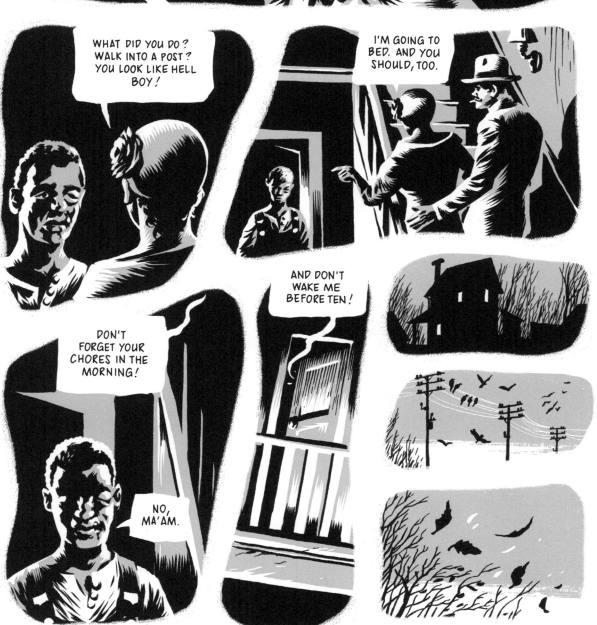

OH, HI!
YOU'RE
EARLY.

MISS
LILLY.

DID YOU HEAR
ABOUT THAT BOY
THEY HANGED OVER
IN TANEYTOWN?

NO?

THEY CAUGHT THAT BOY
STABBING SOME WHITE KID.
THEY STRUNG HIM UP ON
THE OLD TRESTLE BRIDGE,
JUST LIKE THAT!

OH, MY?
A LYNCHING?

GUESS SO! POOR BOY
PLEADED FOR HIS LIFE.
SAID HE JUST FOUND A
BLOODIED KNIFE BY THE
SIDE OF THE TRACKS.

DO YOU HEAR THAT,
CALBERT BROWN?
THAT'S HOW THEY
TREAT US FOLKS OVER
IN TANEYTOWN!

DON'T WORRY, MOMMA. I WON'T EVER GO THERE...
...ANYMORE.
MURDERER...

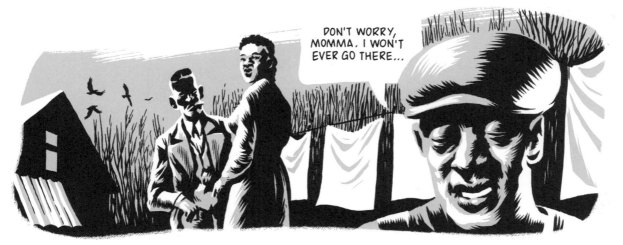

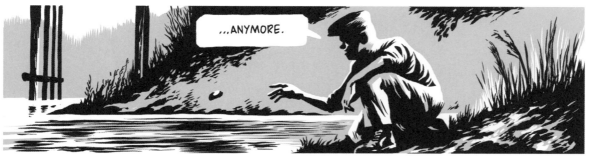

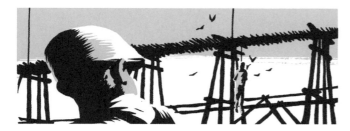

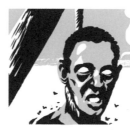

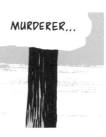

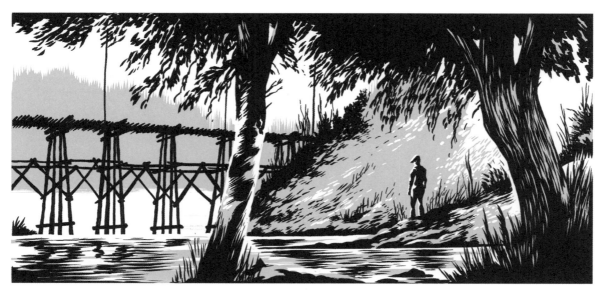

CALEB MEYER

NELLIE!

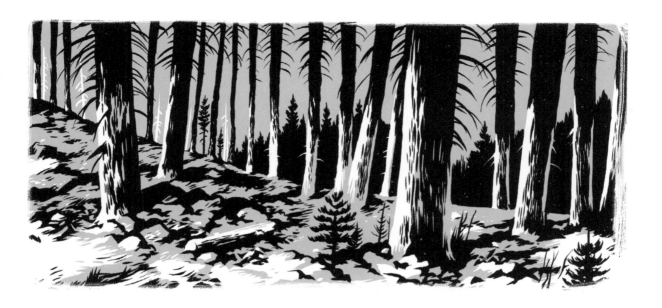

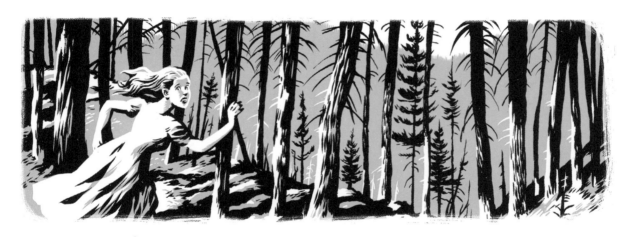

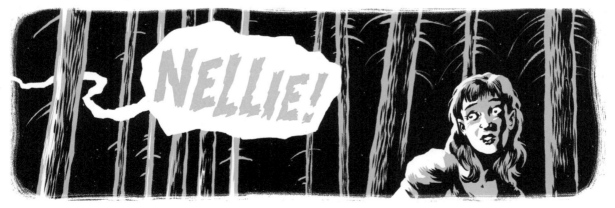

NELLIE!
NELLIE KANE!

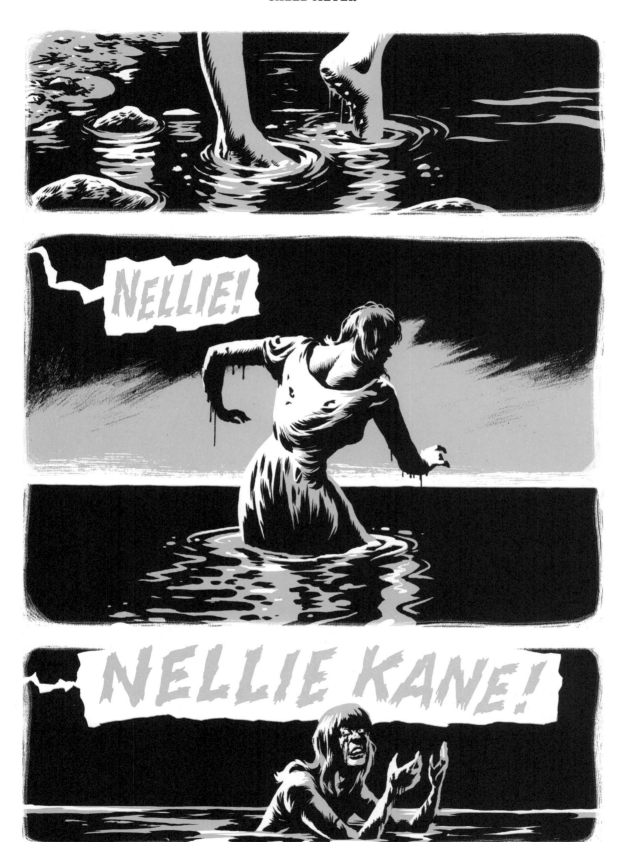

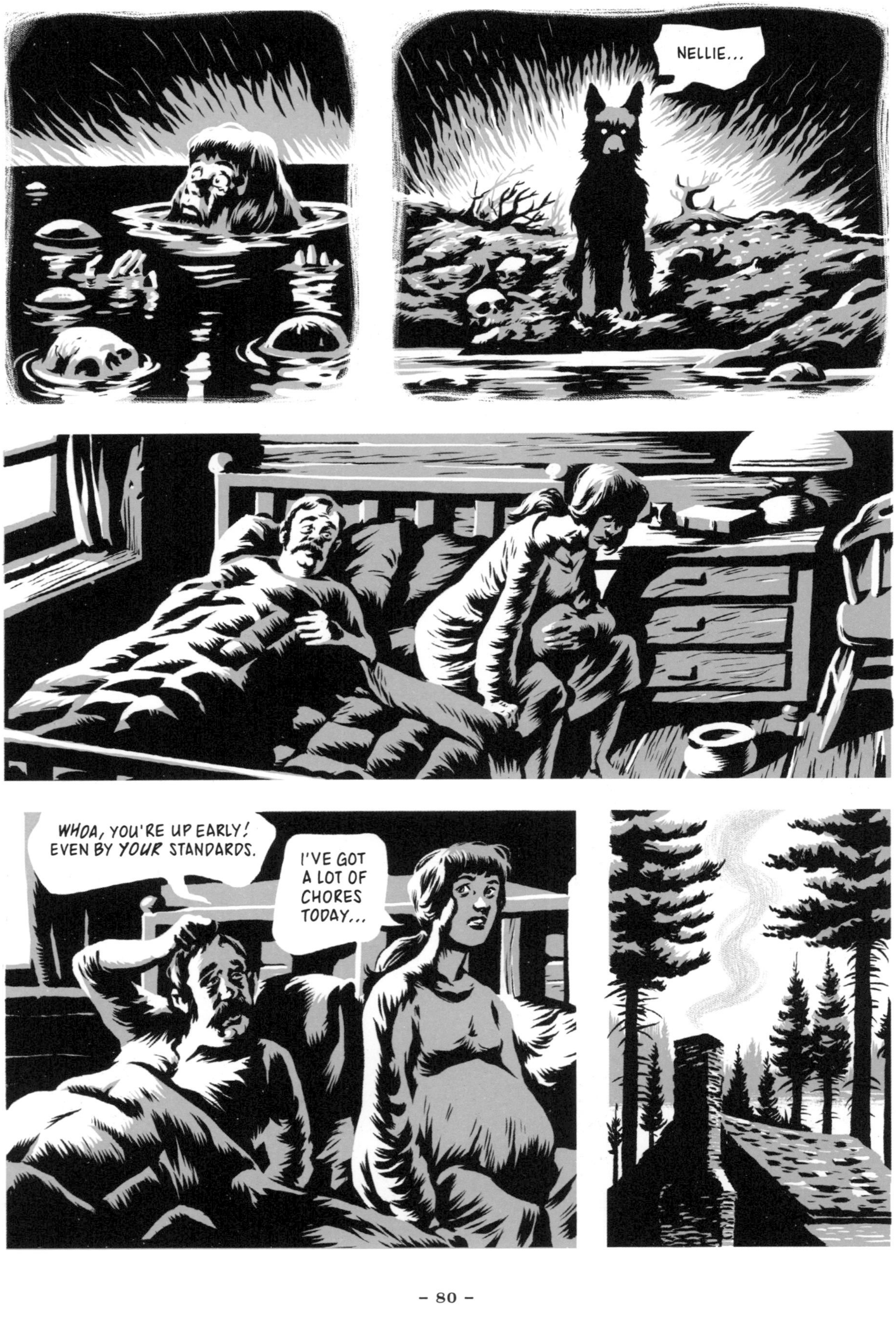
NELLIE...
WHOA, YOU'RE UP EARLY! EVEN BY YOUR STANDARDS.
I'VE GOT A LOT OF CHORES TODAY...

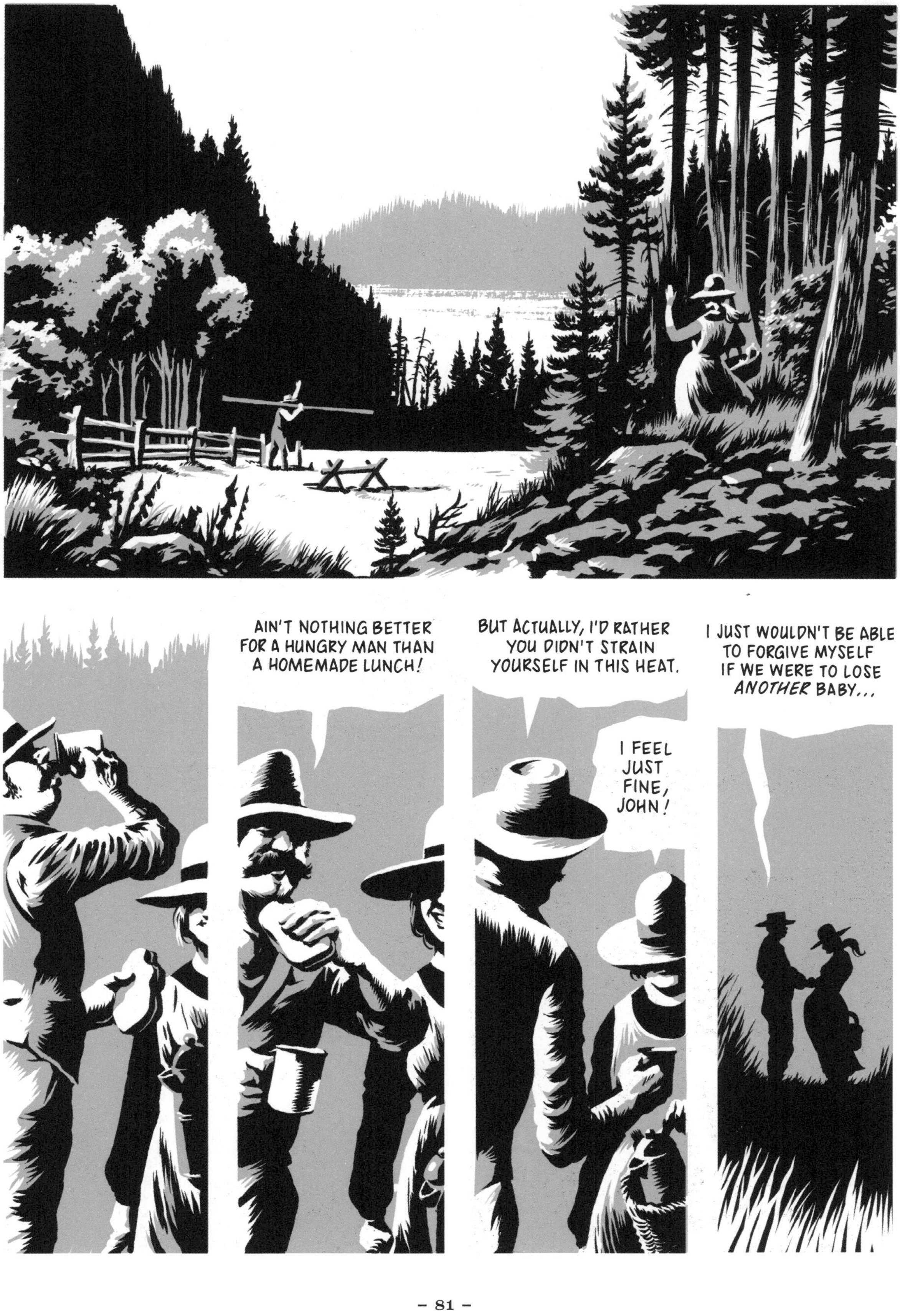
AIN'T NOTHING BETTER FOR A HUNGRY MAN THAN A HOMEMADE LUNCH!
BUT ACTUALLY, I'D RATHER YOU DIDN'T STRAIN YOURSELF IN THIS HEAT.
I FEEL JUST FINE, JOHN!
I JUST WOULDN'T BE ABLE TO FORGIVE MYSELF IF WE WERE TO LOSE *ANOTHER* BABY...

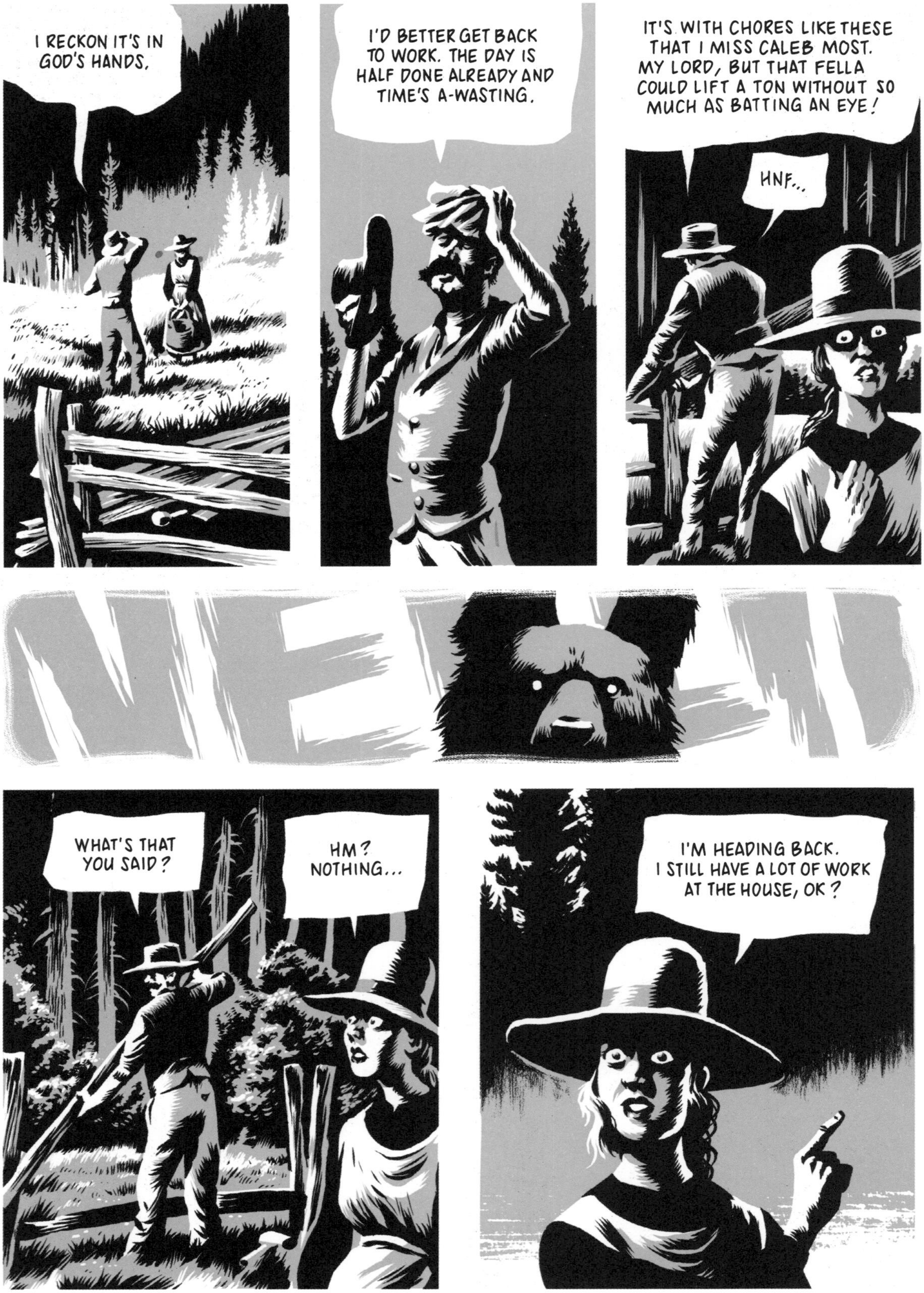
I RECKON IT'S IN GOD'S HANDS,
I'D BETTER GET BACK TO WORK. THE DAY IS HALF DONE ALREADY AND TIME'S A-WASTING.
IT'S WITH CHORES LIKE THESE THAT I MISS CALEB MOST. MY LORD, BUT THAT FELLA COULD LIFT A TON WITHOUT SO MUCH AS BATTING AN EYE!
HNF...
WHAT'S THAT YOU SAID?
HM? NOTHING...
I'M HEADING BACK. I STILL HAVE A LOT OF WORK AT THE HOUSE, OK?

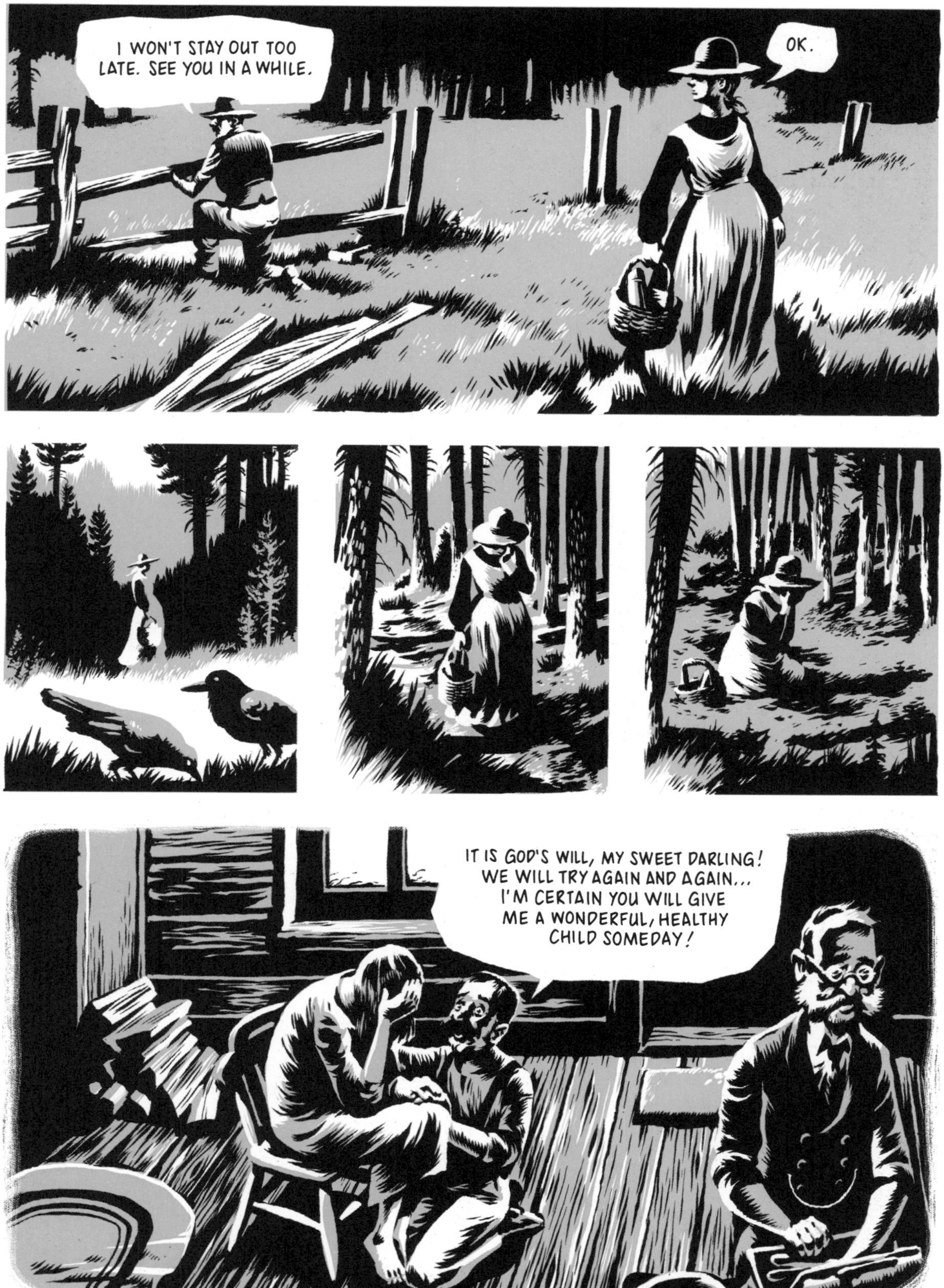
I WON'T STAY OUT TOO LATE. SEE YOU IN A WHILE.
OK.
IT IS GOD'S WILL, MY SWEET DARLING! WE WILL TRY AGAIN AND AGAIN... I'M CERTAIN YOU WILL GIVE ME A WONDERFUL, HEALTHY CHILD SOMEDAY!

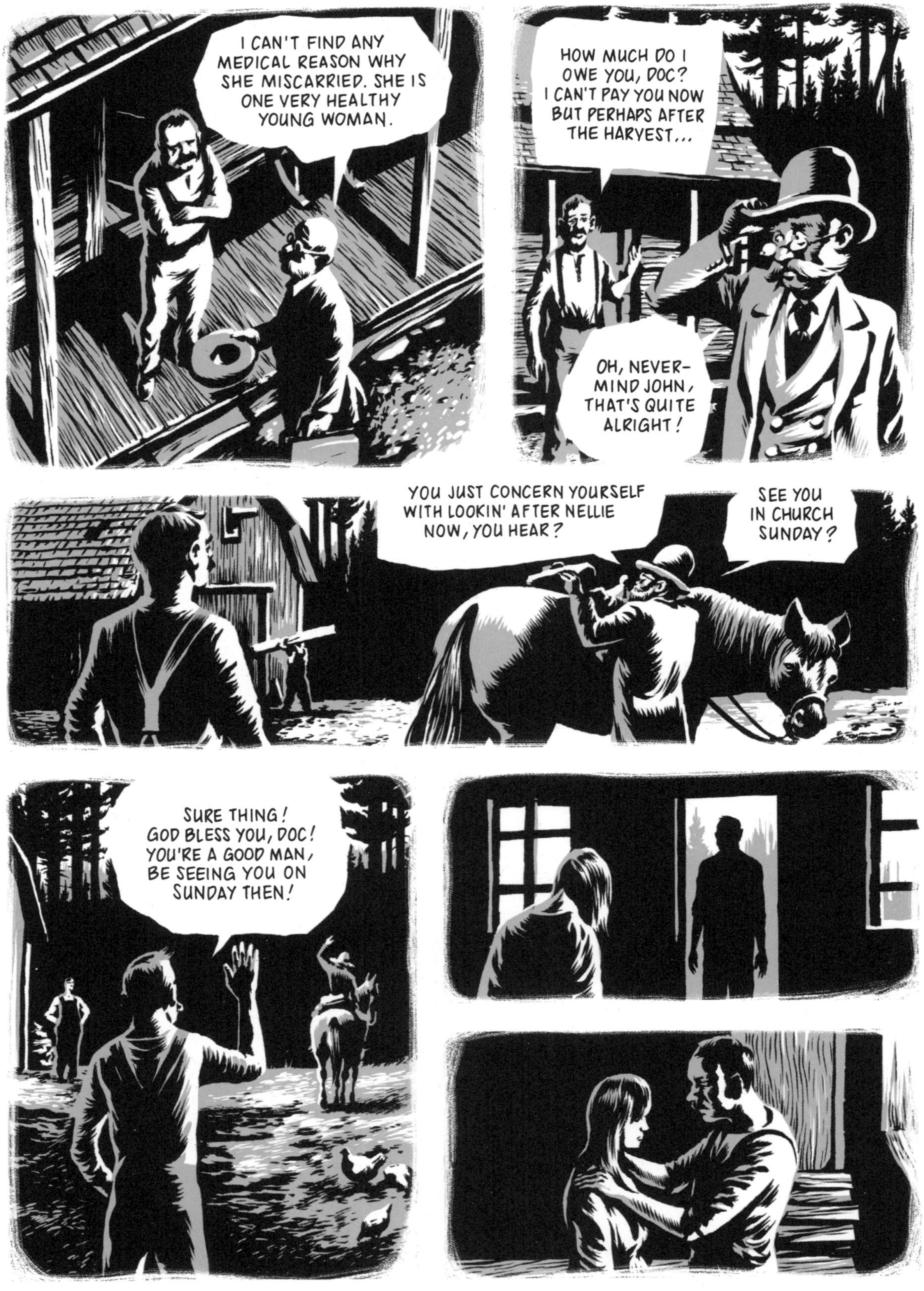
I CAN'T FIND ANY MEDICAL REASON WHY SHE MISCARRIED. SHE IS ONE VERY HEALTHY YOUNG WOMAN.
HOW MUCH DO I OWE YOU, DOC? I CAN'T PAY YOU NOW BUT PERHAPS AFTER THE HARVEST...
OH, NEVER-MIND JOHN, THAT'S QUITE ALRIGHT!
YOU JUST CONCERN YOURSELF WITH LOOKIN' AFTER NELLIE NOW, YOU HEAR?
SEE YOU IN CHURCH SUNDAY?
SURE THING! GOD BLESS YOU, DOC! YOU'RE A GOOD MAN, BE SEEING YOU ON SUNDAY THEN!

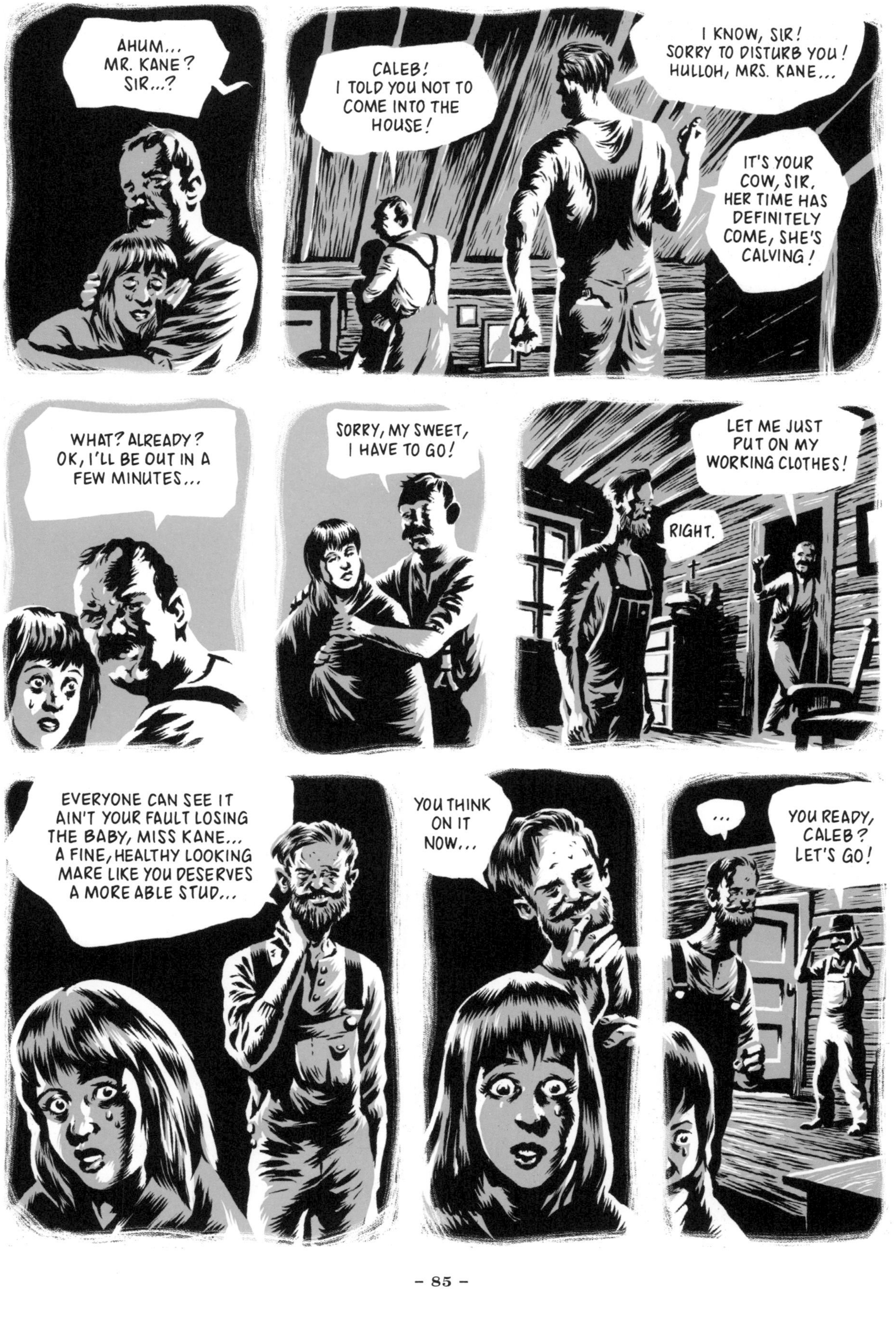
AHUM...
MR. KANE?
SIR...?
CALEB!
I TOLD YOU NOT TO
COME INTO THE
HOUSE!
I KNOW, SIR!
SORRY TO DISTURB YOU!
HULLOH, MRS. KANE...
IT'S YOUR
COW, SIR,
HER TIME HAS
DEFINITELY
COME, SHE'S
CALVING!
WHAT? ALREADY?
OK, I'LL BE OUT IN A
FEW MINUTES...
SORRY, MY SWEET,
I HAVE TO GO!
LET ME JUST
PUT ON MY
WORKING CLOTHES!
RIGHT.
EVERYONE CAN SEE IT
AIN'T YOUR FAULT LOSING
THE BABY, MISS KANE...
A FINE, HEALTHY LOOKING
MARE LIKE YOU DESERVES
A MORE ABLE STUD...
YOU THINK
ON IT
NOW...
...
YOU READY,
CALEB?
LET'S GO!

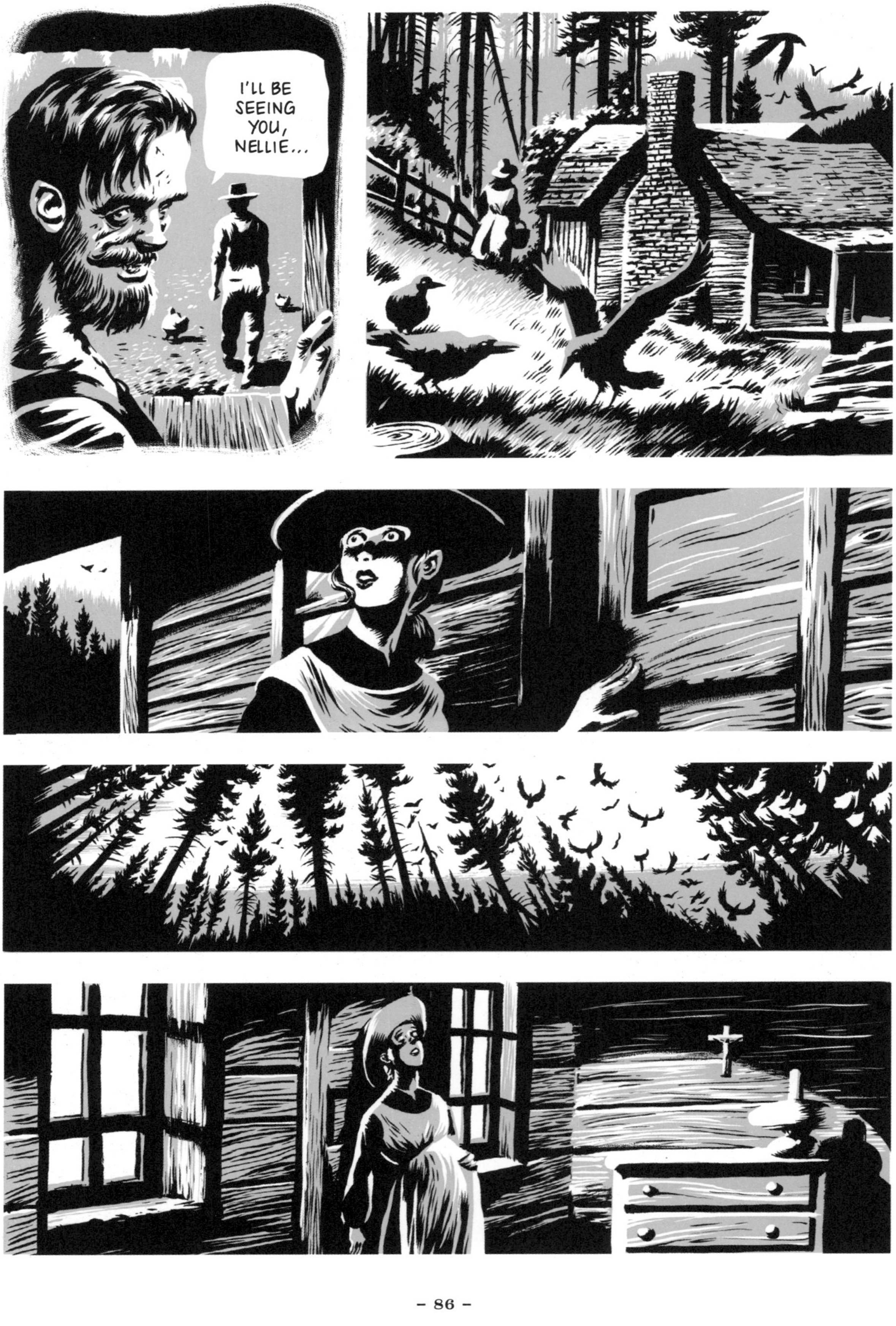
I'LL BE SEEING YOU, NELLIE...

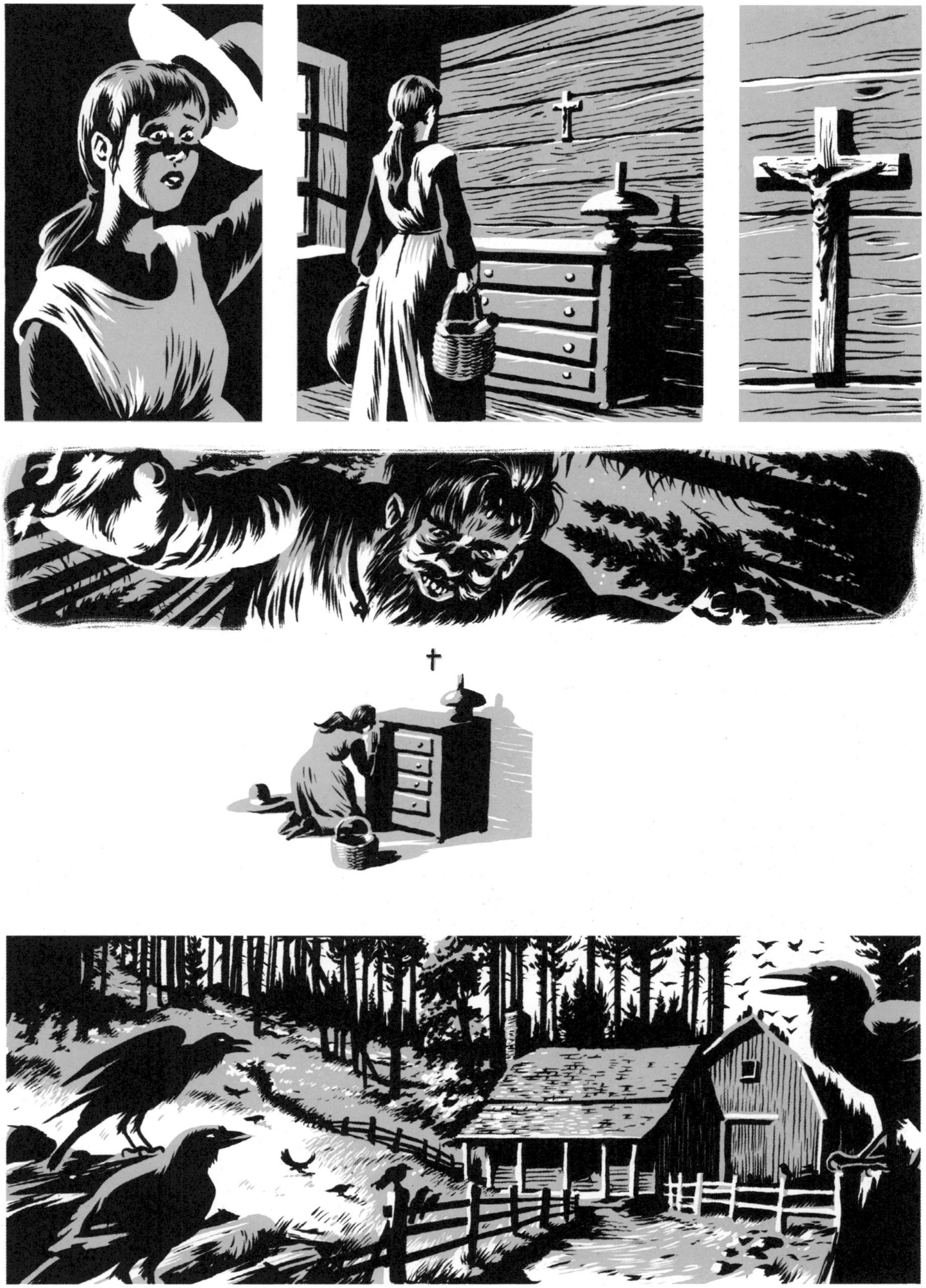

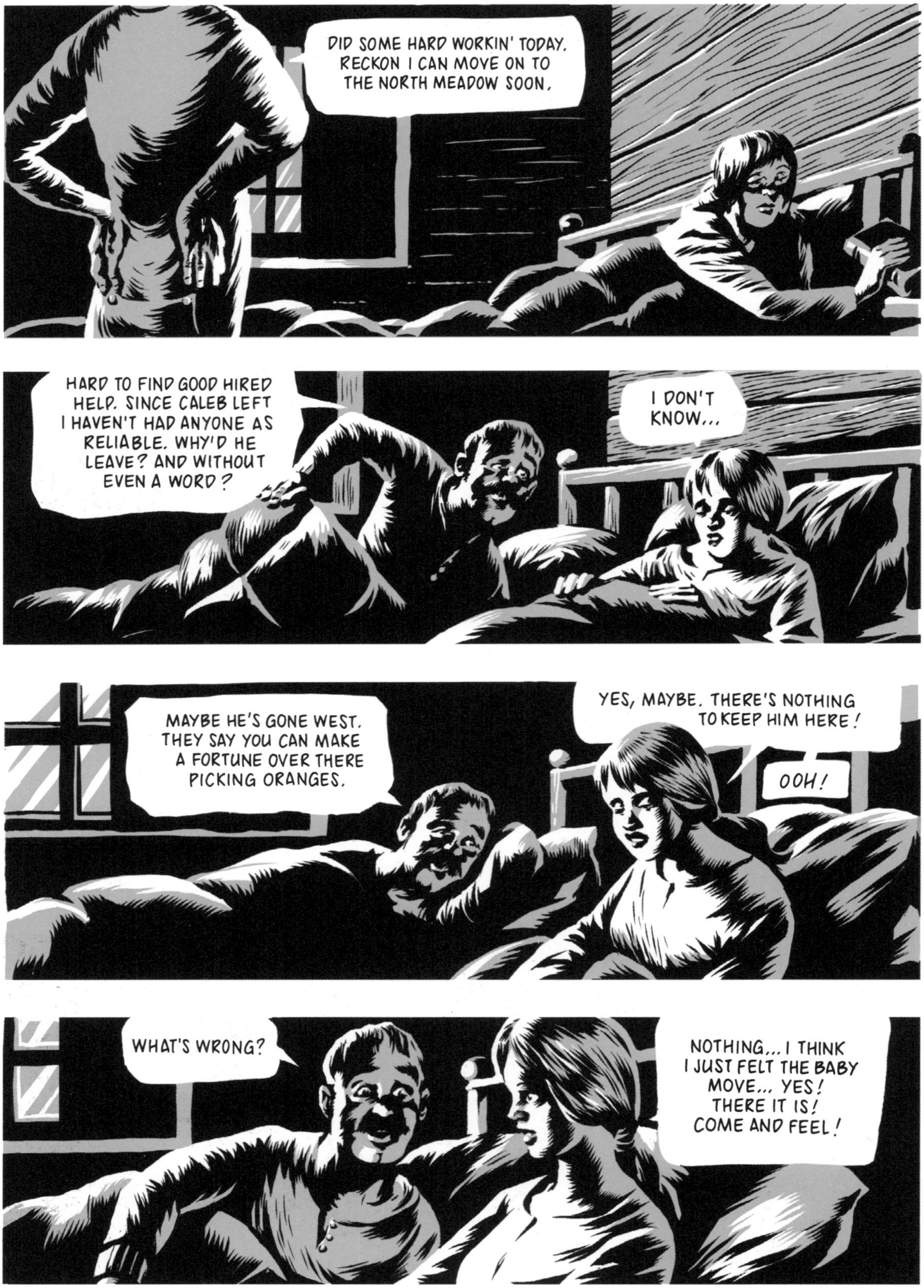
DID SOME HARD WORKIN' TODAY. RECKON I CAN MOVE ON TO THE NORTH MEADOW SOON.
HARD TO FIND GOOD HIRED HELP. SINCE CALEB LEFT I HAVEN'T HAD ANYONE AS RELIABLE. WHY'D HE LEAVE? AND WITHOUT EVEN A WORD?
I DON'T KNOW...
MAYBE HE'S GONE WEST. THEY SAY YOU CAN MAKE A FORTUNE OVER THERE PICKING ORANGES.
YES, MAYBE. THERE'S NOTHING TO KEEP HIM HERE!
OOH!
WHAT'S WRONG?
NOTHING... I THINK I JUST FELT THE BABY MOVE... YES! THERE IT IS! COME AND FEEL!

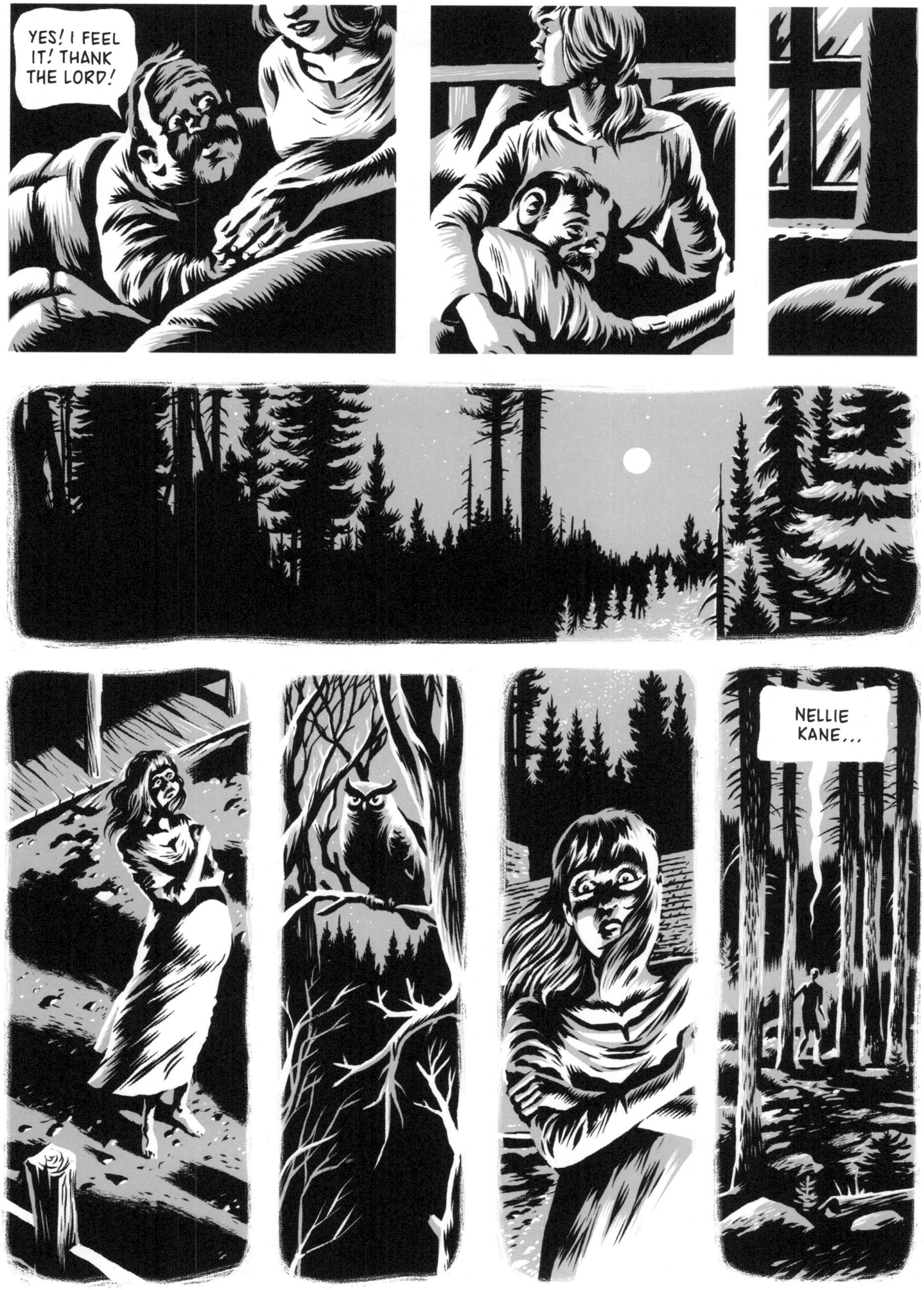
YES! I FEEL IT! THANK THE LORD!
NELLIE KANE...

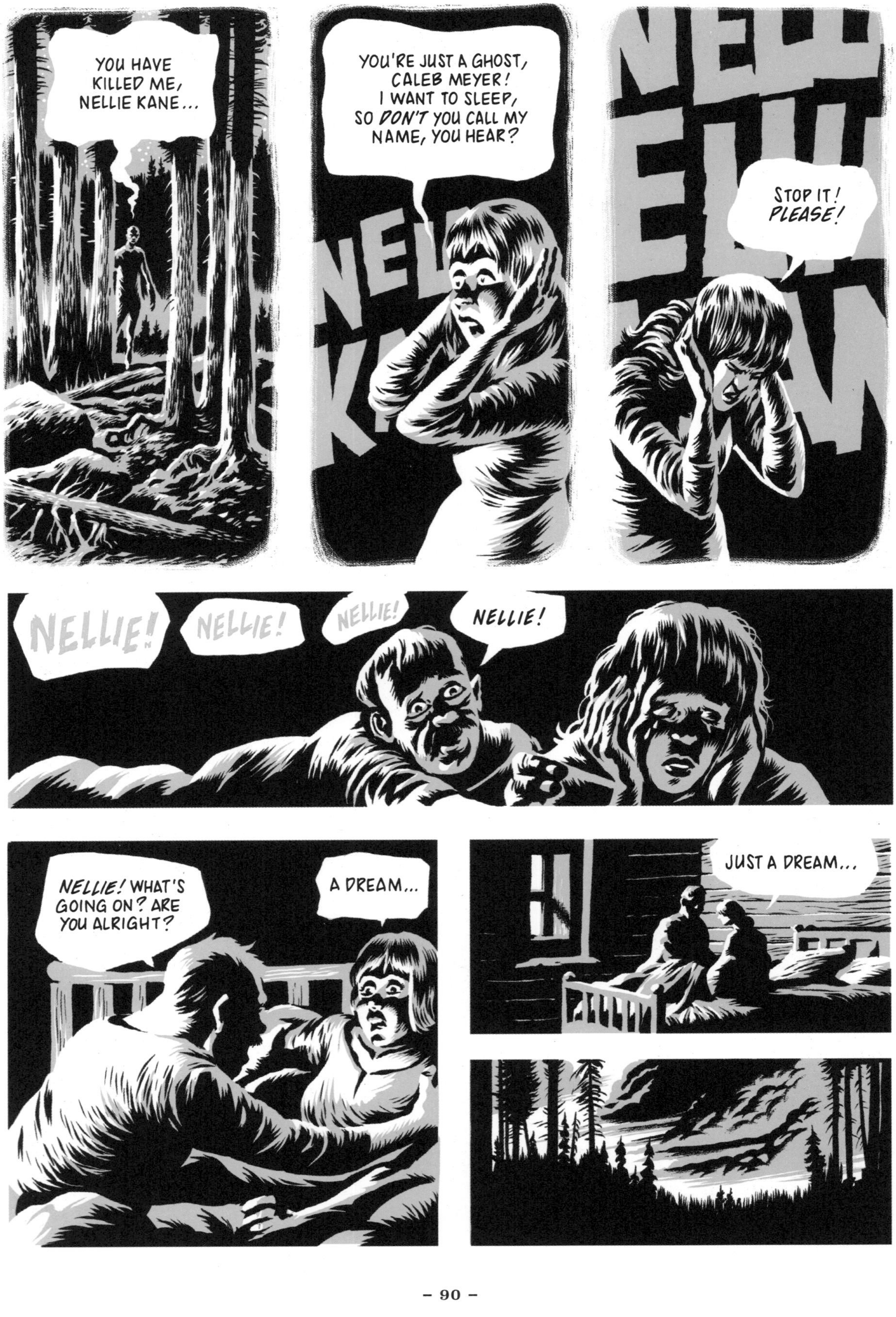
YOU HAVE KILLED ME, NELLIE KANE...
YOU'RE JUST A GHOST, CALEB MEYER! I WANT TO SLEEP, SO *DON'T* YOU CALL MY NAME, YOU HEAR?
STOP IT! *PLEASE!*
NELLIE!
NELLIE!
NELLIE!
NELLIE!
NELLIE! WHAT'S GOING ON? ARE YOU ALRIGHT?
A DREAM...
JUST A DREAM...

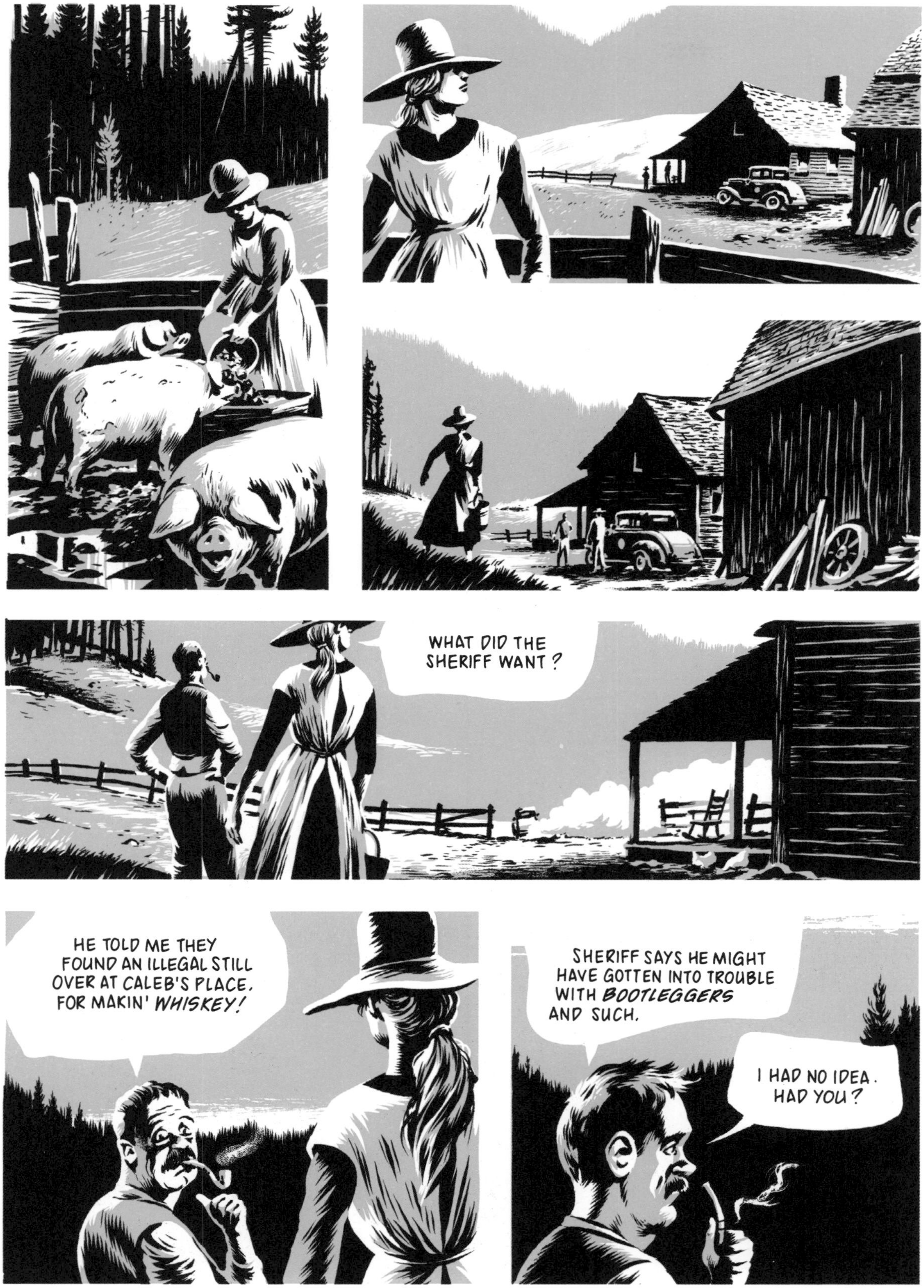
WHAT DID THE SHERIFF WANT?
HE TOLD ME THEY FOUND AN ILLEGAL STILL OVER AT CALEB'S PLACE. FOR MAKIN' WHISKEY!
SHERIFF SAYS HE MIGHT HAVE GOTTEN INTO TROUBLE WITH BOOTLEGGERS AND SUCH.
I HAD NO IDEA. HAD YOU?

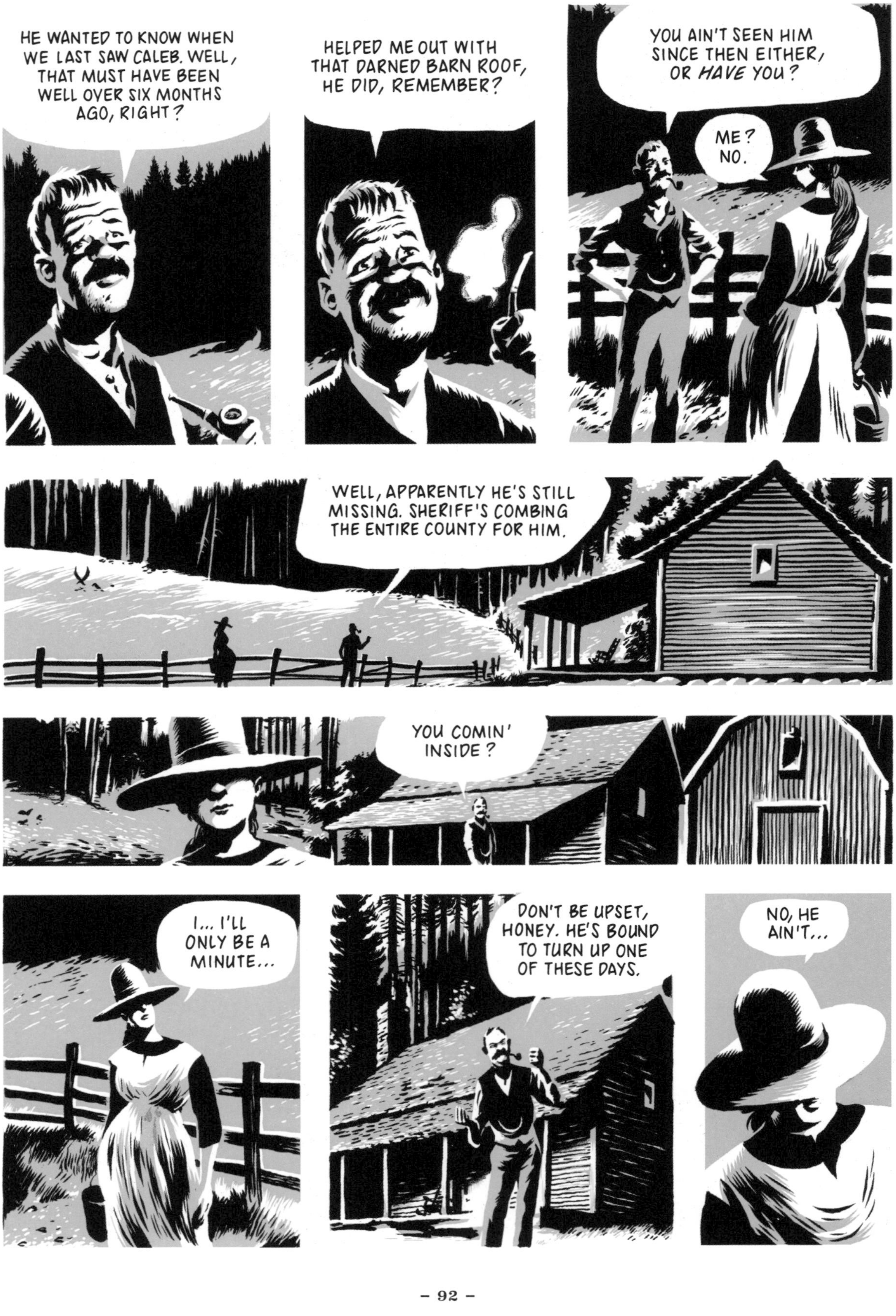
HE WANTED TO KNOW WHEN WE LAST SAW CALEB. WELL, THAT MUST HAVE BEEN WELL OVER SIX MONTHS AGO, RIGHT?
HELPED ME OUT WITH THAT DARNED BARN ROOF, HE DID, REMEMBER?
YOU AIN'T SEEN HIM SINCE THEN EITHER, OR *HAVE* YOU?
ME? NO.
WELL, APPARENTLY HE'S STILL MISSING. SHERIFF'S COMBING THE ENTIRE COUNTY FOR HIM.
YOU COMIN' INSIDE?
I... I'LL ONLY BE A MINUTE...
DON'T BE UPSET, HONEY. HE'S BOUND TO TURN UP ONE OF THESE DAYS.
NO, HE AIN'T...

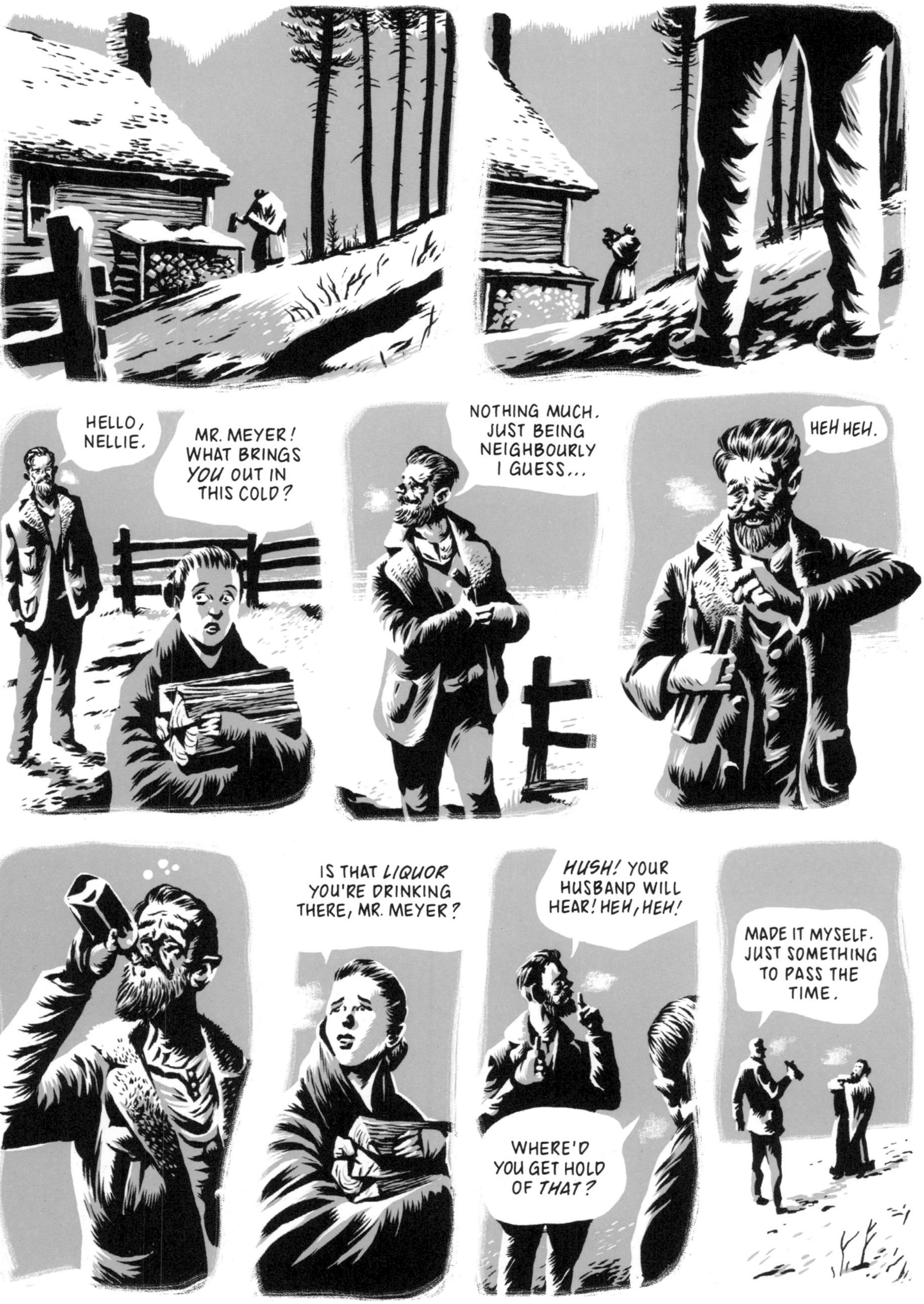
HELLO, NELLIE.
MR. MEYER! WHAT BRINGS YOU OUT IN THIS COLD?
NOTHING MUCH. JUST BEING NEIGHBOURLY I GUESS...
HEH HEH.
IS THAT LIQUOR YOU'RE DRINKING THERE, MR. MEYER?
HUSH! YOUR HUSBAND WILL HEAR! HEH, HEH!
WHERE'D YOU GET HOLD OF THAT?
MADE IT MYSELF. JUST SOMETHING TO PASS THE TIME.

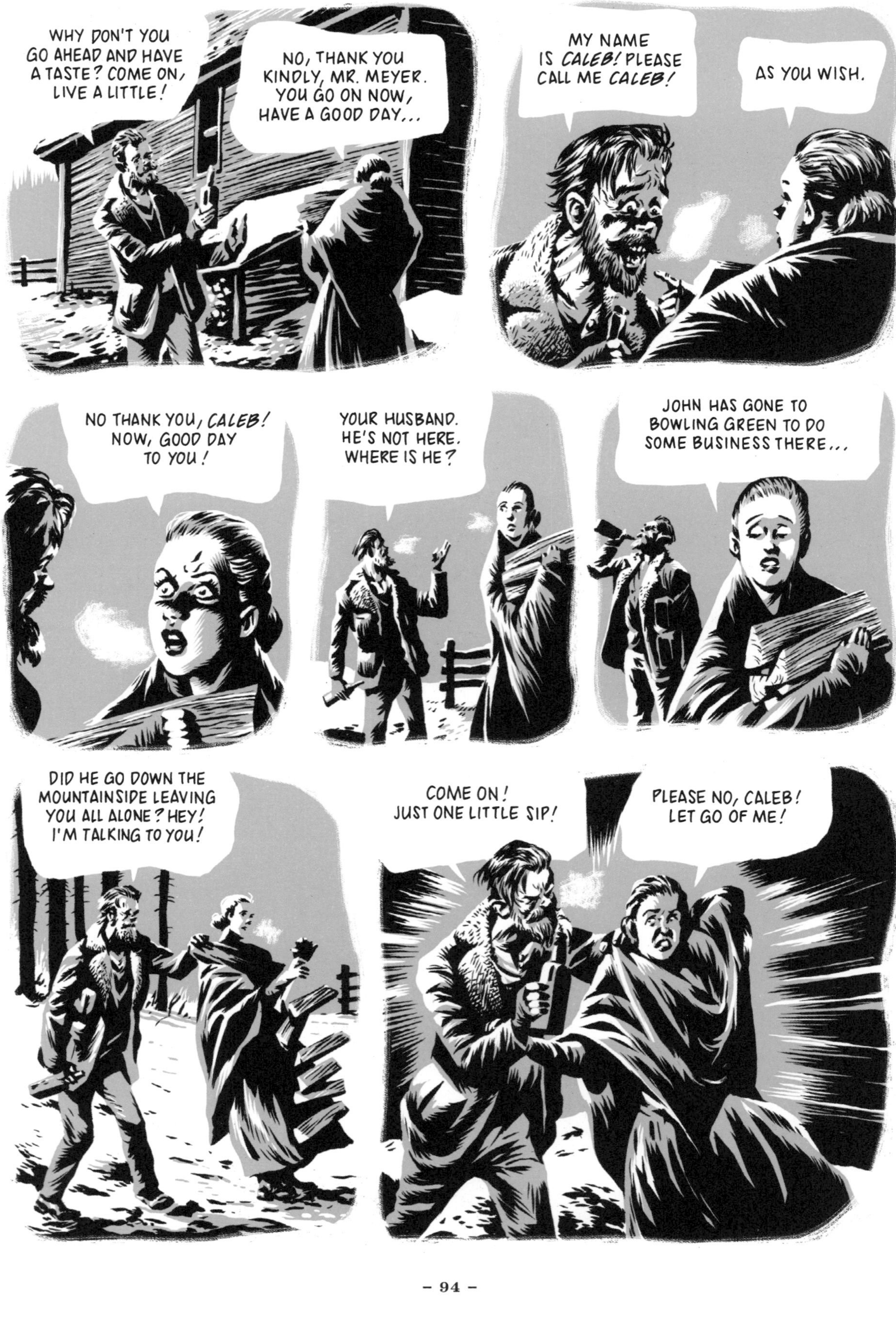
WHY DON'T YOU GO AHEAD AND HAVE A TASTE? COME ON, LIVE A LITTLE!
NO, THANK YOU KINDLY, MR. MEYER. YOU GO ON NOW, HAVE A GOOD DAY...
MY NAME IS CALEB! PLEASE CALL ME CALEB!
AS YOU WISH.
NO THANK YOU, CALEB! NOW, GOOD DAY TO YOU!
YOUR HUSBAND. HE'S NOT HERE. WHERE IS HE?
JOHN HAS GONE TO BOWLING GREEN TO DO SOME BUSINESS THERE...
DID HE GO DOWN THE MOUNTAINSIDE LEAVING YOU ALL ALONE? HEY! I'M TALKING TO YOU!
COME ON! JUST ONE LITTLE SIP!
PLEASE NO, CALEB! LET GO OF ME!

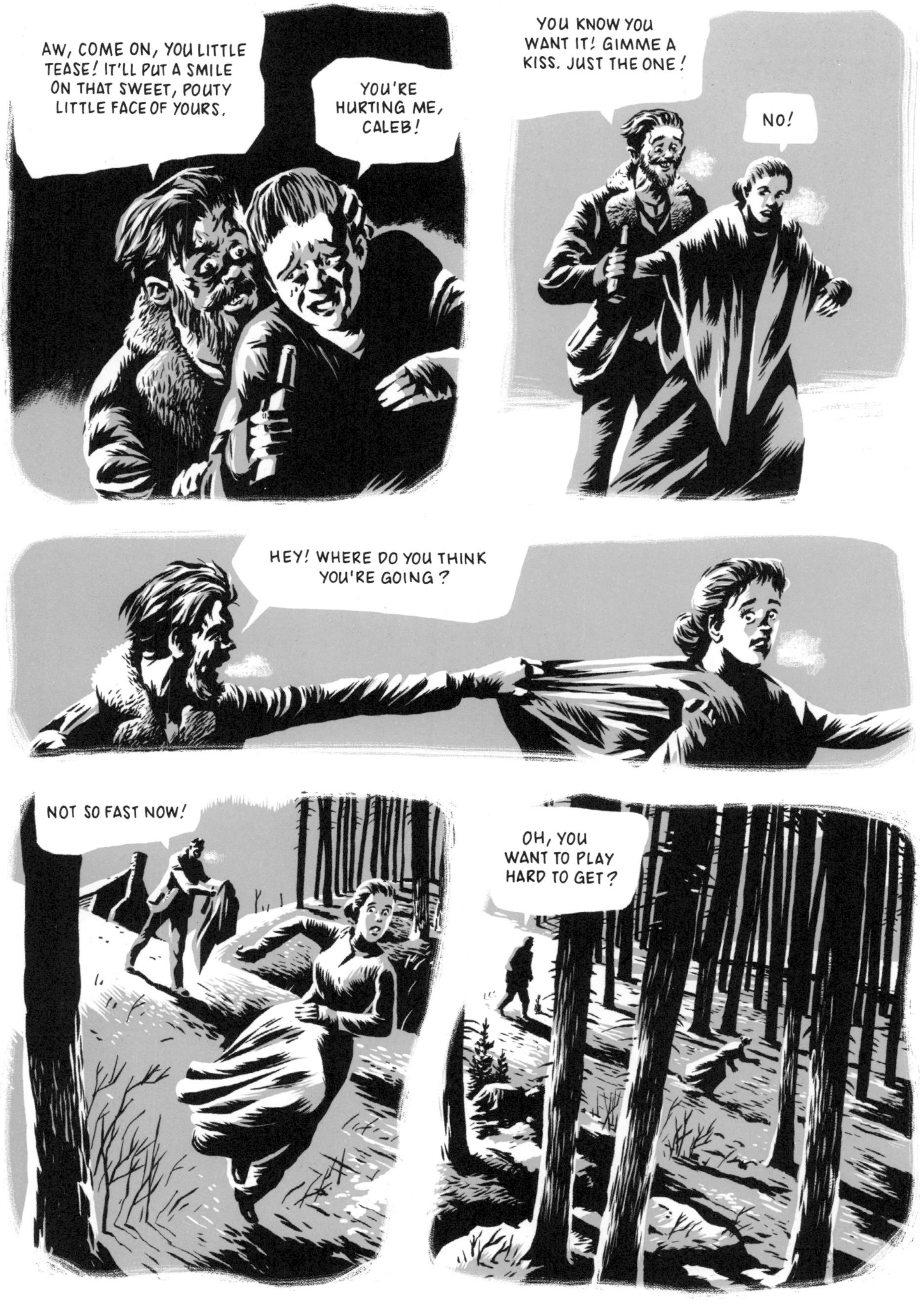
AW, COME ON, YOU LITTLE TEASE! IT'LL PUT A SMILE ON THAT SWEET, POUTY LITTLE FACE OF YOURS.
YOU'RE HURTING ME, CALEB!
YOU KNOW YOU WANT IT! GIMME A KISS. JUST THE ONE!
NO!
HEY! WHERE DO YOU THINK YOU'RE GOING?
NOT SO FAST NOW!
OH, YOU WANT TO PLAY HARD TO GET?

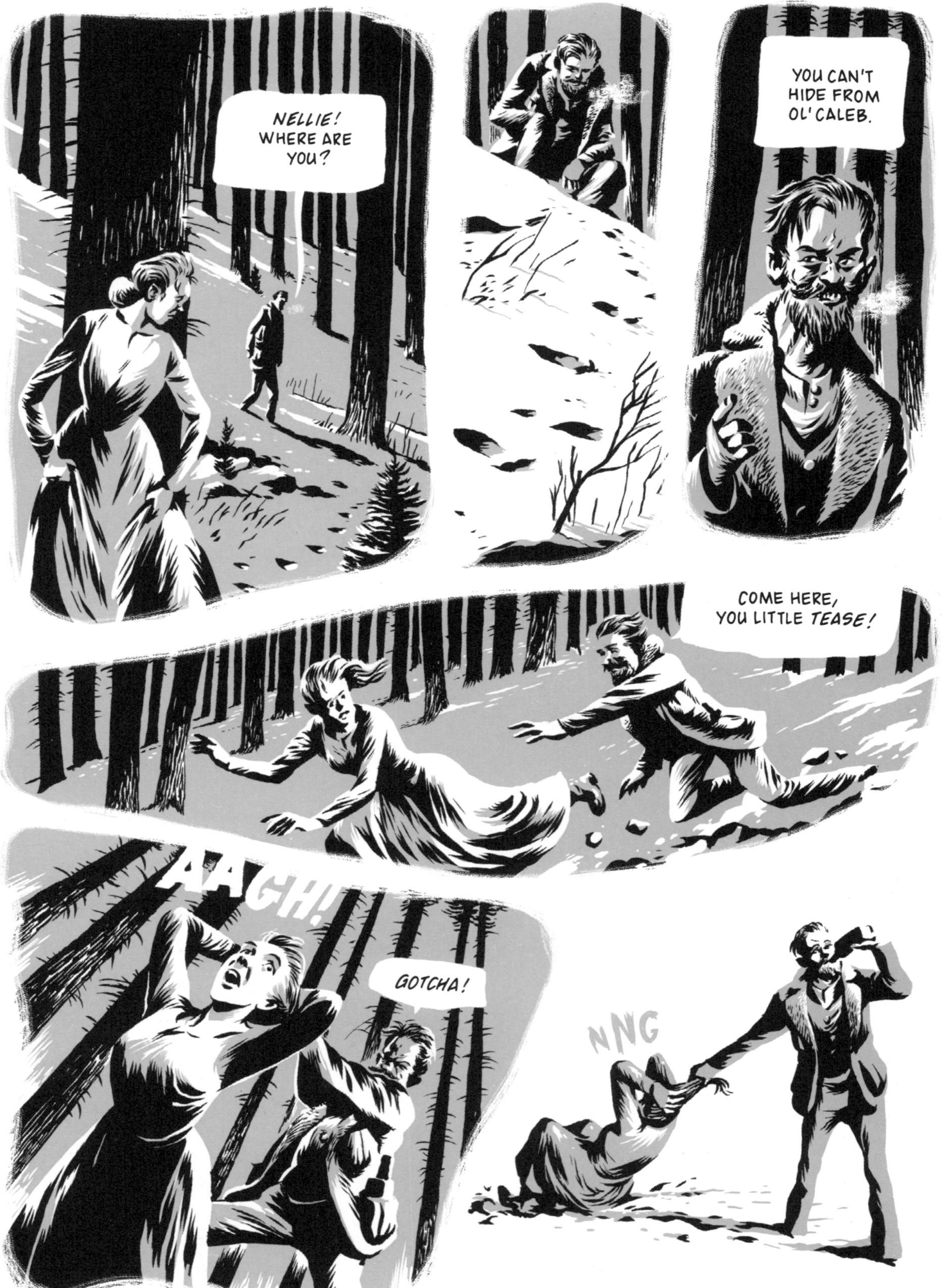
NELLIE! WHERE ARE YOU?
YOU CAN'T HIDE FROM OL' CALEB.
COME HERE, YOU LITTLE TEASE!
AAGH!
GOTCHA!
NNG

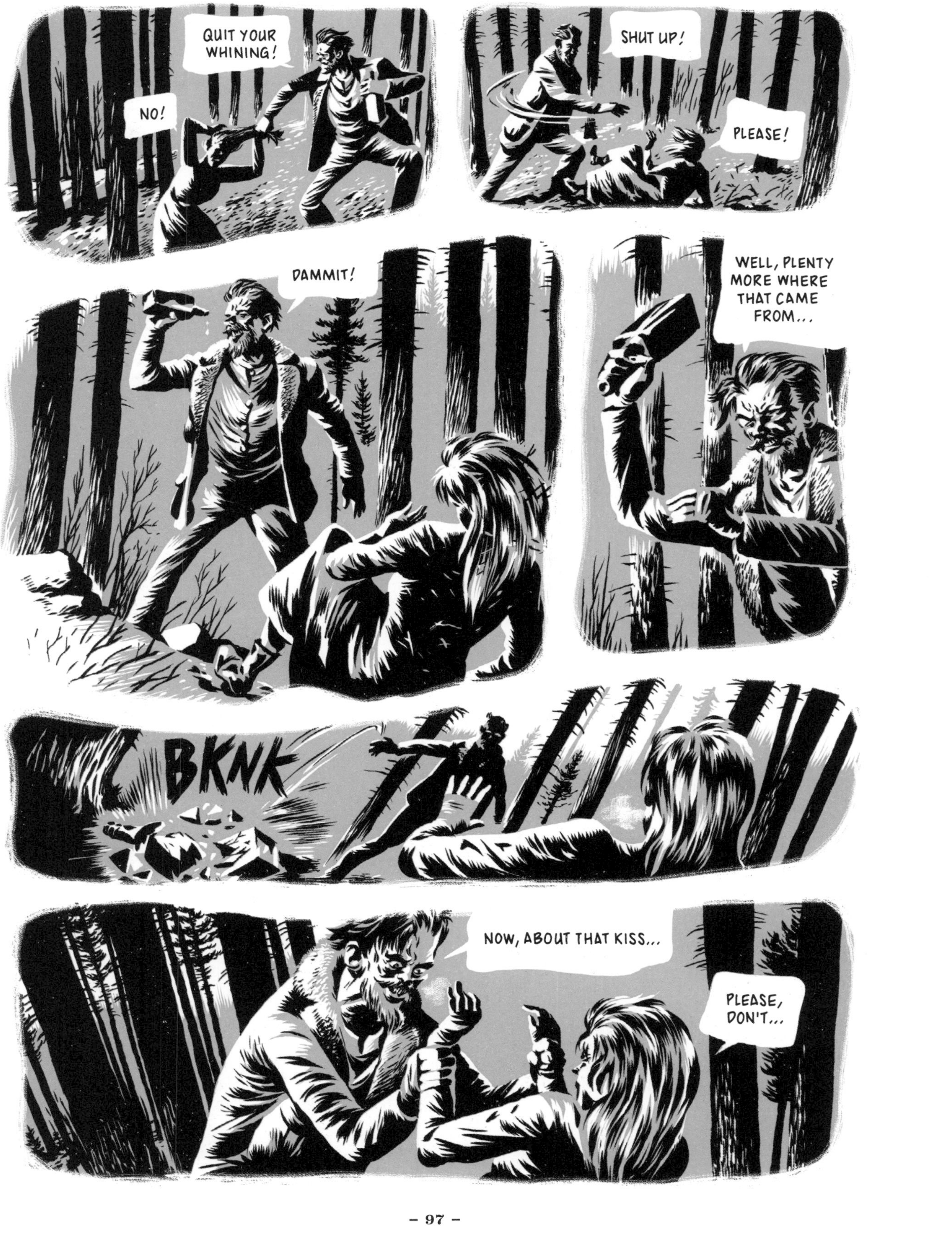
QUIT YOUR WHINING!
NO!
SHUT UP!
PLEASE!
DAMMIT!
WELL, PLENTY MORE WHERE THAT CAME FROM...
BKNK
NOW, ABOUT THAT KISS...
PLEASE, DON'T...

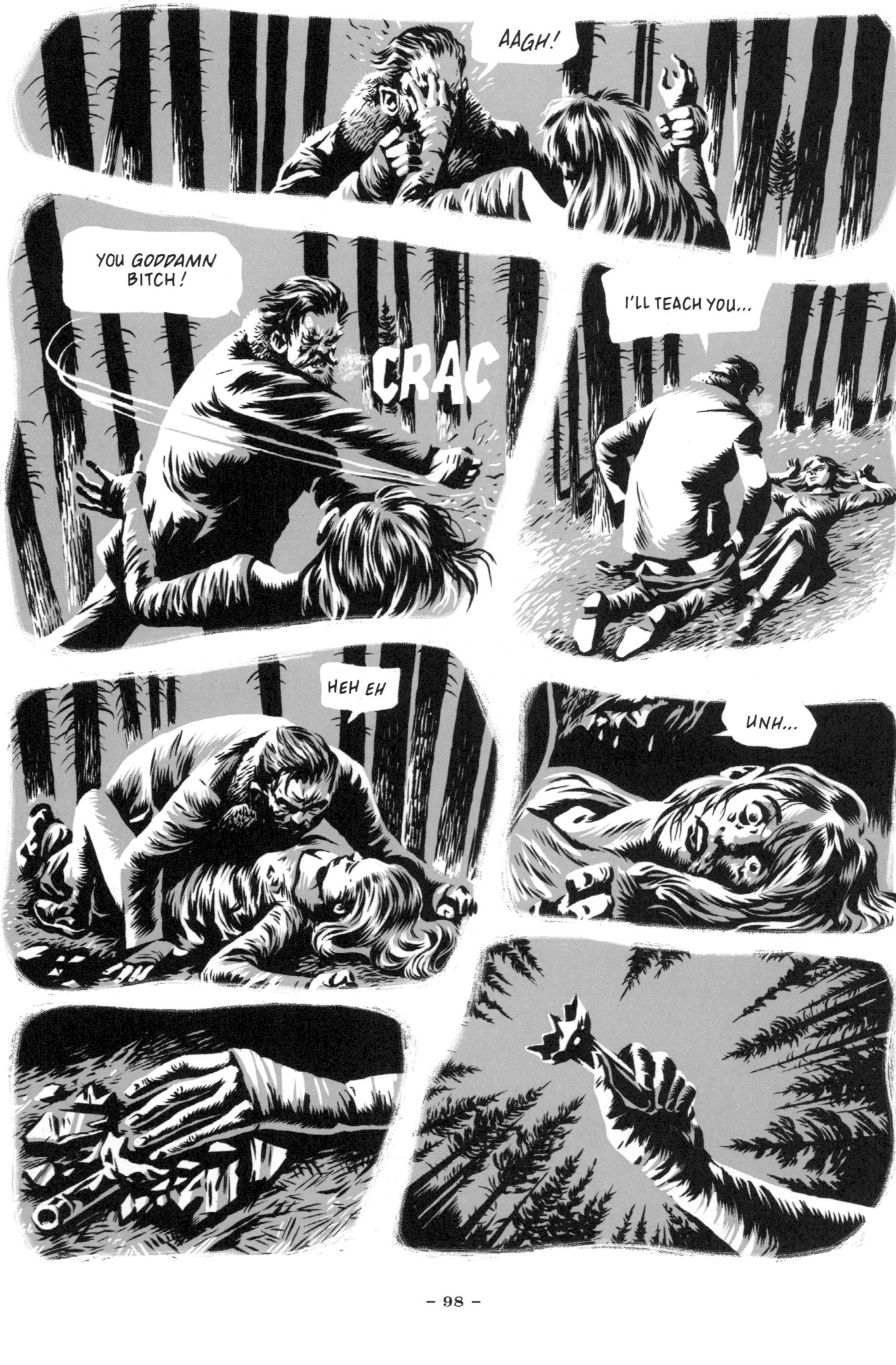
AAGH!
YOU GODDAMN BITCH!
CRAC
I'LL TEACH YOU...
HEH EH
UNH...

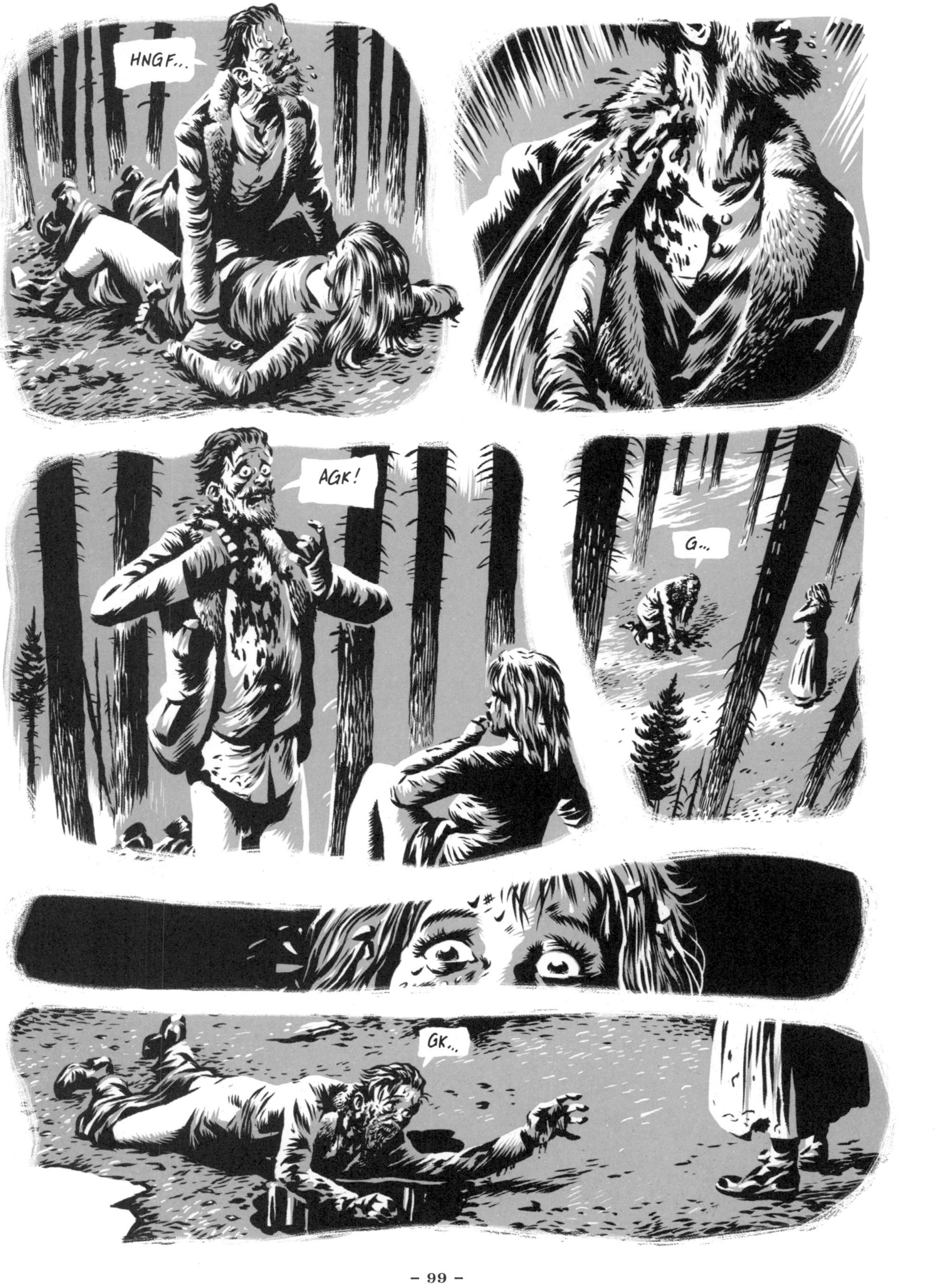
HNGF...
AGK!
G...
GK...

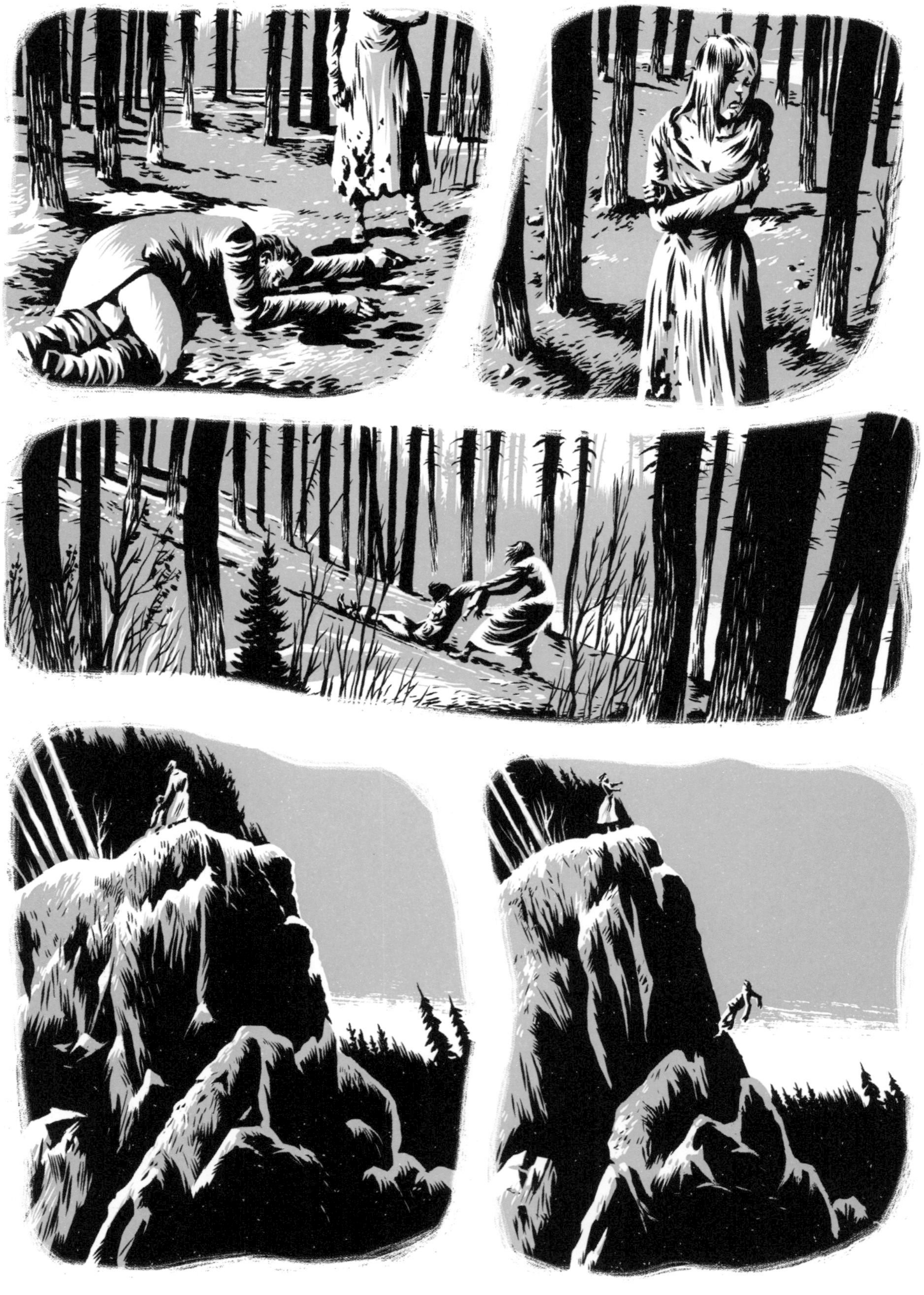

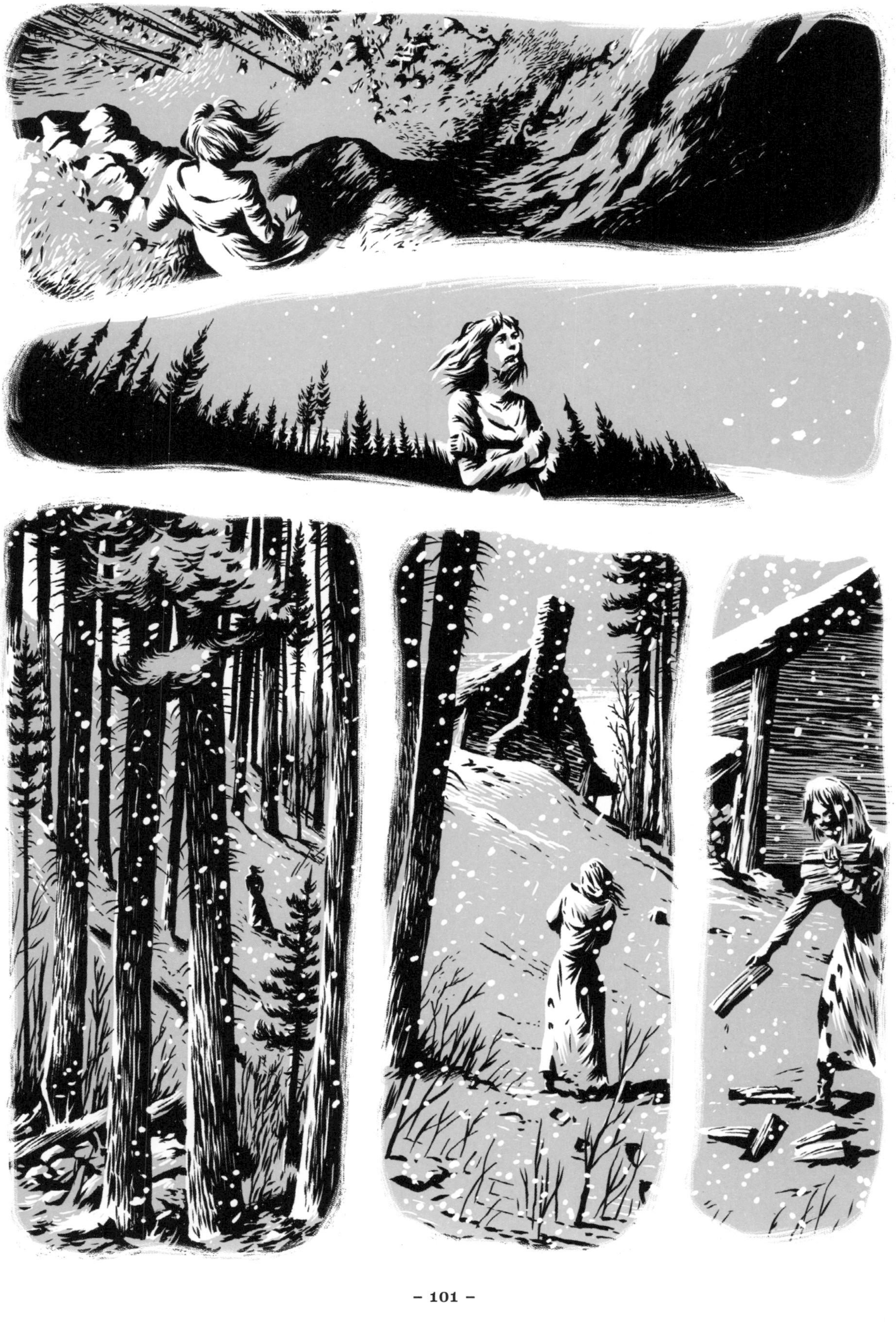

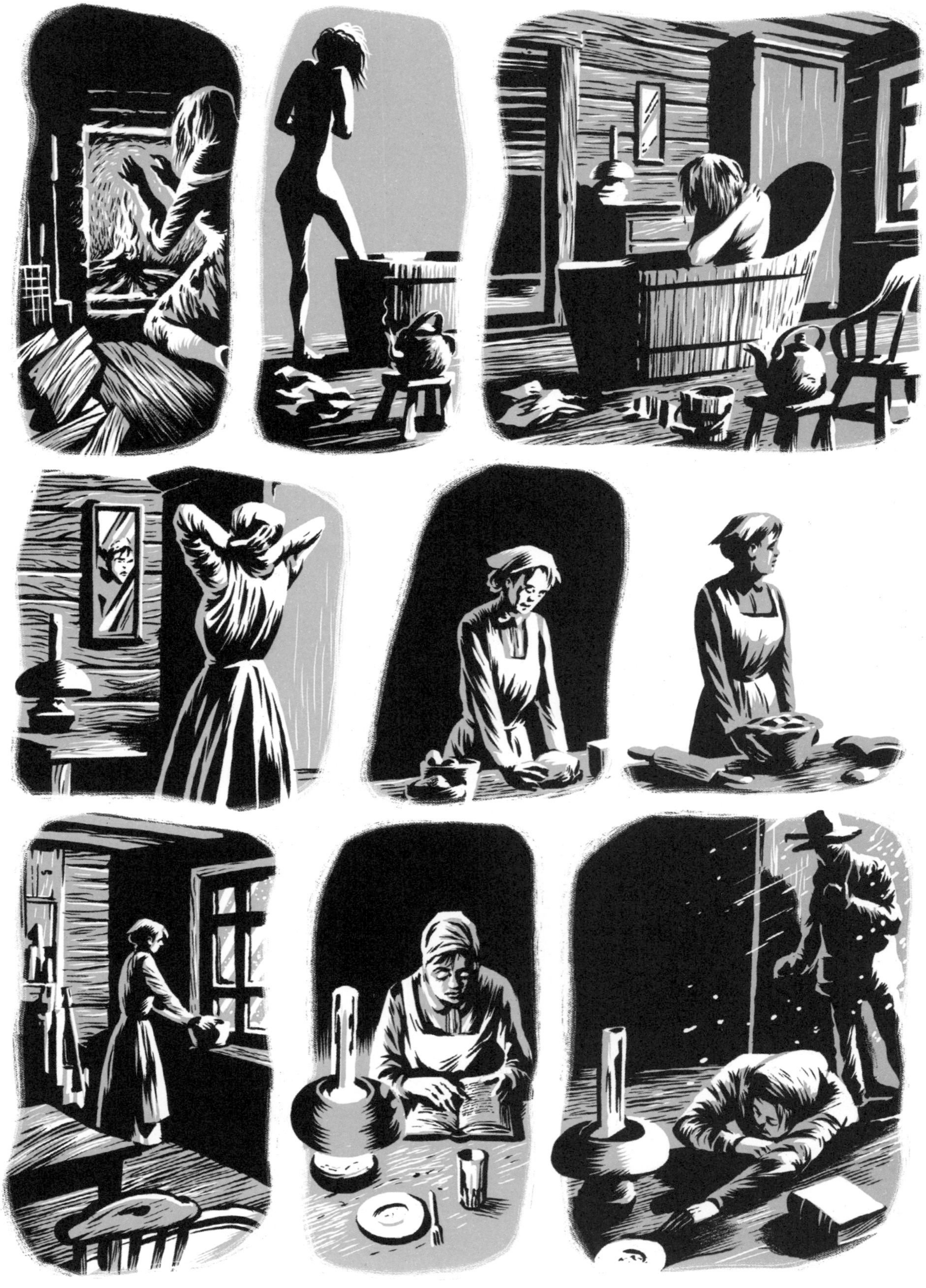

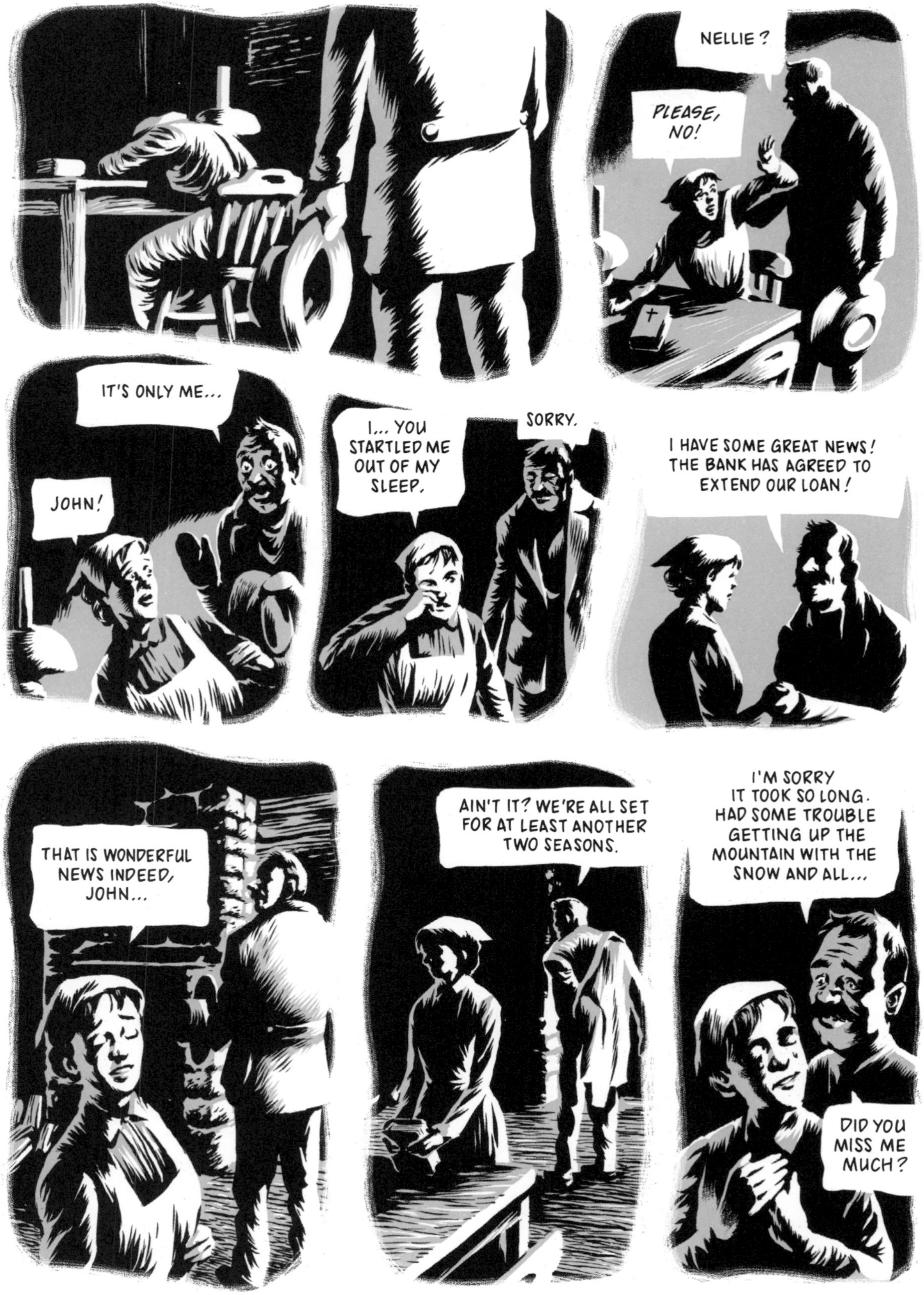
NELLIE?
PLEASE, NO!
IT'S ONLY ME...
JOHN!
I... YOU STARTLED ME OUT OF MY SLEEP.
SORRY.
I HAVE SOME GREAT NEWS! THE BANK HAS AGREED TO EXTEND OUR LOAN!
THAT IS WONDERFUL NEWS INDEED, JOHN...
AIN'T IT? WE'RE ALL SET FOR AT LEAST ANOTHER TWO SEASONS.
I'M SORRY IT TOOK SO LONG. HAD SOME TROUBLE GETTING UP THE MOUNTAIN WITH THE SNOW AND ALL...
DID YOU MISS ME MUCH?

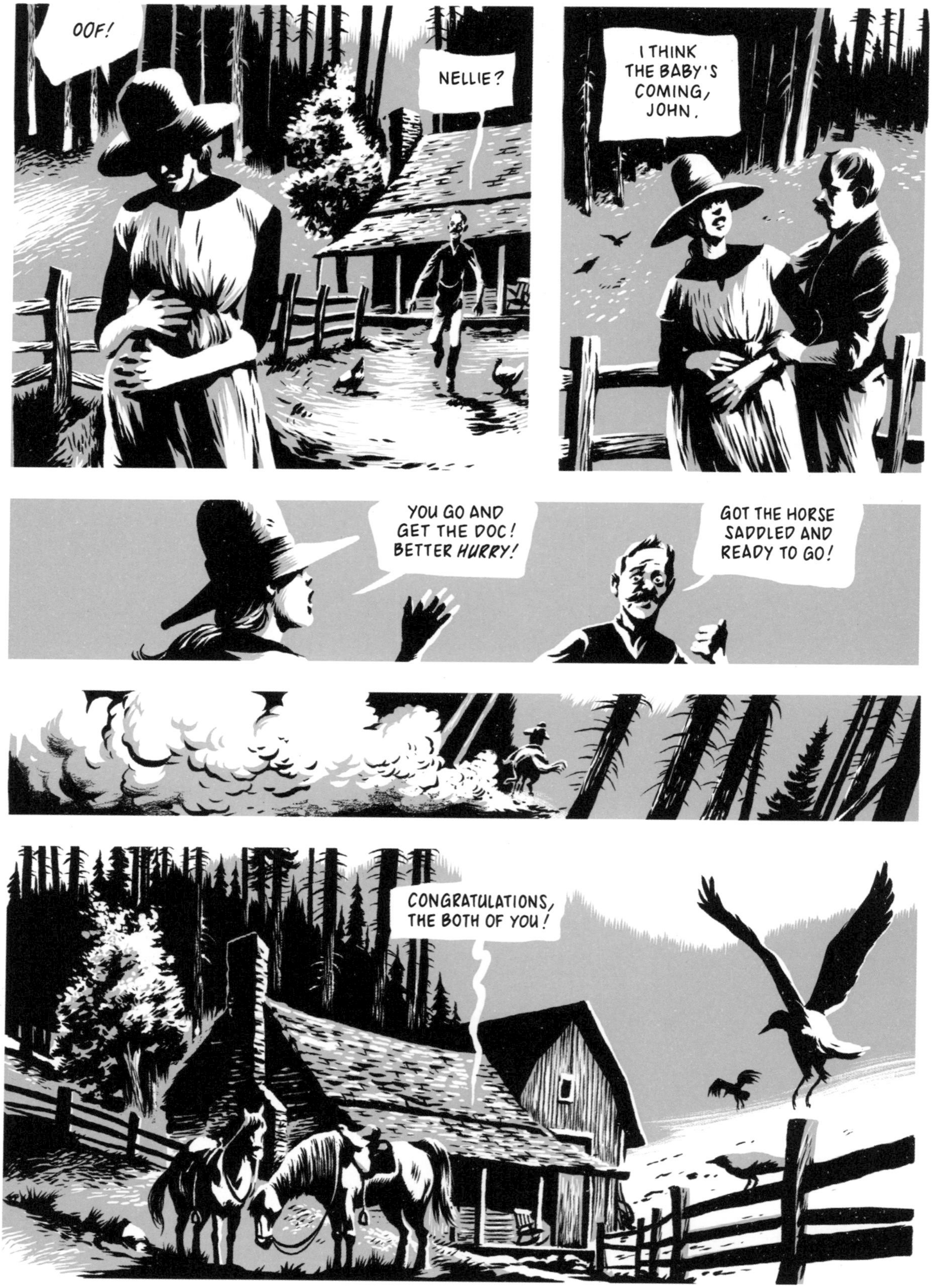
OOF!
NELLIE?
I THINK THE BABY'S COMING, JOHN.
YOU GO AND GET THE DOC! BETTER *HURRY!*
GOT THE HORSE SADDLED AND READY TO GO!
CONGRATULATIONS, THE BOTH OF YOU!

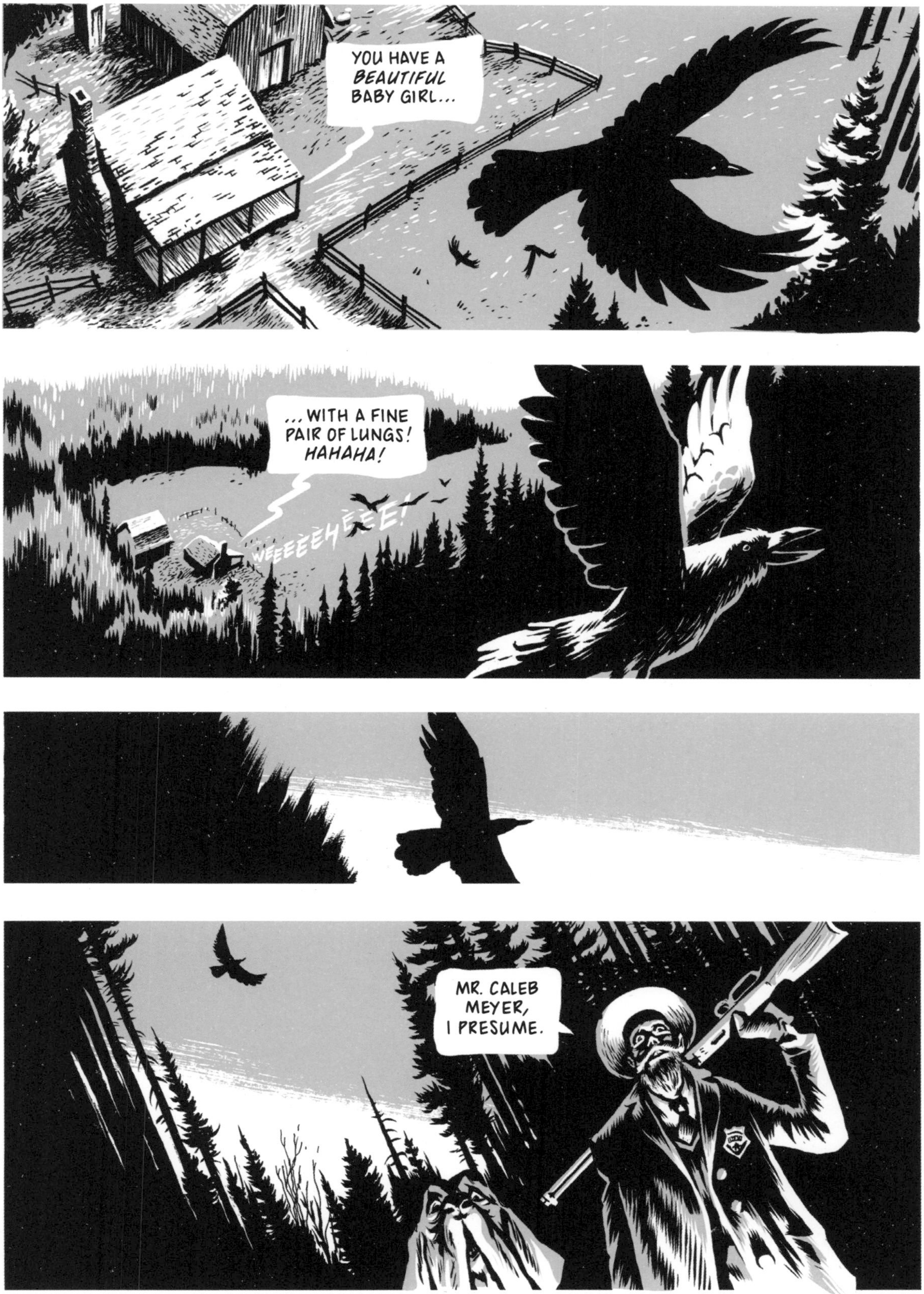
YOU HAVE A BEAUTIFUL BABY GIRL...
...WITH A FINE PAIR OF LUNGS! HAHAHA!
WEEEEEEHEEEE!
MR. CALEB MEYER, I PRESUME.

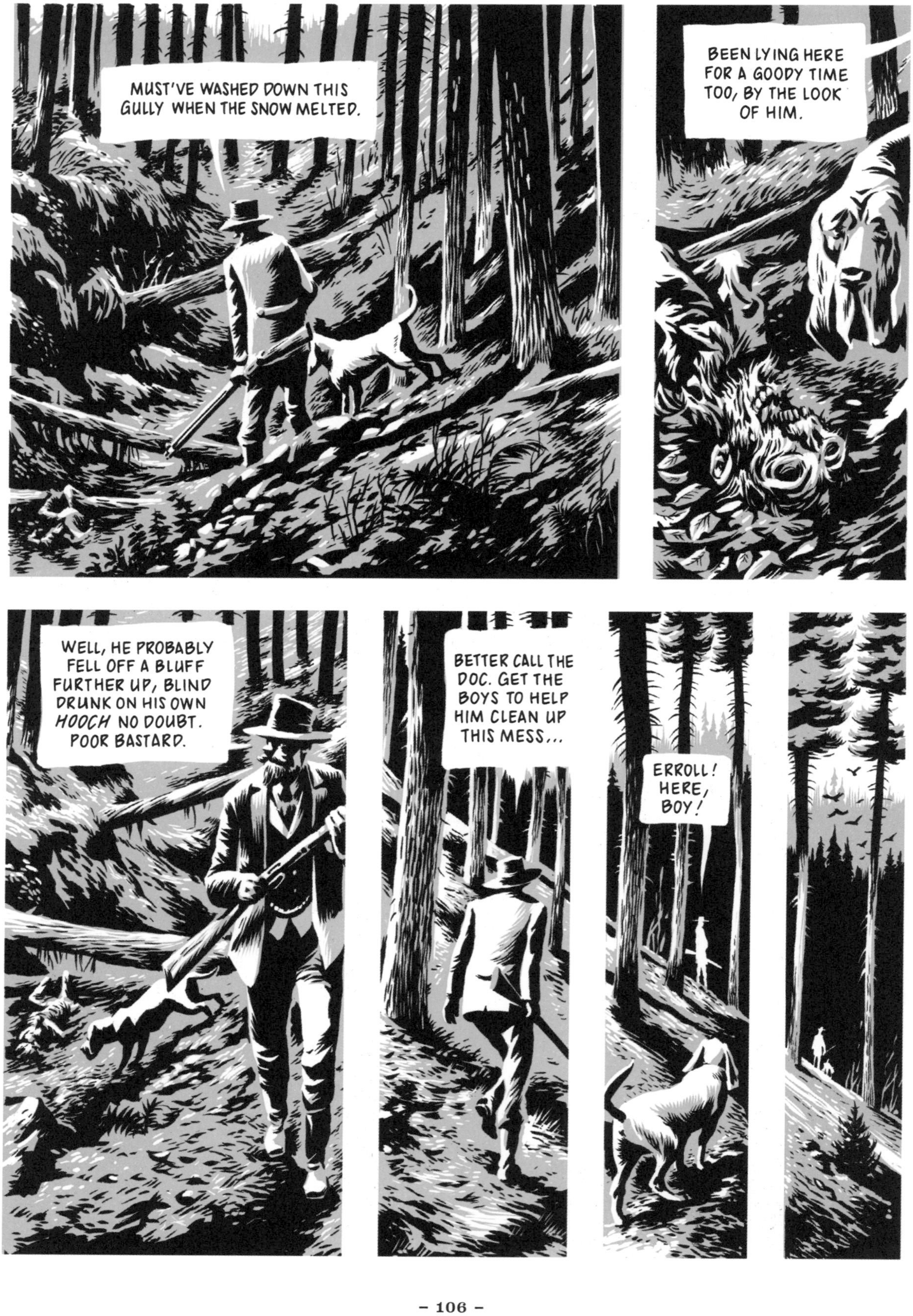
MUST'VE WASHED DOWN THIS GULLY WHEN THE SNOW MELTED.
BEEN LYING HERE FOR A GOODY TIME TOO, BY THE LOOK OF HIM.
WELL, HE PROBABLY FELL OFF A BLUFF FURTHER UP, BLIND DRUNK ON HIS OWN *HOOCH* NO DOUBT. POOR BASTARD.
BETTER CALL THE DOC. GET THE BOYS TO HELP HIM CLEAN UP THIS MESS...
ERROLL! HERE, BOY!

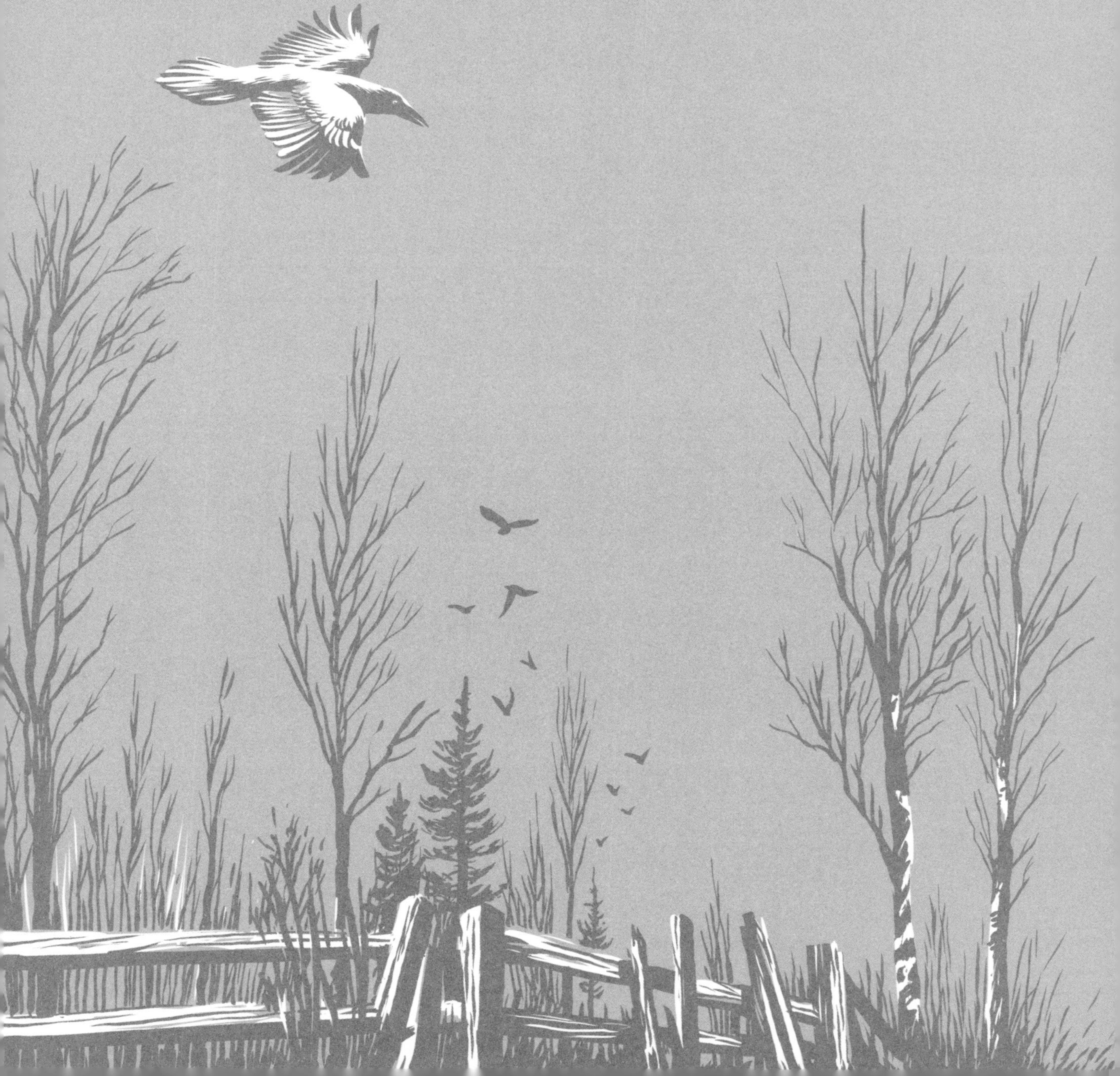

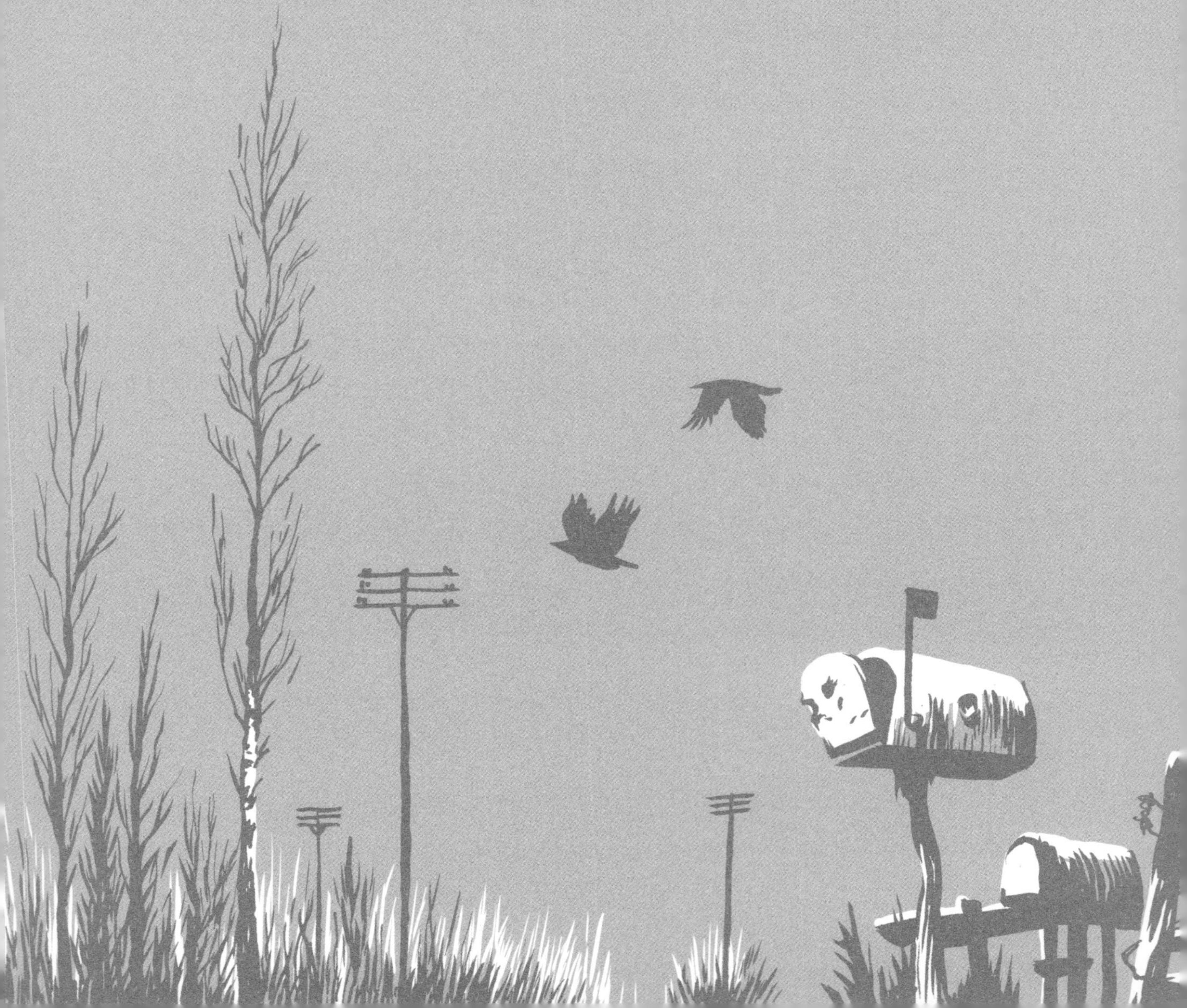

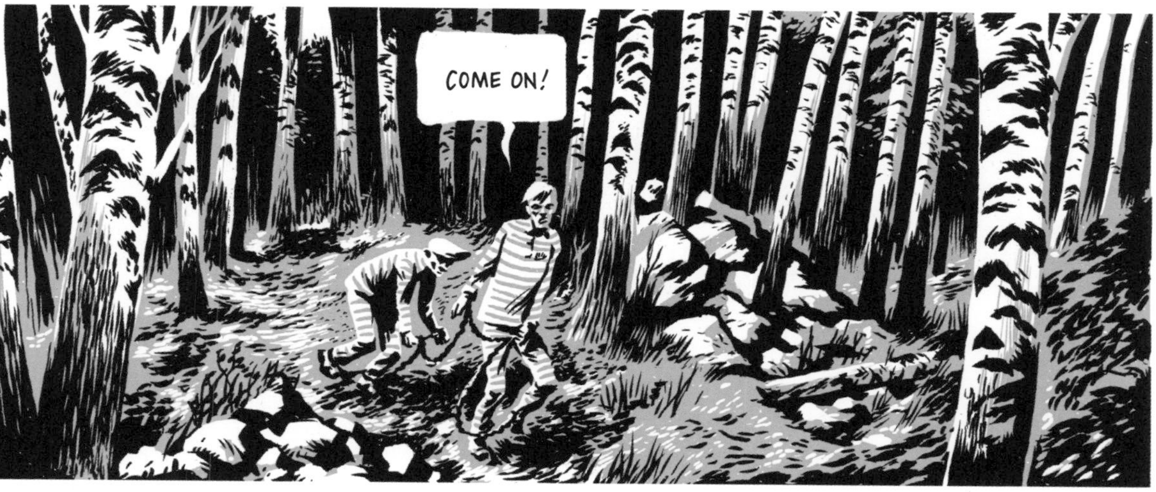
COME ON!

WHERE THE WILD ROSES GROW

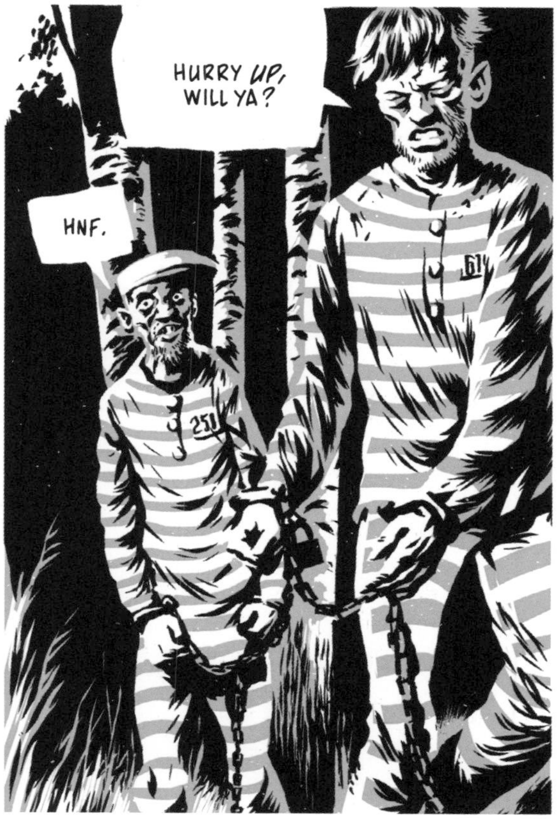
HURRY UP, WILL YA?
HNF.

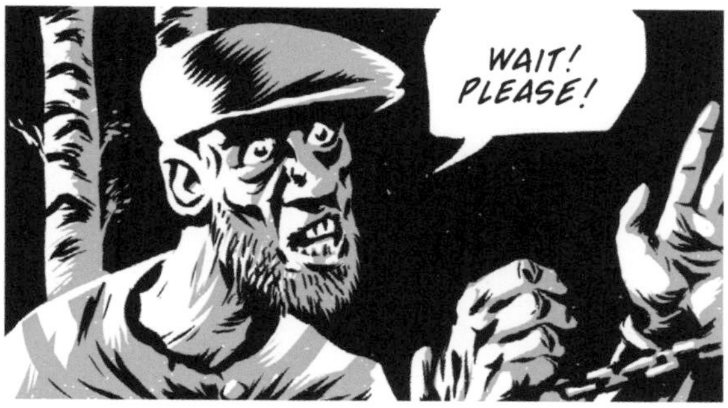
WAIT! PLEASE!

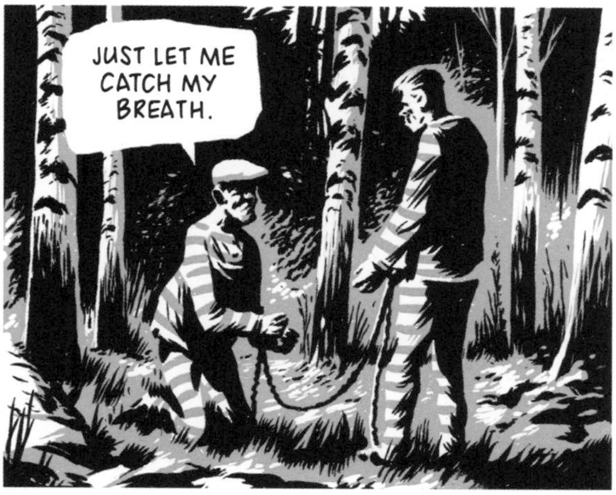
JUST LET ME CATCH MY BREATH.

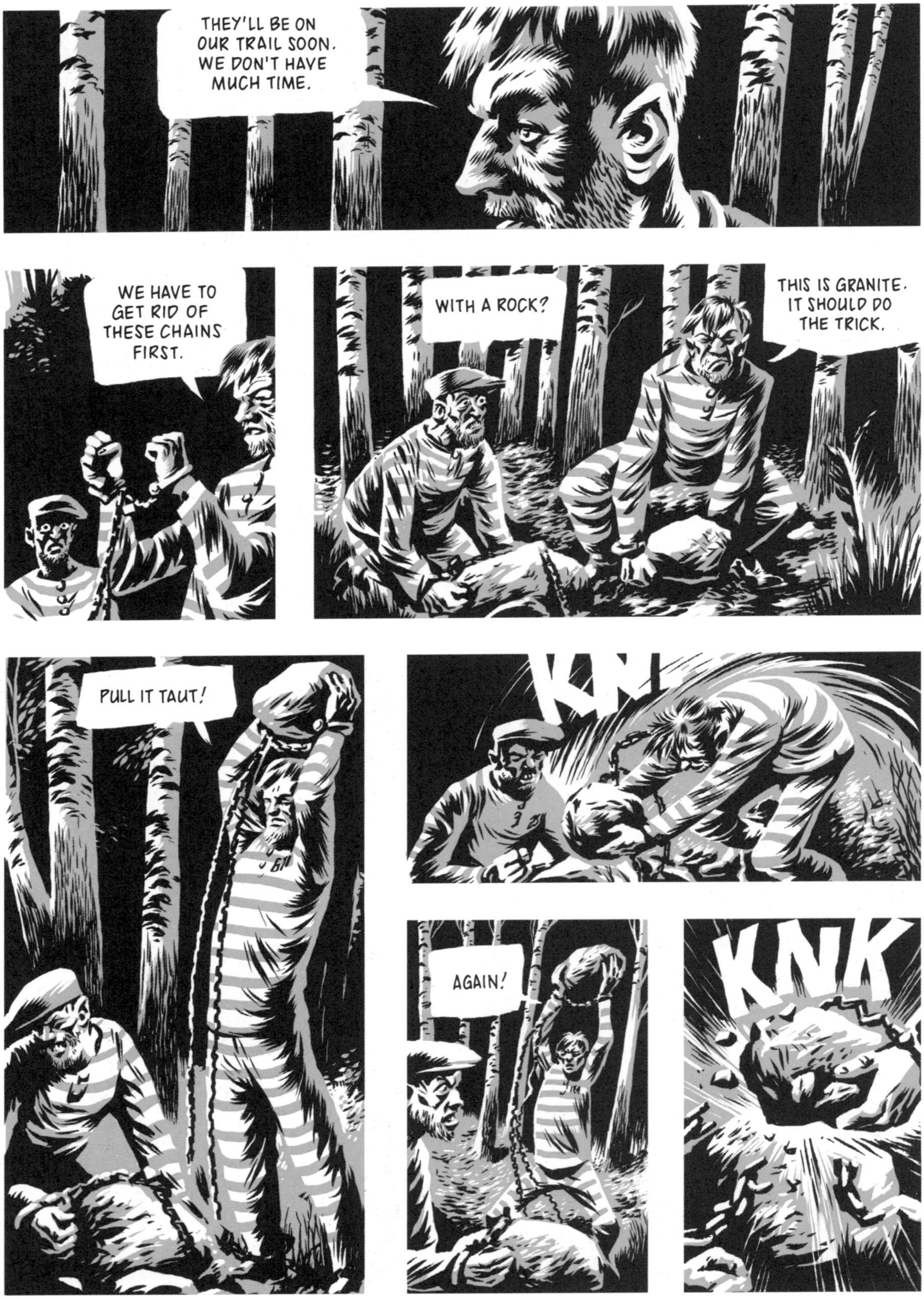
THEY'LL BE ON OUR TRAIL SOON. WE DON'T HAVE MUCH TIME.
WE HAVE TO GET RID OF THESE CHAINS FIRST.
WITH A ROCK?
THIS IS GRANITE. IT SHOULD DO THE TRICK.
PULL IT TAUT!
AGAIN!
KNK

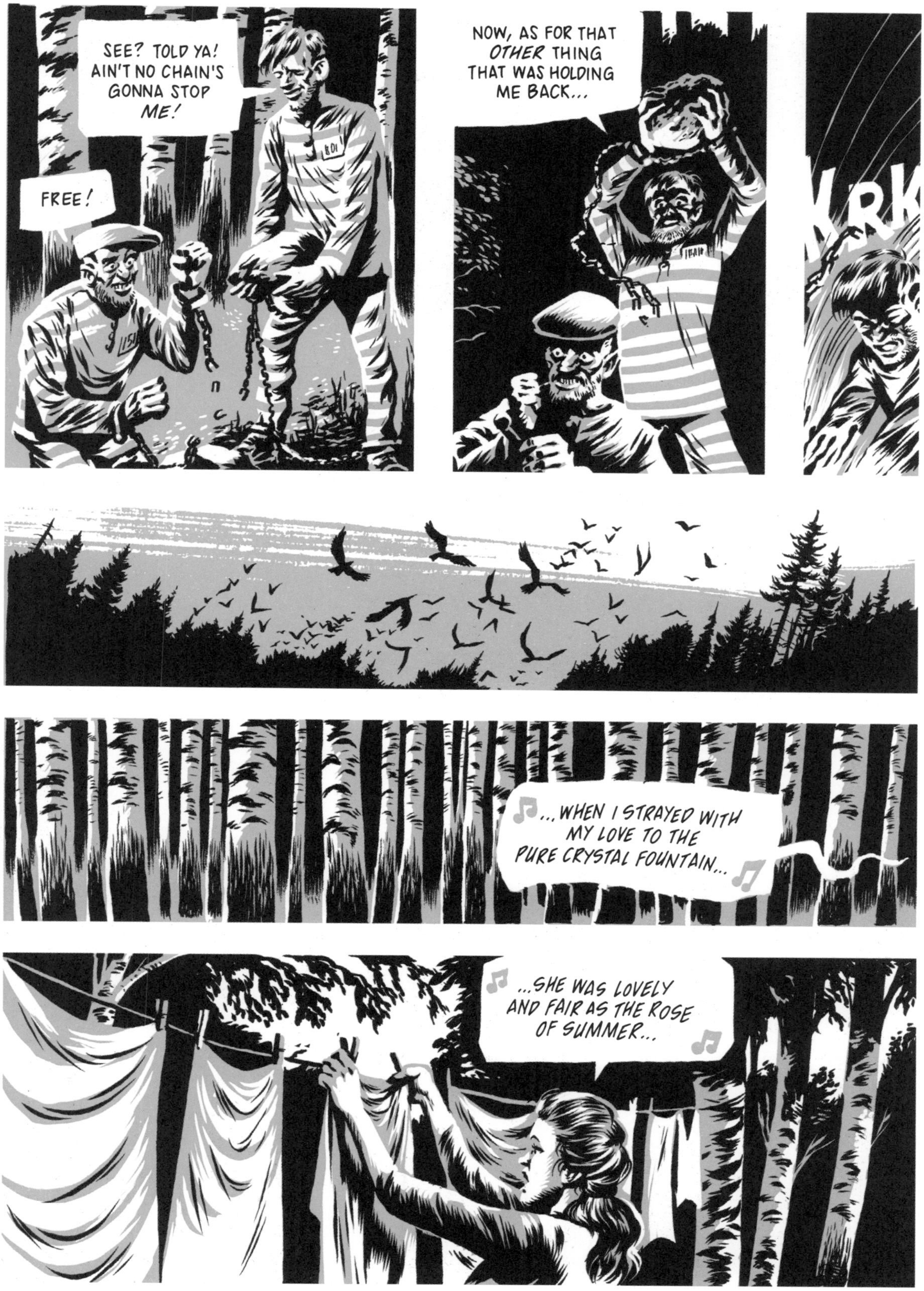
SEE? TOLD YA! AIN'T NO CHAIN'S GONNA STOP ME!
FREE!
NOW, AS FOR THAT OTHER THING THAT WAS HOLDING ME BACK...
...WHEN I STRAYED WITH MY LOVE TO THE PURE CRYSTAL FOUNTAIN...
...SHE WAS LOVELY AND FAIR AS THE ROSE OF SUMMER...

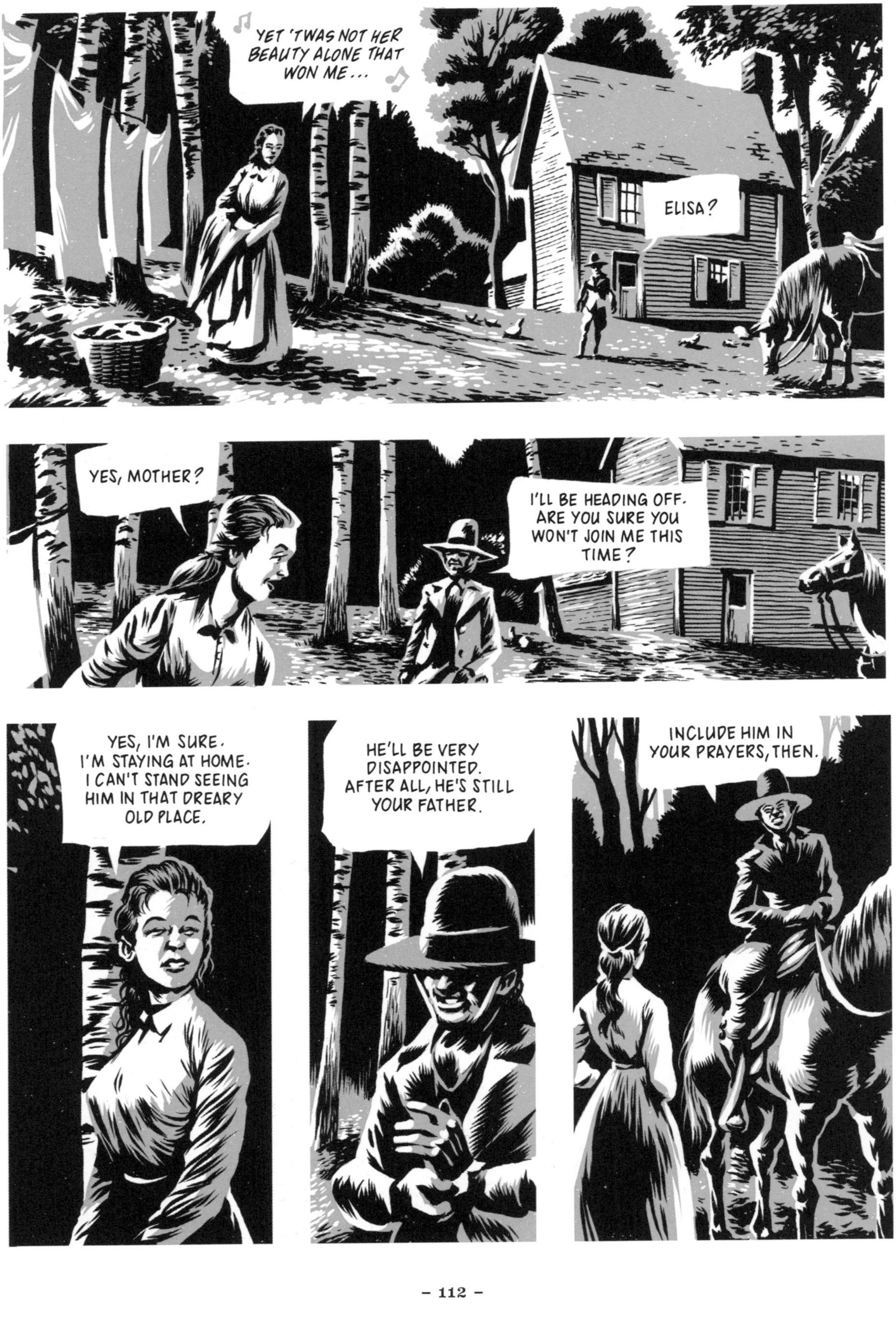
YET 'TWAS NOT HER BEAUTY ALONE THAT WON ME ...
ELISA?
YES, MOTHER?
I'LL BE HEADING OFF. ARE YOU SURE YOU WON'T JOIN ME THIS TIME?
YES, I'M SURE. I'M STAYING AT HOME. I CAN'T STAND SEEING HIM IN THAT DREARY OLD PLACE.
HE'LL BE VERY DISAPPOINTED. AFTER ALL, HE'S STILL YOUR FATHER.
INCLUDE HIM IN YOUR PRAYERS, THEN.

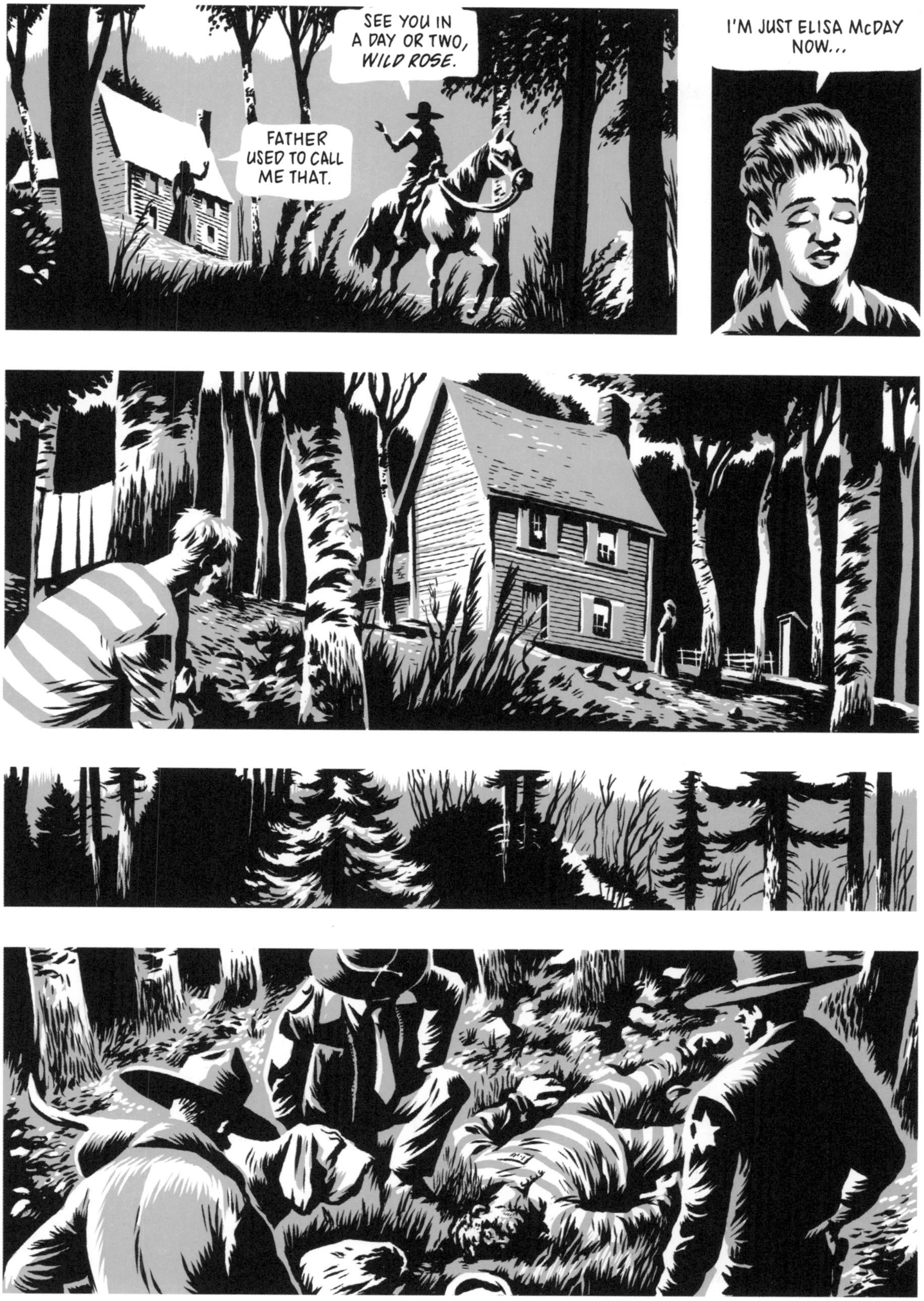
SEE YOU IN
A DAY OR TWO,
WILD ROSE.
FATHER
USED TO CALL
ME THAT.
I'M JUST ELISA McDAY
NOW...

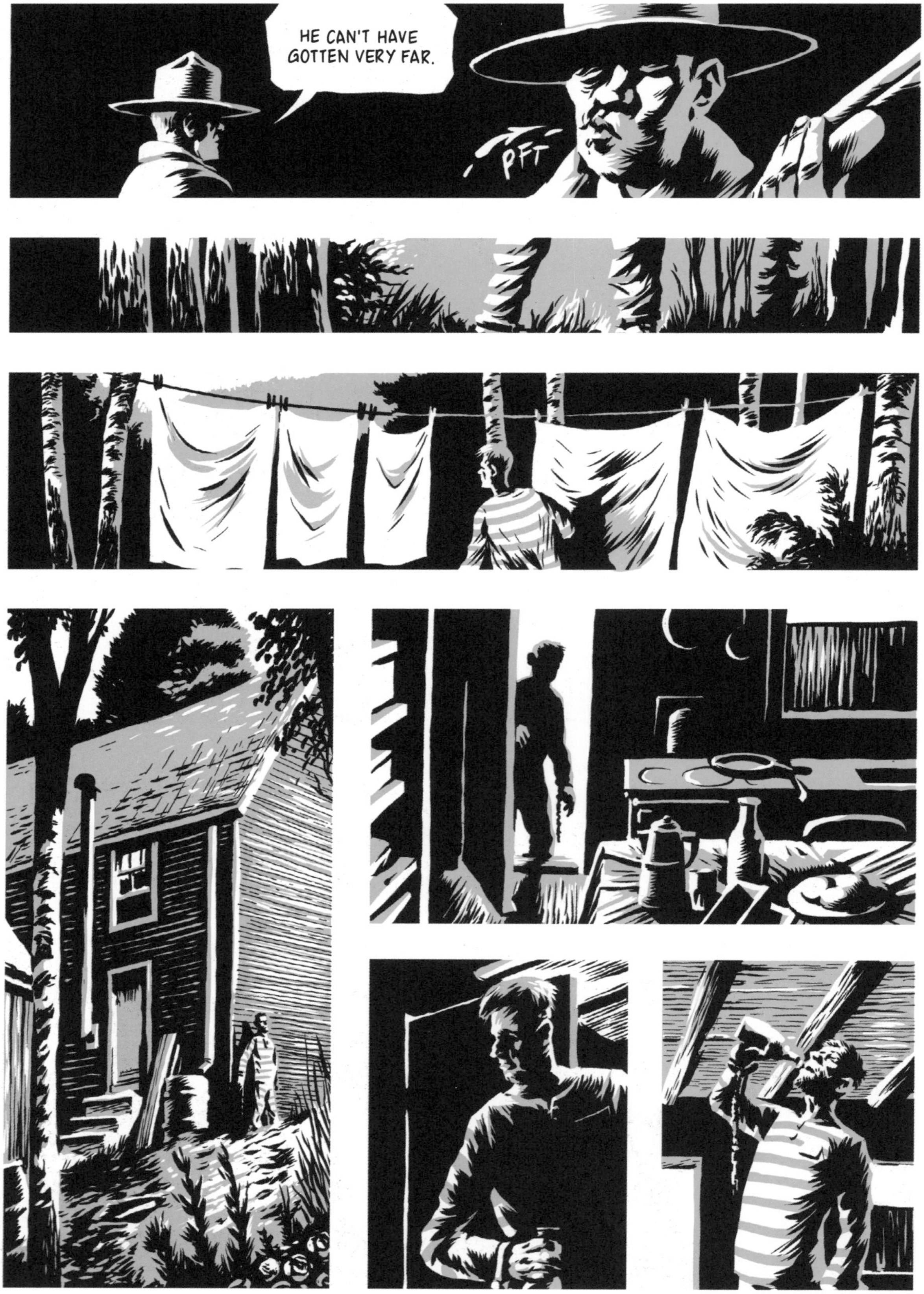
HE CAN'T HAVE GOTTEN VERY FAR.
PFT

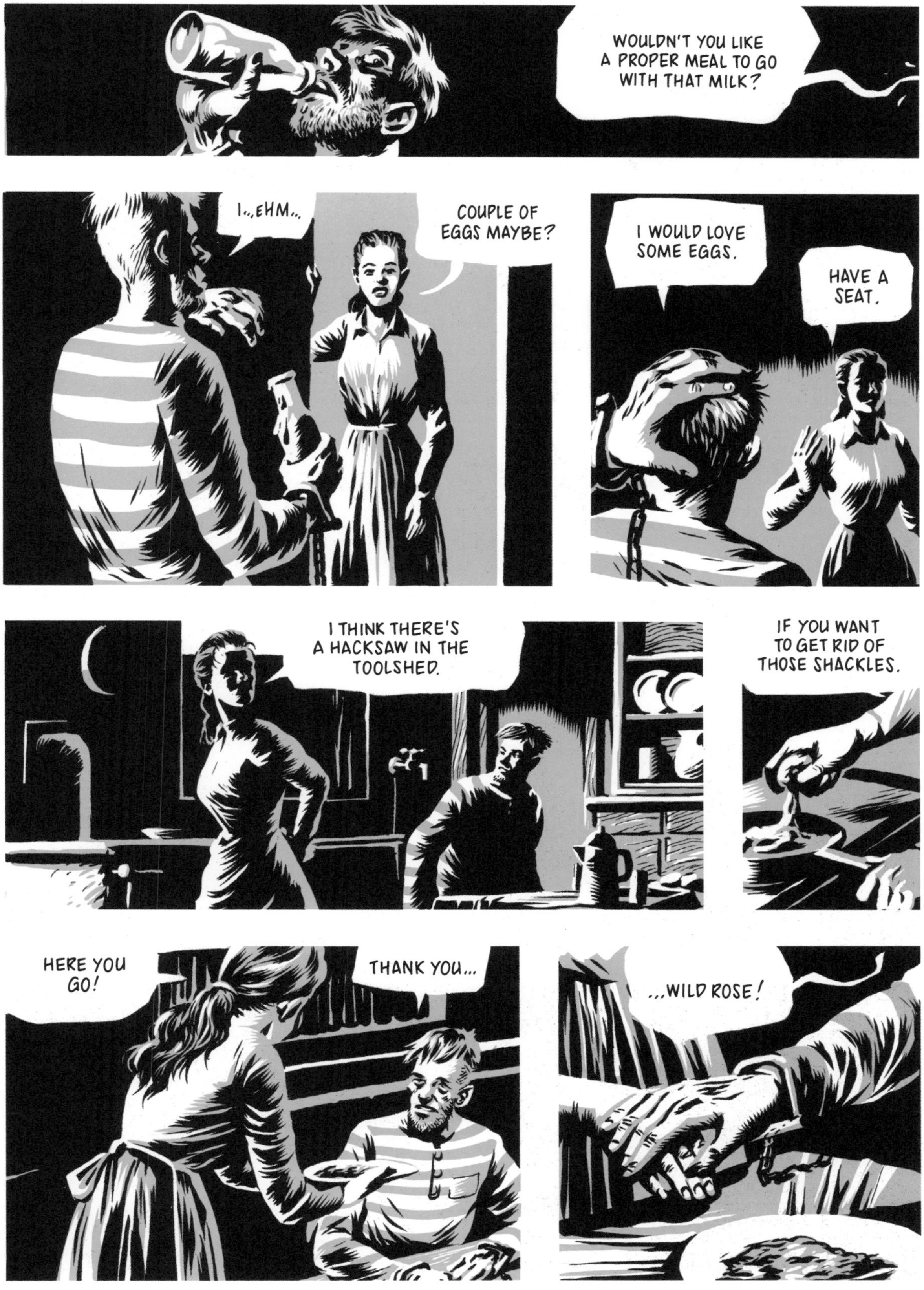
WOULDN'T YOU LIKE A PROPER MEAL TO GO WITH THAT MILK?
I...EHM...
COUPLE OF EGGS MAYBE?
I WOULD LOVE SOME EGGS.
HAVE A SEAT.
I THINK THERE'S A HACKSAW IN THE TOOLSHED.
IF YOU WANT TO GET RID OF THOSE SHACKLES.
HERE YOU GO!
THANK YOU...
...WILD ROSE!

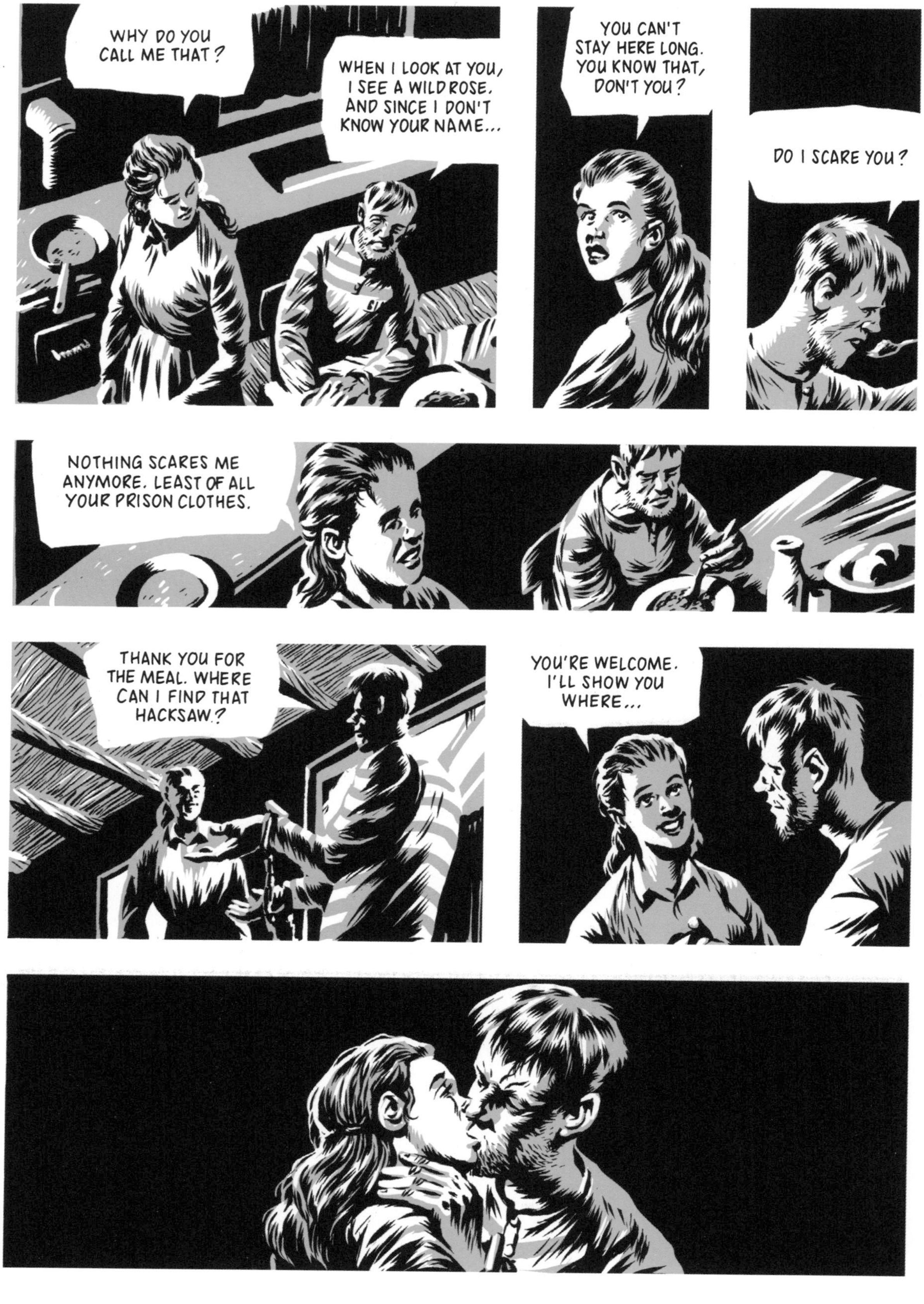
WHY DO YOU CALL ME THAT?
WHEN I LOOK AT YOU, I SEE A WILD ROSE. AND SINCE I DON'T KNOW YOUR NAME...
YOU CAN'T STAY HERE LONG. YOU KNOW THAT, DON'T YOU?
DO I SCARE YOU?
NOTHING SCARES ME ANYMORE. LEAST OF ALL YOUR PRISON CLOTHES.
THANK YOU FOR THE MEAL. WHERE CAN I FIND THAT HACKSAW?
YOU'RE WELCOME. I'LL SHOW YOU WHERE...

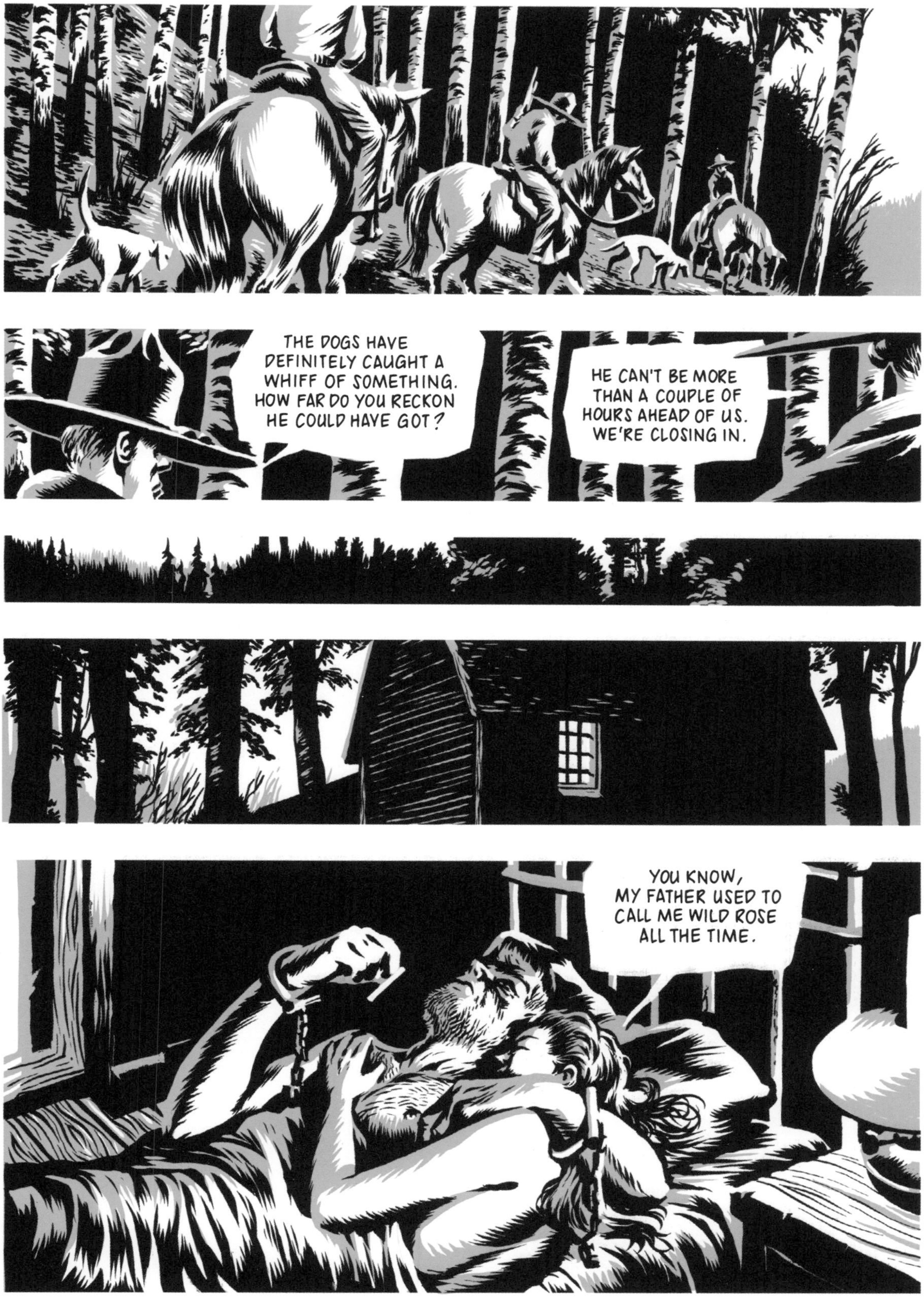
THE DOGS HAVE DEFINITELY CAUGHT A WHIFF OF SOMETHING. HOW FAR DO YOU RECKON HE COULD HAVE GOT?
HE CAN'T BE MORE THAN A COUPLE OF HOURS AHEAD OF US. WE'RE CLOSING IN.
YOU KNOW, MY FATHER USED TO CALL ME WILD ROSE ALL THE TIME.

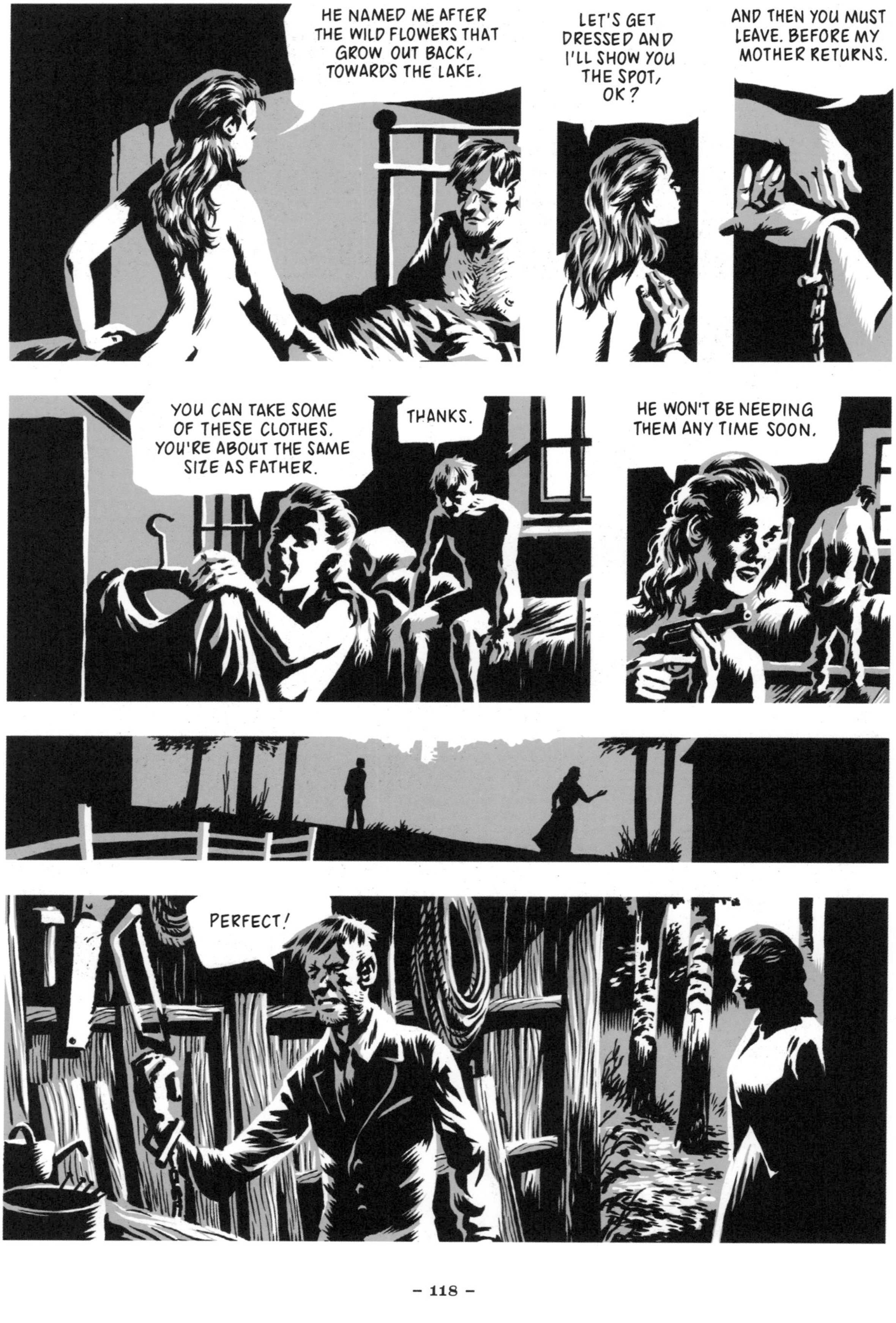
HE NAMED ME AFTER THE WILD FLOWERS THAT GROW OUT BACK, TOWARDS THE LAKE.
LET'S GET DRESSED AND I'LL SHOW YOU THE SPOT, OK?
AND THEN YOU MUST LEAVE. BEFORE MY MOTHER RETURNS.
YOU CAN TAKE SOME OF THESE CLOTHES. YOU'RE ABOUT THE SAME SIZE AS FATHER.
THANKS.
HE WON'T BE NEEDING THEM ANY TIME SOON.
PERFECT!

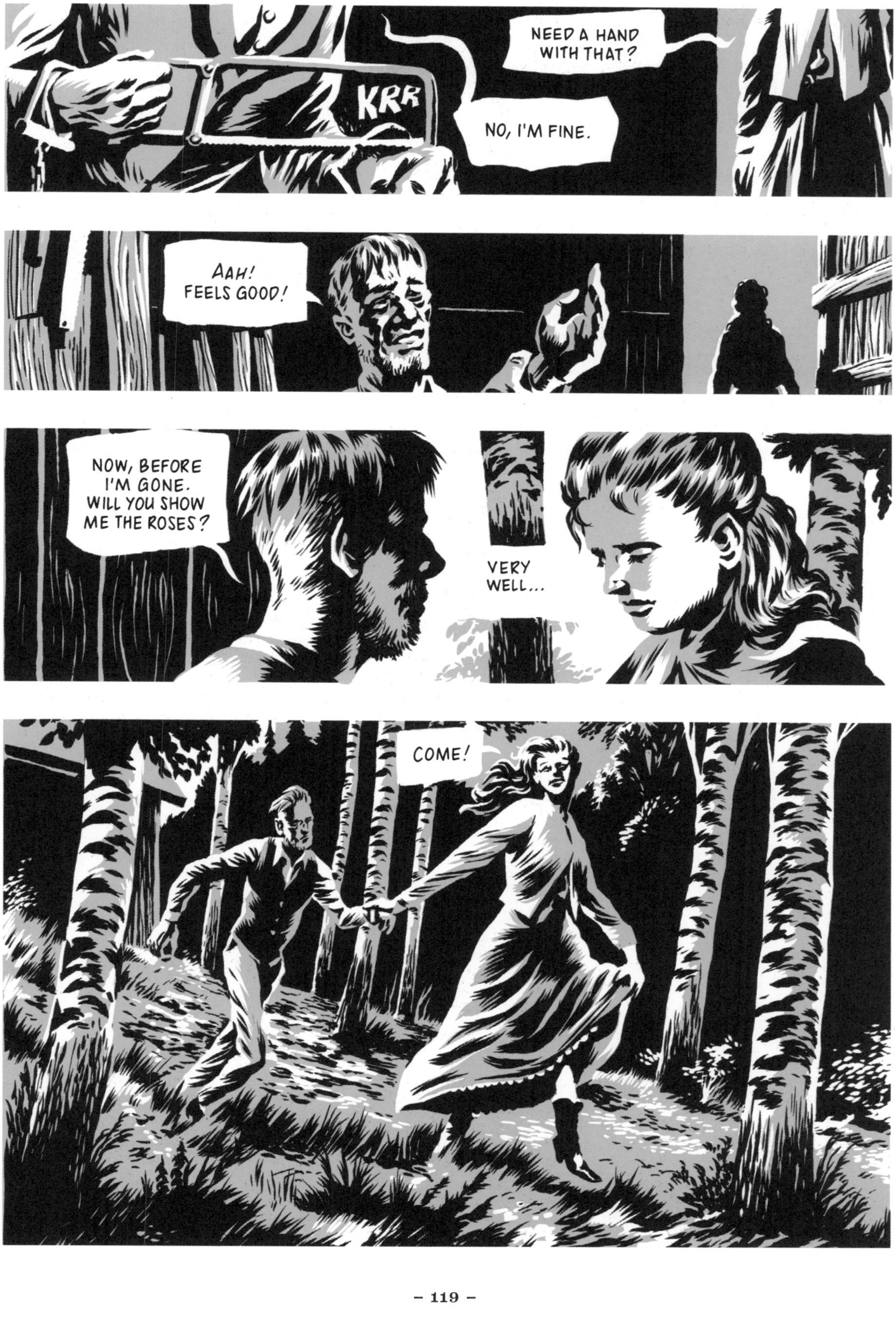
KRR
NEED A HAND WITH THAT?
NO, I'M FINE.
AAH! FEELS GOOD!
NOW, BEFORE I'M GONE. WILL YOU SHOW ME THE ROSES?
VERY WELL...
COME!

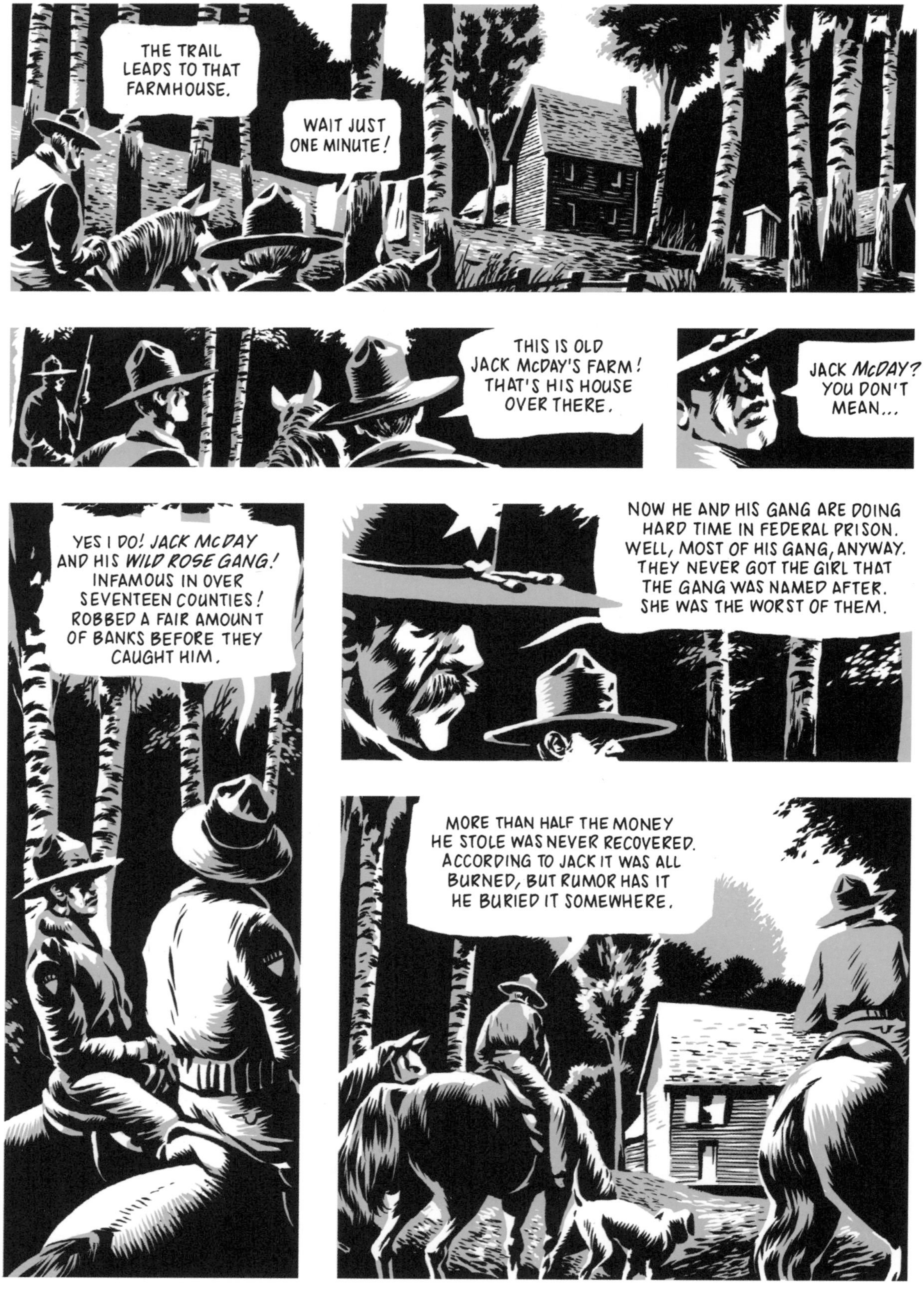
THE TRAIL LEADS TO THAT FARMHOUSE.
WAIT JUST ONE MINUTE!
THIS IS OLD JACK McDAY'S FARM! THAT'S HIS HOUSE OVER THERE.
JACK McDAY? YOU DON'T MEAN...
YES I DO! JACK McDAY AND HIS WILD ROSE GANG! INFAMOUS IN OVER SEVENTEEN COUNTIES! ROBBED A FAIR AMOUNT OF BANKS BEFORE THEY CAUGHT HIM.
NOW HE AND HIS GANG ARE DOING HARD TIME IN FEDERAL PRISON. WELL, MOST OF HIS GANG, ANYWAY. THEY NEVER GOT THE GIRL THAT THE GANG WAS NAMED AFTER. SHE WAS THE WORST OF THEM.
MORE THAN HALF THE MONEY HE STOLE WAS NEVER RECOVERED. ACCORDING TO JACK IT WAS ALL BURNED, BUT RUMOR HAS IT HE BURIED IT SOMEWHERE.

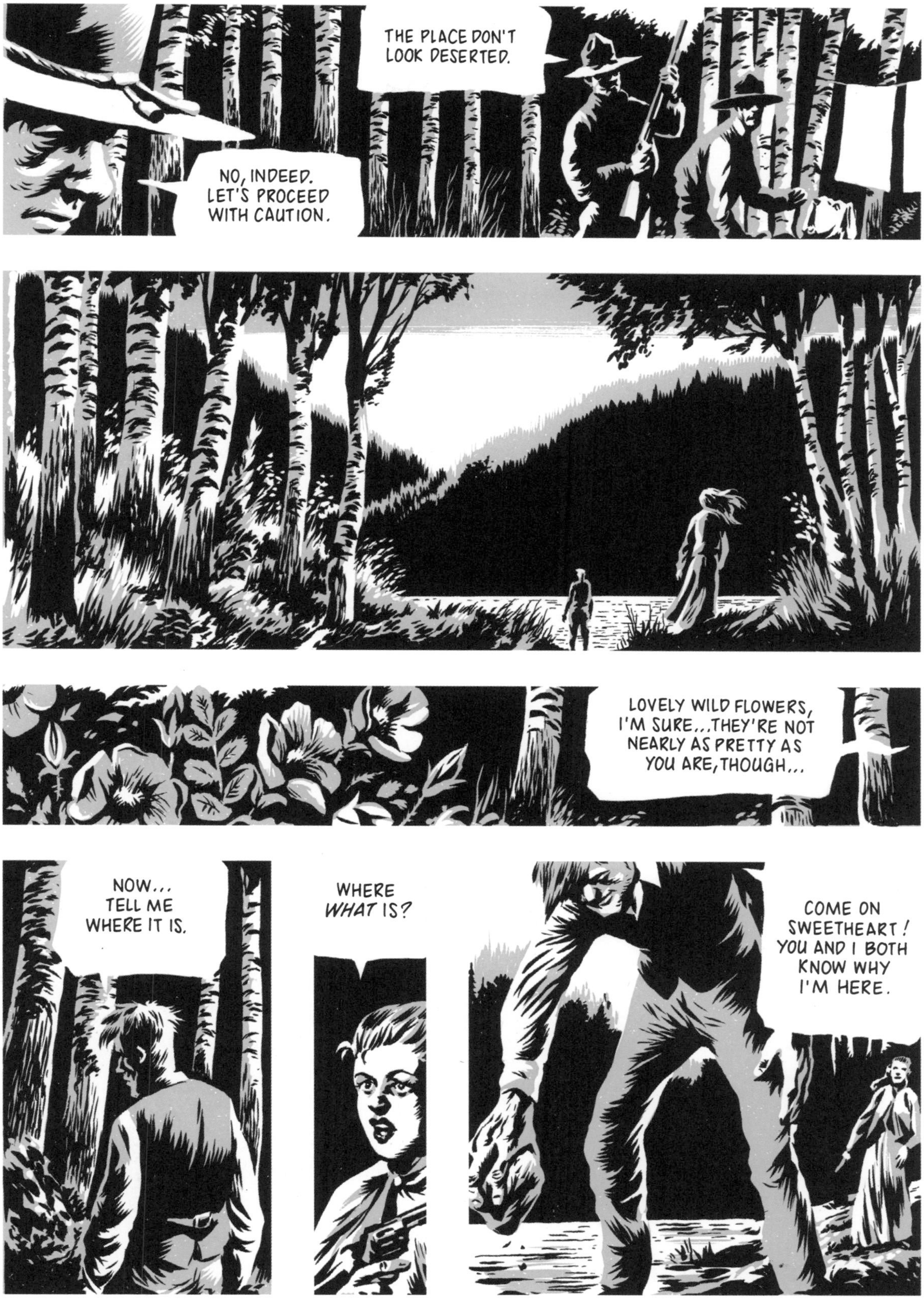
THE PLACE DON'T LOOK DESERTED.
NO, INDEED. LET'S PROCEED WITH CAUTION.
LOVELY WILD FLOWERS, I'M SURE... THEY'RE NOT NEARLY AS PRETTY AS YOU ARE, THOUGH...
NOW... TELL ME WHERE IT IS.
WHERE *WHAT* IS?
COME ON SWEETHEART! YOU AND I BOTH KNOW WHY I'M HERE.

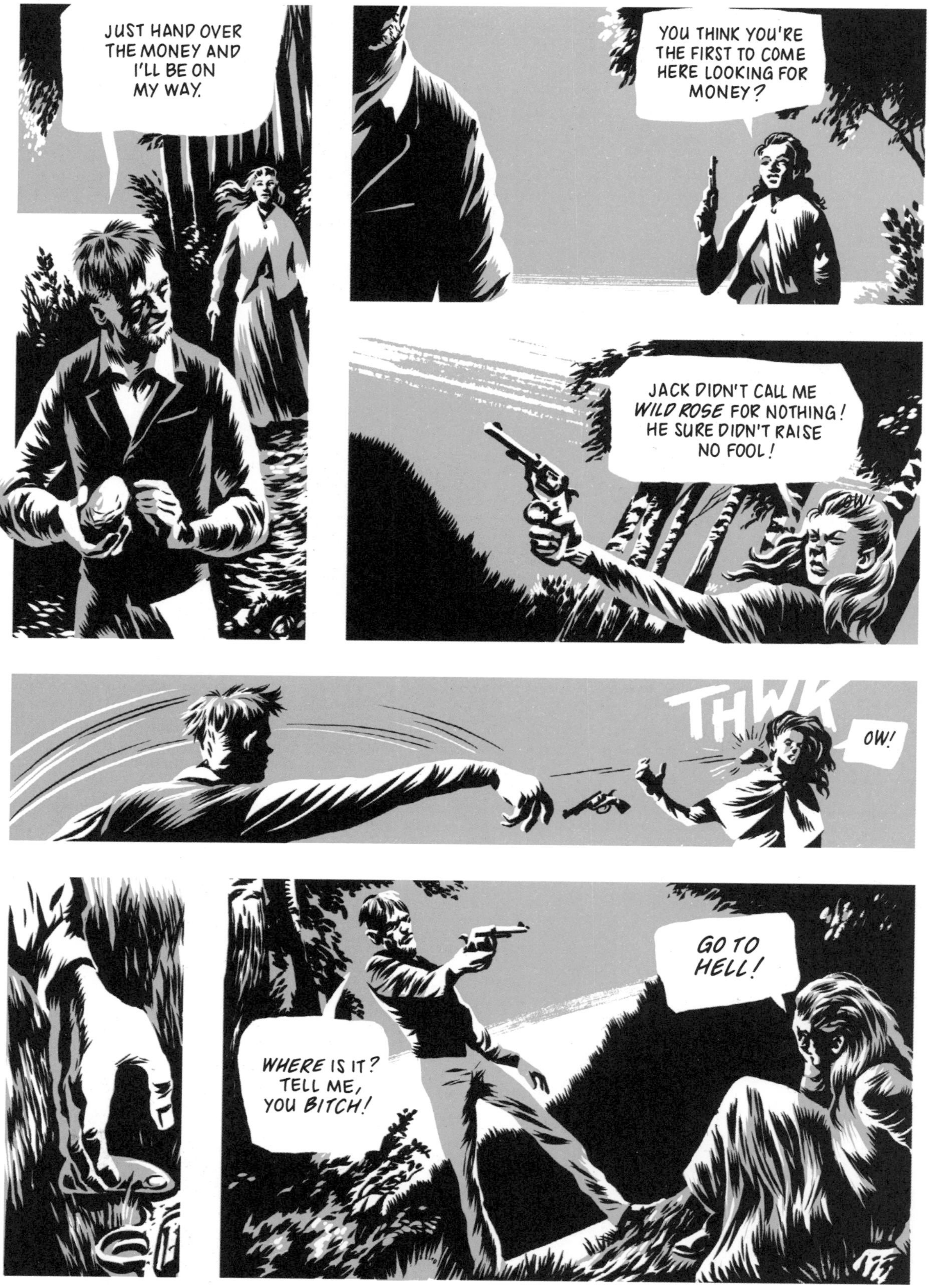
JUST HAND OVER THE MONEY AND I'LL BE ON MY WAY.
YOU THINK YOU'RE THE FIRST TO COME HERE LOOKING FOR MONEY?
JACK DIDN'T CALL ME WILD ROSE FOR NOTHING! HE SURE DIDN'T RAISE NO FOOL!
OW!
THWK
OW!
GO TO HELL!
WHERE IS IT? TELL ME, YOU BITCH!

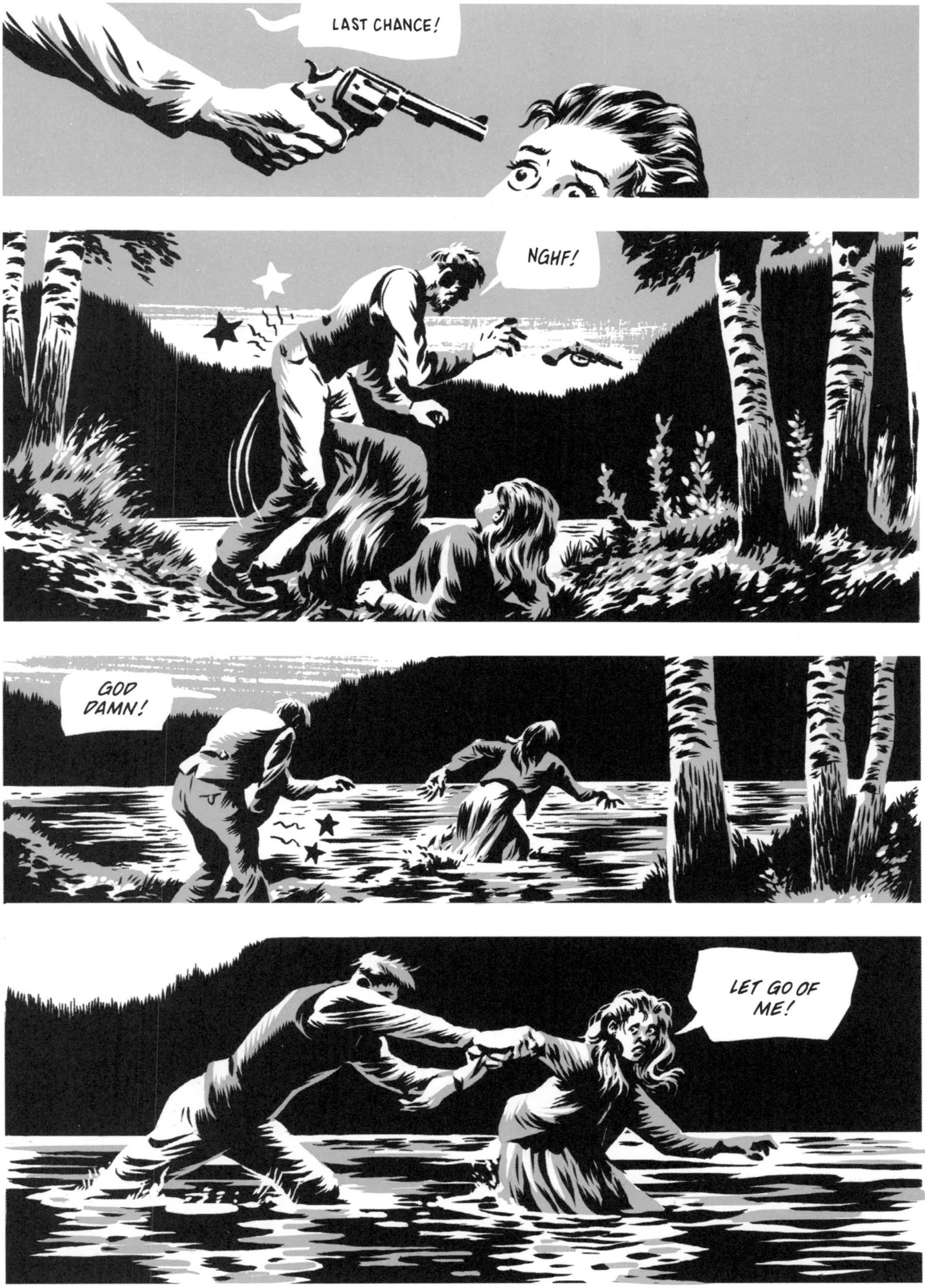
LAST CHANCE!
NGHF!
GOD DAMN!
LET GO OF ME!

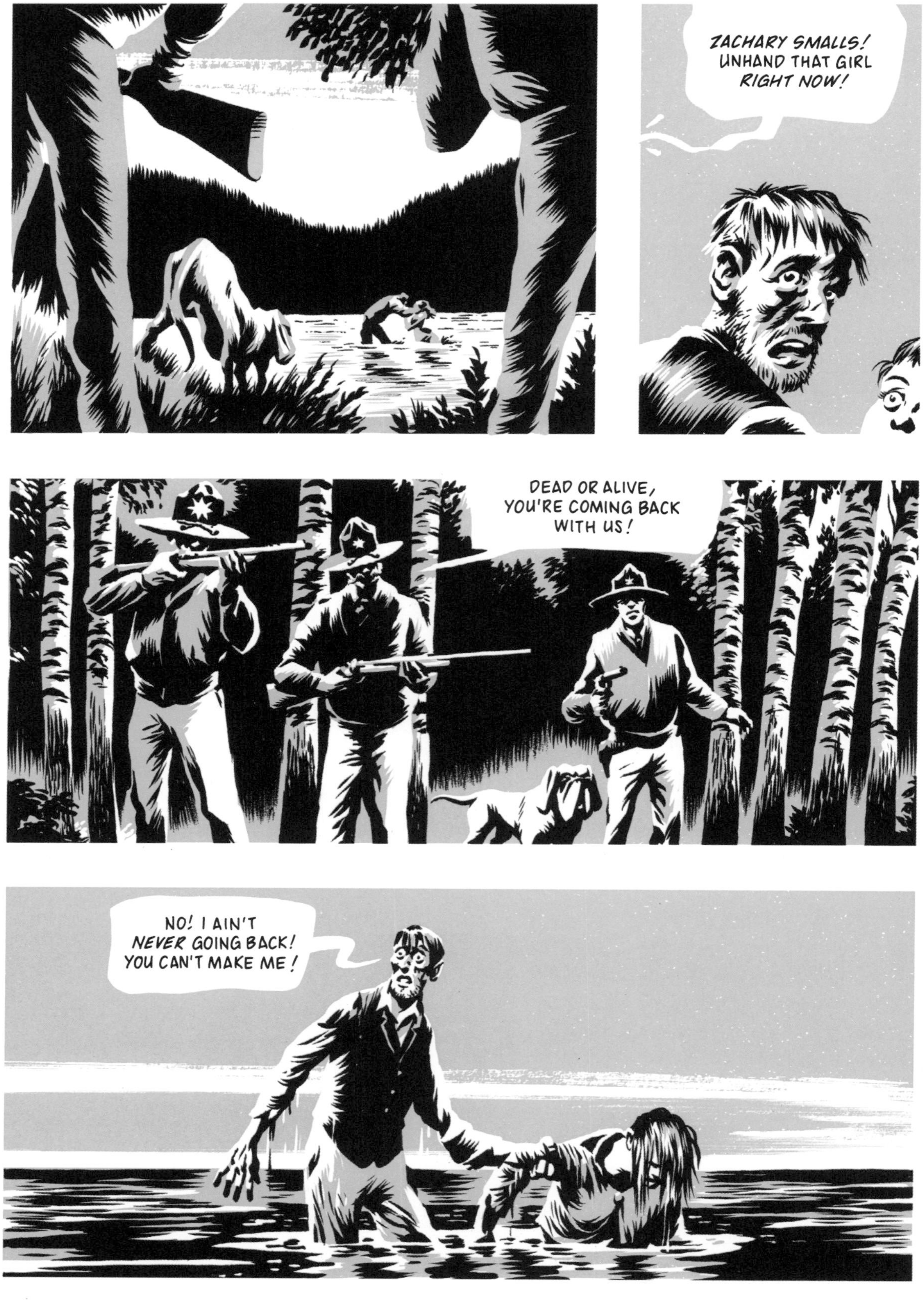
ZACHARY SMALLS! UNHAND THAT GIRL RIGHT NOW!
DEAD OR ALIVE, YOU'RE COMING BACK WITH US!
NO! I AIN'T NEVER GOING BACK! YOU CAN'T MAKE ME!

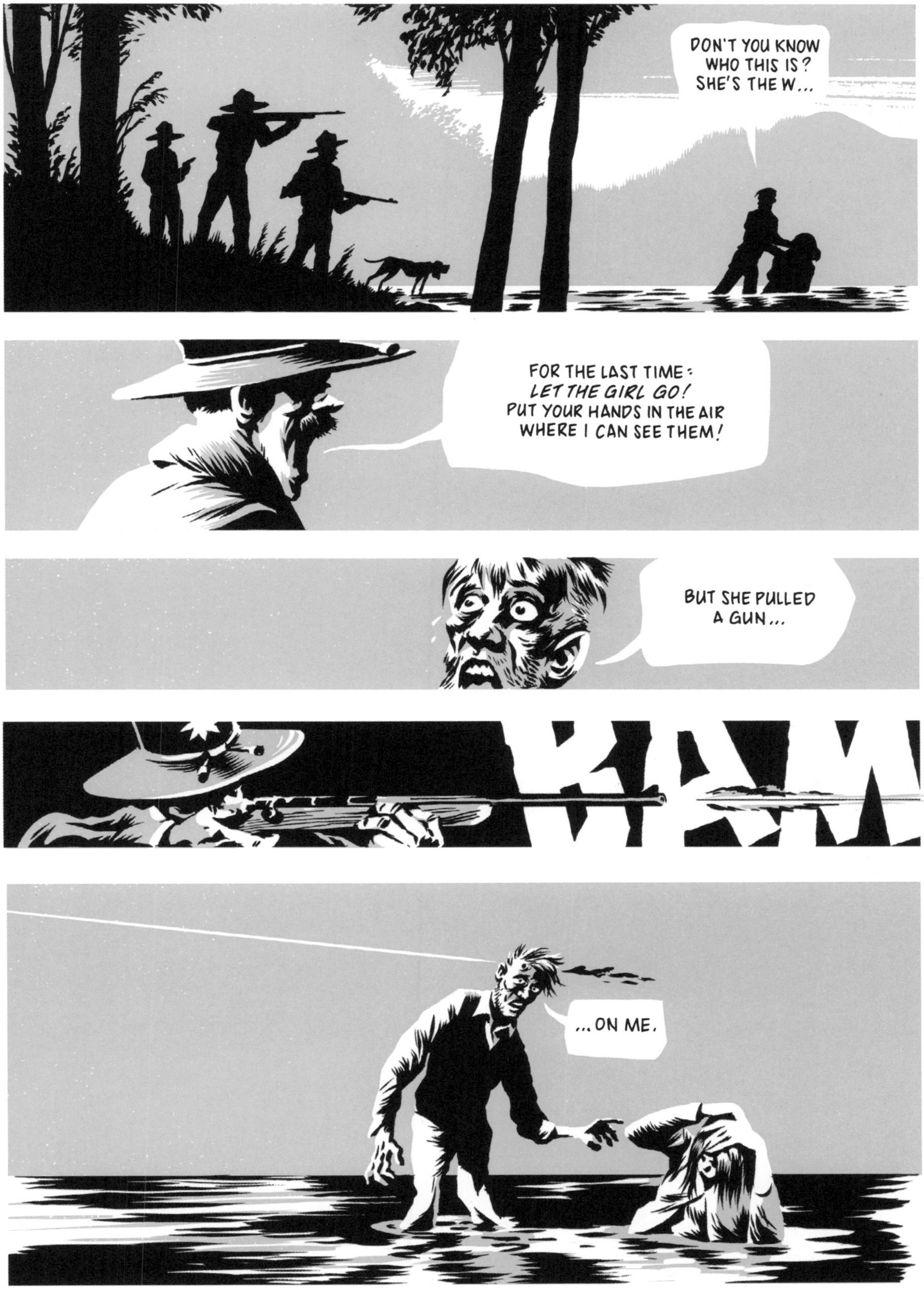
DON'T YOU KNOW WHO THIS IS? SHE'S THE W...
FOR THE LAST TIME: LET THE GIRL GO! PUT YOUR HANDS IN THE AIR WHERE I CAN SEE THEM!
BUT SHE PULLED A GUN...
...ON ME.

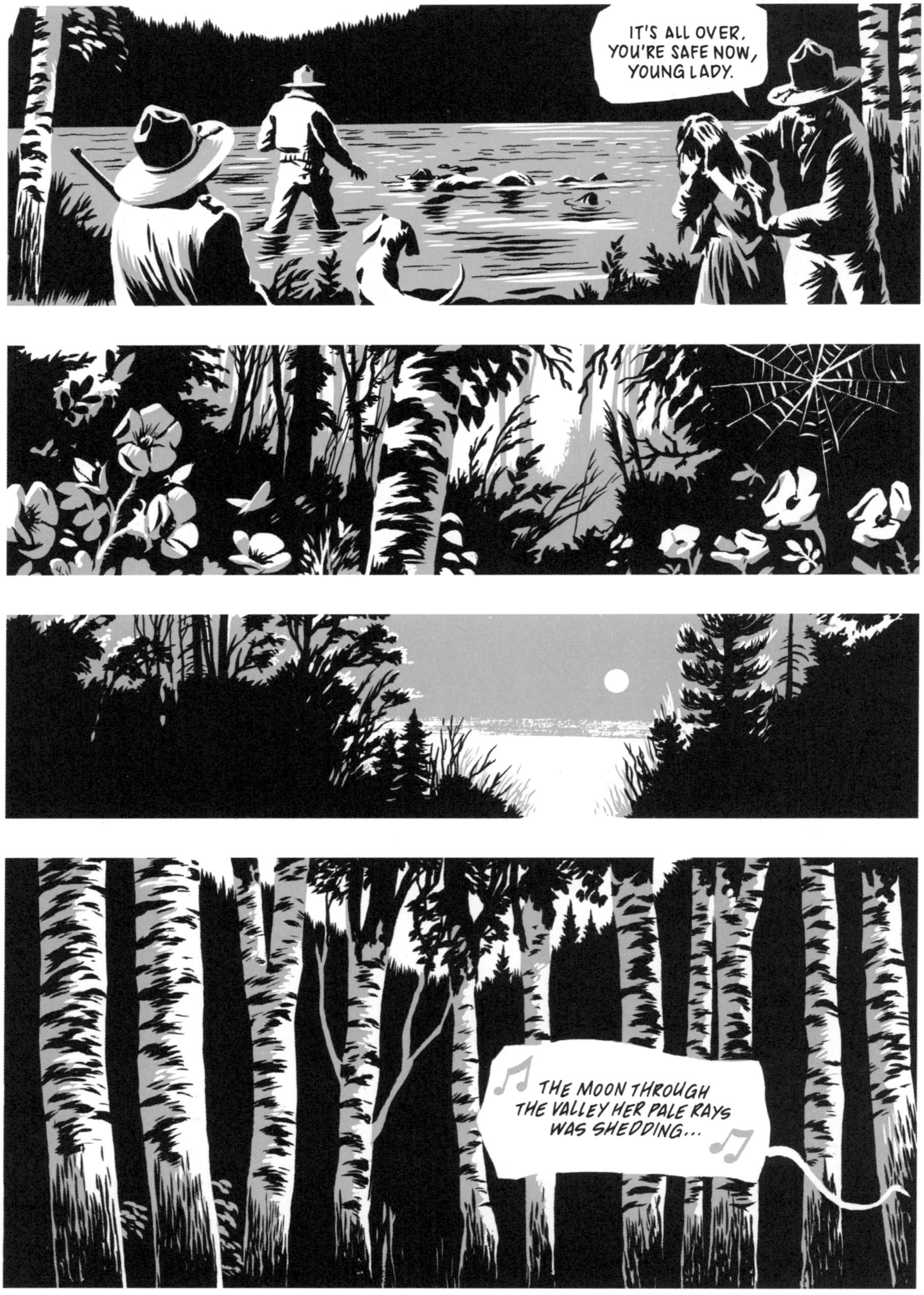
IT'S ALL OVER. YOU'RE SAFE NOW, YOUNG LADY.
THE MOON THROUGH THE VALLEY HER PALE RAYS WAS SHEDDING...

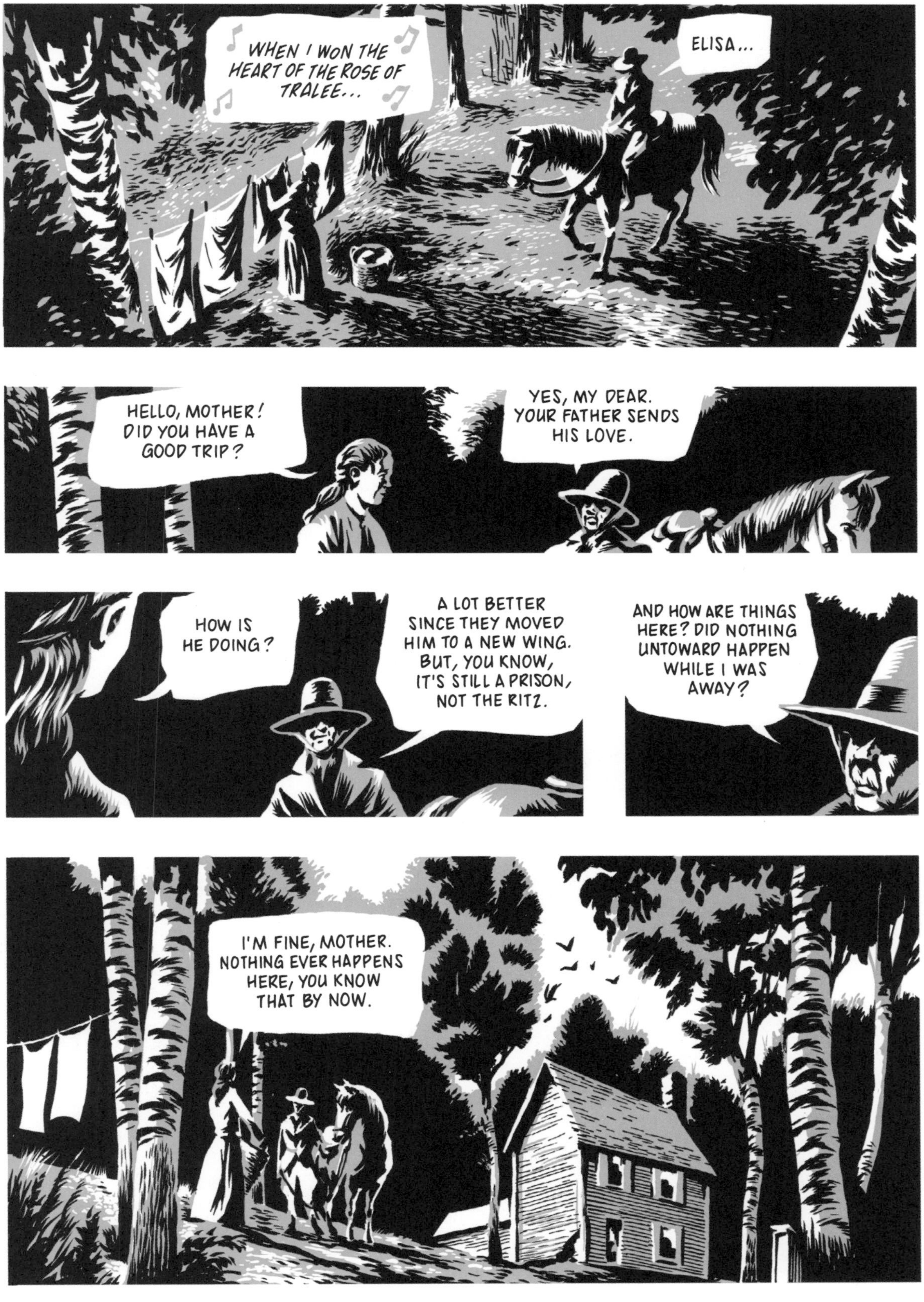
WHEN I WON THE HEART OF THE ROSE OF TRALEE...
ELISA...
HELLO, MOTHER! DID YOU HAVE A GOOD TRIP?
YES, MY DEAR. YOUR FATHER SENDS HIS LOVE.
HOW IS HE DOING?
A LOT BETTER SINCE THEY MOVED HIM TO A NEW WING. BUT, YOU KNOW, IT'S STILL A PRISON, NOT THE RITZ.
AND HOW ARE THINGS HERE? DID NOTHING UNTOWARD HAPPEN WHILE I WAS AWAY?
I'M FINE, MOTHER. NOTHING EVER HAPPENS HERE, YOU KNOW THAT BY NOW.

MURDER BALLADS

by Jan Donkers

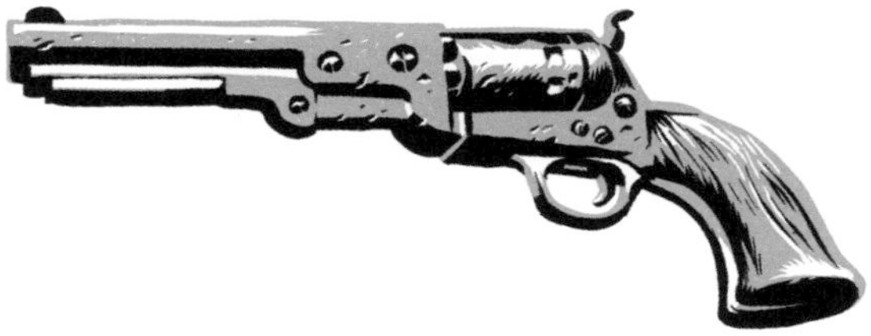

Murder Ballads? But isn't that the title of a Nick Cave album? Indeed it is, and the album is a gem of the genre, but the term stands for a lot more. Murder ballads were (and still are) an important element of the Great American Songbook — the unofficial anthology of American popular music — and a sub-genre of the traditional ballad. The lyrics of these ballads all deal with a murder, but the way the story is told can differ considerably. Sometimes we follow that story from the point of view of the murderer, sometimes from the point of view of the victim, but more often from the point of view of an observing third person — the narrator/singer. The development of the drama comes in different forms as well, but often the killer doesn't escape his (or her) fate and ends up on the gallows or behind bars, and the singer concludes with a moralistic argument: don't do it, 'cause see where it will lead you! The ballads are a fine depiction of nineteenth-century America, where gun violence and religiously-inspired moralism tried to balance each other out.

Yet, this is not strictly an American genre, because many of the ballads originated in England, Scotland, and Scandinavia, and were brought to the US by immigrants and adapted, passed down orally, and recycled in the form of song to recount gruesome incidents.

Erik Kriek has taken five of these ballads — recent as well as traditional — as starting points for his graphic stories, drawn in his characteristically suspenseful and nightmarish style. But he has done much more than adapt a song into a comic strip. Kriek has taken the lyrics as a starting point and delved into their history, as well as his own imagination, and taken the liberty of turning them into his own, broader pictorial stories — thereby giving us new, independent works of art.

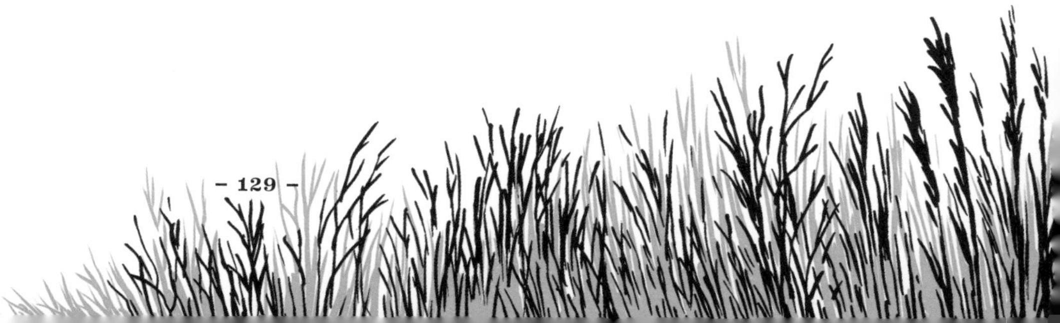

The first story, PRETTY POLLY, is a good example of that process. The song, with its multiple points of view, has been performed by a variety of artists, ranging from The Stanley Brothers to The Byrds, from Sandy Denny to Judy Collins. All of them have limited themselves to the abridged version of the song, which does not include the things the future has in store for Willie. He is not a murderer who arouses mixed feelings: the fact that (in the song) he has already dug the grave for pregnant Polly before killing her makes him, according to Rennie Sparks (half of The Handsome Family, who have created memorable contributions to the genre themselves), a "creep," a "snickering psycho," and a present day killer comparable to Ted Bundy. For his interpretation of this ballad, Kriek has chosen the original English version, which dates back to the first half of the eighteenth century and was known as "The Gosport Tragedy" or "The Cruel Ship's Carpenter." In this text, Willie is indeed a ship's carpenter who brings down a curse upon the ship on which he sails. It was common superstition among British sailors at the time that the ship was doomed if there was a murderer on board.

LONG BLACK VEIL, probably the best known of these five ballads, has a much shorter history and is not based upon just one historic event. The song was written by Marijohn Wilkin and Danny Dill in 1959 and was made into a country and western hit when Lefty Frizzell recorded his version. The songwriters combined three events into a tragic ballad about a man who — the noose already around his neck — refuses to reveal his alibi: protecting the honor of his lover is more important to him than his urge to survive. The unresolved murder of a priest was one of the events, and the mystery of the veiled woman, who visited the grave of movie star/heartbreaker Rudolph Valentino almost every day, gave the song its gloomy yet romantic coda. "Long Black Veil" is a song that is part of the standard repertoire of many an Americana artist but has been adopted by artists outside of the genre, too. The version by The Band is the best known, but the song was also covered by Johnny Cash, Mick Jagger with The Chieftains, Nick Cave, The Grateful Dead, Chip Taylor, Jason and The Scorchers... The entire list would fill almost a whole page.

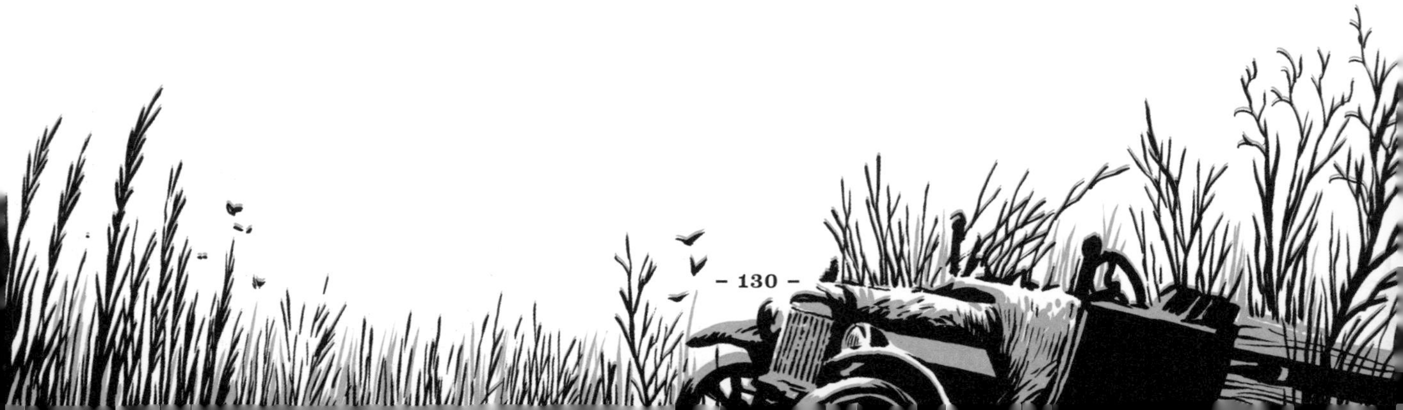

TANEYTOWN is not based upon a historic event but was invented by Steve Earle, who not only found inspiration for the song, but also for a short story of the same title in his book, *Doghouse Roses*. The song came first, but it was after finishing the story and giving his characters more flesh and blood that the song took on its final shape. "The premise of the song is that rednecks are everywhere, not just in the Southern United States," Earle himself said. In Kriek's version, justice is done beautifully to the "flesh and blood" of the story. More than an interpretation of the song on paper, Kriek adapts the essence of the song as well.

CALEB MEYER is a murder ballad written by Gillian Welch, a singer who has many devoted fans among Americana aficionados, and especially those who are attracted by the retro element that characterizes Welch's repertoire. "Caleb Meyer" can be found on *Hell Among the Yearlings*, an album steeped in darkness and Biblical references, and "Caleb Meyer" is most certainly not an incongruous item there. Yet, this is not an entirely gloomy song: after all, Caleb Meyer ultimately gets what he deserves.

WHERE THE WILD ROSES GROW is no traditional murder ballad either. Nick Cave did base the song, which he recorded with Kylie Minogue, upon an event which is recounted in "The Willow Garden," the flip-side of his single, which was a hit in 1996. However, no background story is explained in either of the two songs. Why the man kills the Wild Rose with a rock (in "The Willow Garden" he uses a sabre) is not made clear, except for his murderous opinion that "all beauty must die." In Erik Kriek's version, things happen differently: here the would-be murderer is an escaped convict, Zachary Smalls, who is after Elisa's money. She doesn't trust him, and packs a pistol when she takes him to the place where the wild roses grow. But in this version, he throws the rock, striking her and causing her to drop the gun, which is used in the song to kill her. With a sigh of relief, we can verify that she has survived the terrible incident and the sheriff's men arrive in the nick of time. The coda is great: "Has anything happened while I was gone?" Elisa's mother asks after returning from a visit to the prison where her husband is locked up. "No, nothing ever happens here," Elisa McDay can answer. Not quite truthfully, as we know.

In the Pines is a splendid collection of graphic stories; after reading them I wanted more. If one accepts a broad interpretation of the genre, quite a lot of recent contributions to the Great American Songbook would be fit for graphic adaptation. I would be curious to see Kriek's version of Bob Dylan's "The Lonesome Death of Hattie Carroll", which is based upon a historic event. Or "There Is Something On Your Mind" (originally by Big Jay McNeely, but a hit for Bobby Marchan in 1960) in which the murderer first kills the lover of his adulterous wife, but hesitates to shoot her too. He decides to forgive her, but at that very moment another admirer steps in. And the singer, he can't help himself... From "Hey Joe," to "Delia's Gone," "Stagger Lee," "Little Sadie," Lyle Lovett's "L.A. County," and "Tom Dooley," many a song has supplied a picture of the darker side of the American Dream.

America has hardly become less trigger-happy since the era of the Wild West, the years when the first murder ballads were written. Have there been songs written about Jeffrey Dahmer and all those other psycho-pathic killers? There's a lot more work ahead for Erik Kriek...

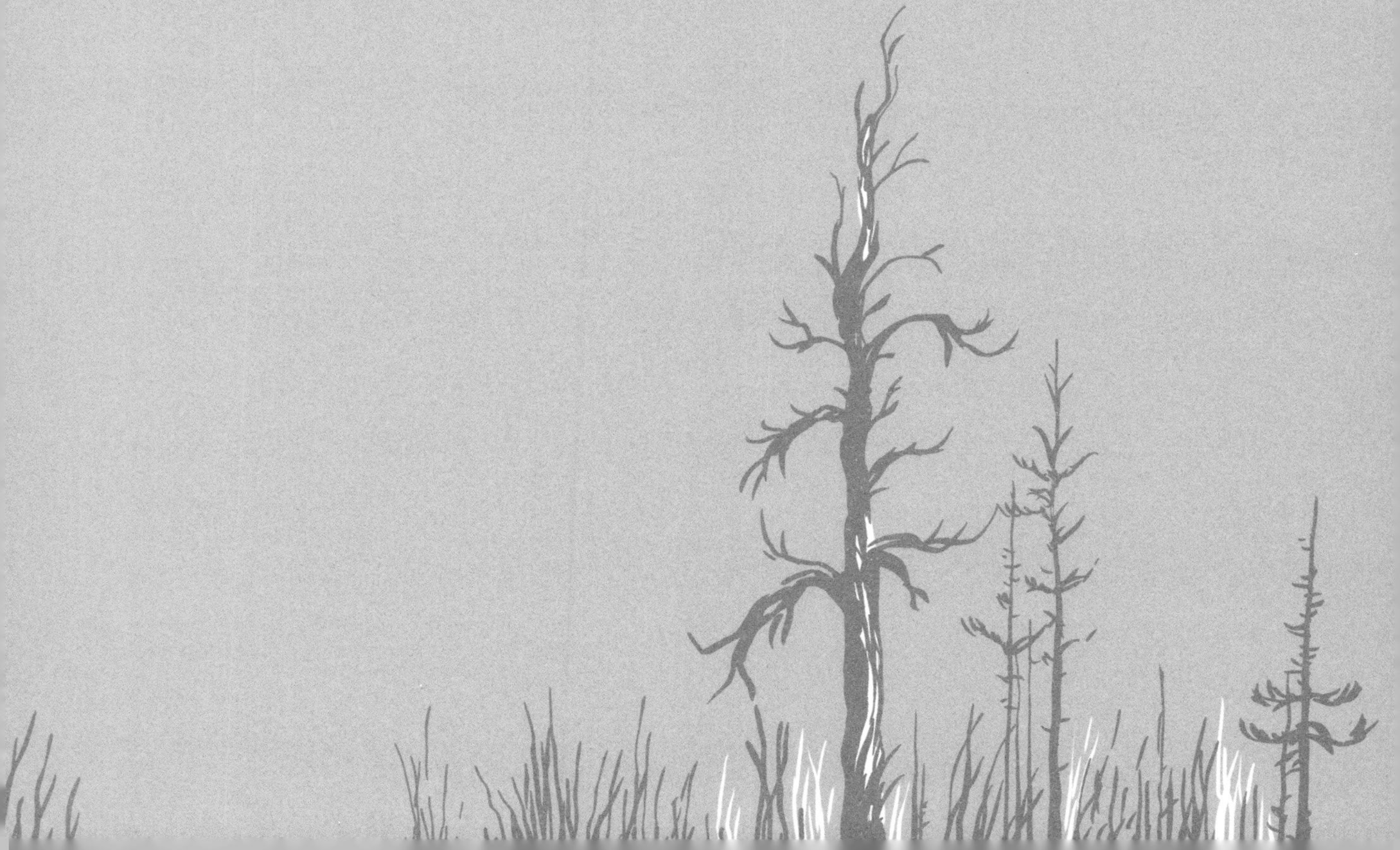

Erik Kriek (Amsterdam, 1966) is best known in his native Holland for the wordless adventures of faux-superhero Gutsman and his girlfriend Tigra. His 2012 publication *Het Onzienbare (From Beyond)*, a selection of adaptations of stories by H.P Lovecraft, introduced his name to an international audience.

Aside from making comics, Kriek is a prolific illustrator, working for a variety of national and international media, magazines and newspapers. He has also recently started illustrating children's books, taking his work into hitherto uncharted territories.

Erik Kriek lives and works in Amsterdam, the Netherlands, together with his wife Stans and their son, Clovis.

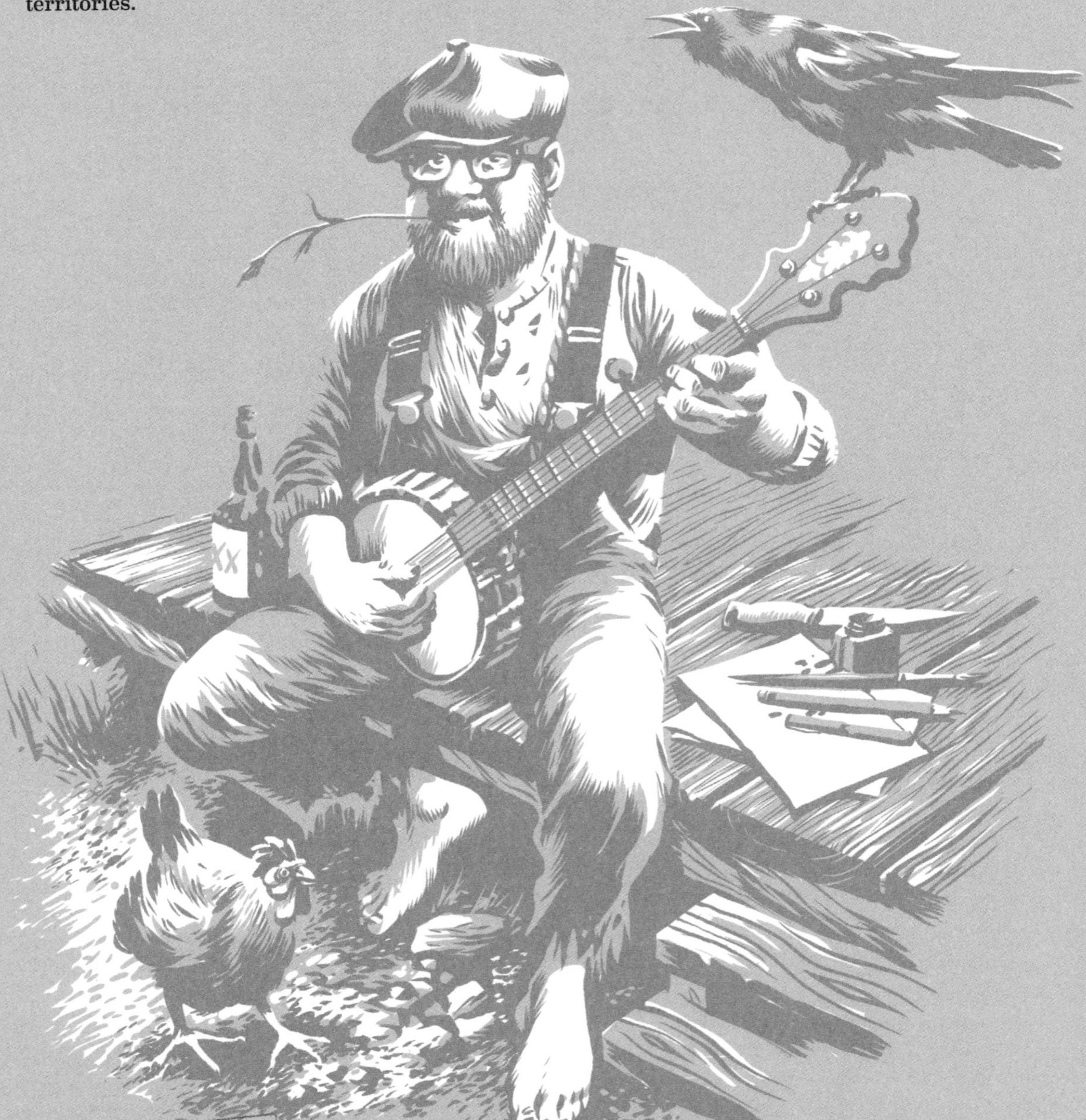

XX

Thank you to Hansje Joustra, Wiebe Mokken, Jan Donkers, my fellow studio-mates at Pelikaen Studios, the Blue Grass Boogiemen, Sophie ter Schure, Annita Langereis, Excelsior Recordings and my dearest, ever faithful yet critical proofreader, Stans.

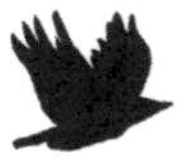

In the Pines is dedicated to my father,
Erik Kriek, Sr. (1931–2013) who, sadly,
only saw the first sketches for this book.

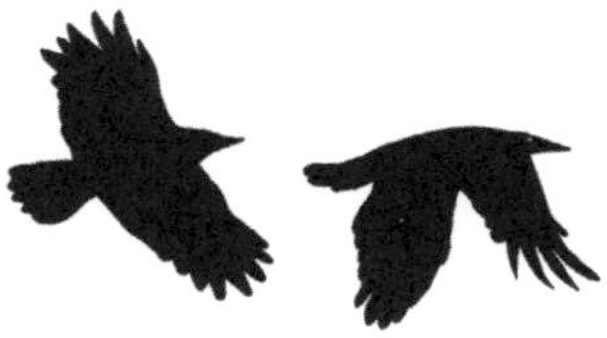

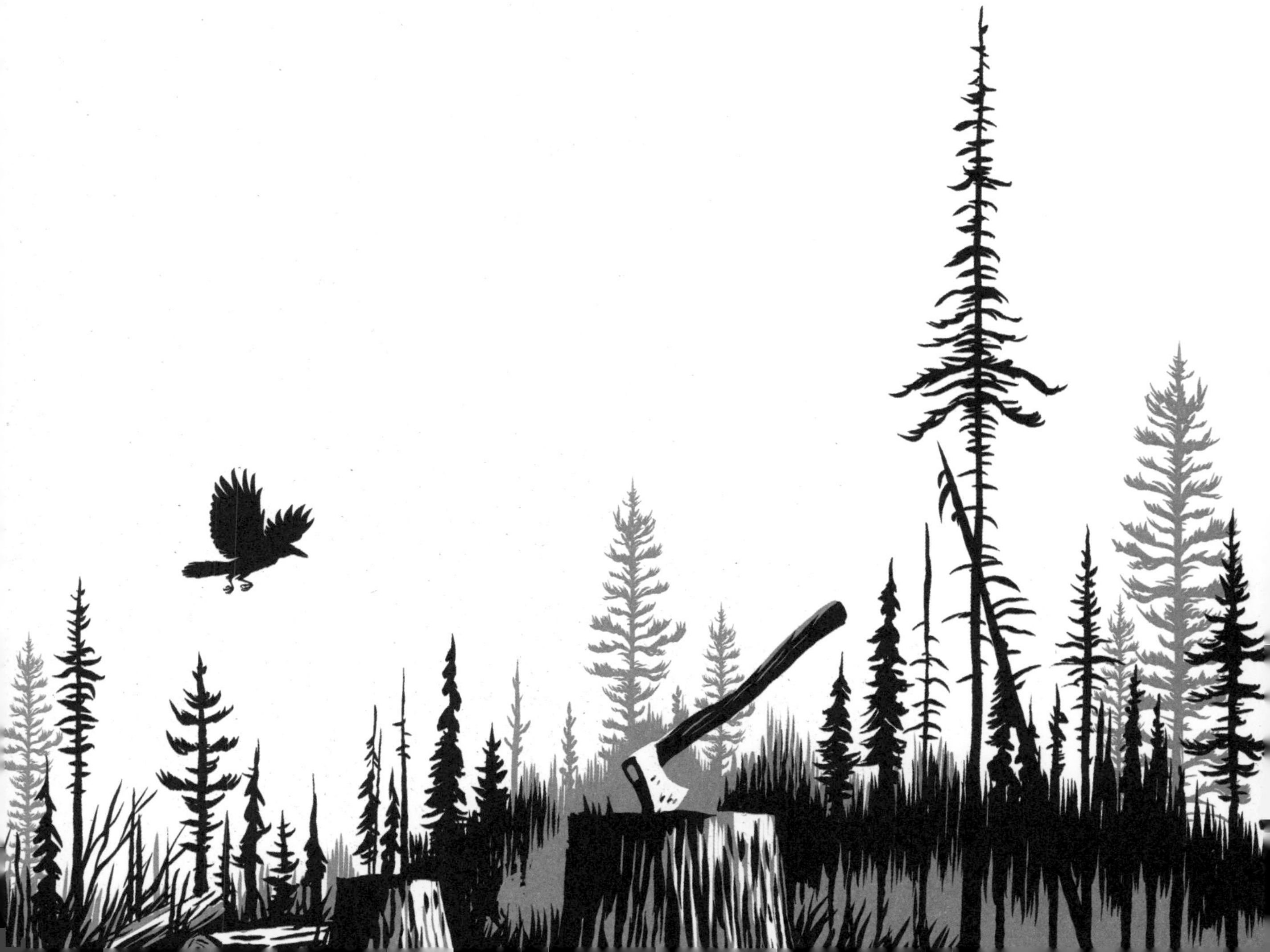

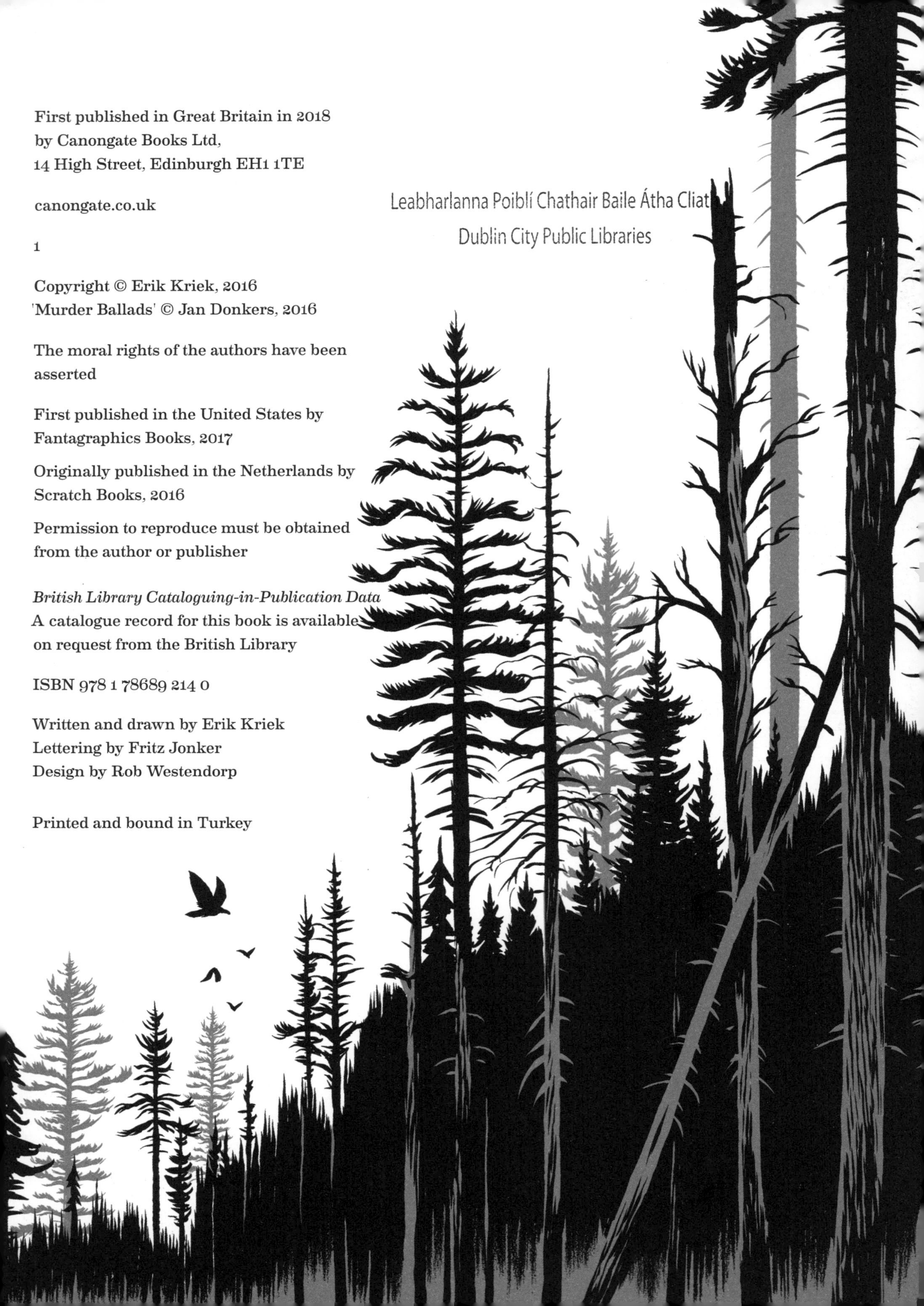

First published in Great Britain in 2018
by Canongate Books Ltd,
14 High Street, Edinburgh EH1 1TE

canongate.co.uk

1

First published in the United States by Fantagraphics Books, 2017

Originally published in the Netherlands by Scratch Books, 2016

British Library Cataloguing-in-Publication Data
A catalogue record for this book is available on request from the British Library

ISBN 978 1 78689 214 0

Written and drawn by Erik Kriek
Lettering by Fritz Jonker
Design by Rob Westendorp

Printed and bound in Turkey